-Acknowledgments-

Without help and encouragement from the following people I would never have written, or if I had written I would never have published, these tales. In no particular order muchas gracias to: John Clevenger, Pam Pryzbylo, Billy Finn, Paul Maritz, David Lundquist, Zola Stoltz, Luigi Chiarani, Tim Roska, Dori Vialpando, Tadeo Poderes, Chris and Kathleen Talbot, John McAfee, Bill Cummings, Kenny Brown, John Kemmeries and the Circuit Writers of Portal, Arizona. Gracias amigos! Special thanks to Gordon Stitt for many great photos.

78th edition copyright 2008 by John Quinn Olson

ISBN 0-9820703-2-2 Paperback
ISBN 0-9820703-3-0 Hardcover

Published for you by

Dust Devil Press

Rodeo, NM

Cover art by David Lundquist
www.EagleEyesStudio.com

Cover photo by the author
*Headed for Mt. Whitney

Tales From The Wild Blue Yonder

Recipes For Disaster

By John Q. Olson

This book is dedicated to people who believe that flying and reading are for fun. This book is not dedicated to the pathetic bureaucrats at the Federal Aviation Administration AFS-610, who really know how to take the fun out of flying and reading too.

Table Of Contents

Either write something worth reading
or do something worth writing.
--Benjamin Franklin

I remember when sex was safe
and hang gliding was dangerous.
--Confucius

Banished... for GOOD or, Busted On KT-22

The Gringo's Last Day of Skiing was the First Day of the Rest of His Life...

Snow was falling at the rate of about six inches per hour and conditions were near-whiteout as Walter clipped into the wisdom of his Solomons. He hustled up to the KT-22 lift and watched as a few chairs appeared from the mist, swung around the bull wheel, and disappeared again up the mountain. He couldn't believe his good fortune at being the first in line, the very first. It had paid to rise and shine early today; the whole of the KT-22 chair would be his for making those first luscious tracks. The whole of Squaw Valley for that matter; any skier's dream come true. Well... any foul weather skier, that is. A spring storm was blanketing the High Sierra, but there were few takers.

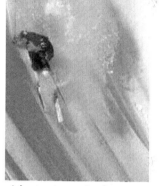

The lift operator turned the CLOSED sign around and opened the maze. Walter slid forward and caught the very first chair. Now, the sky was the limit. He wedged his poles between the chair uprights to avoid slipping out of his snowy perch, and settled in for the cosmic ride, a magical mystery tour of inclement weather. There was no wind however, hardly any sound at all but the buzzing of the lift, and the soft flutter of snow falling straight down, coating everything with its weight. Now and then a tree limb, sagging under a foot of powder, would spring up as the snow fell away.

Otherwise, there was no movement around him, just the falling snow and the lift towers sliding past like silent sentinels.

On the way up, Walter noticed reassuring evidence of the bomb-squad that had preceded him. Dark, powder-blackened holes in the snow revealed their work and above the holes, ski tracks where they had stopped to toss those bombs indicated their passage just minutes past. Good! The snow had been stabilized by human effort and high explosives. Walter would follow those tracks to safety, even as they were quickly disappearing under fresh cover.

Soon the top lift shack came into view and Walter thrilled with anticipation. He knocked the accumulation of powder from his goggles and slid off the chair. Silky snow caressed his legs as he eagerly pointed along the traverse to the West Face of KT-22 and gained speed.

With a soothing, almost sensual rhythm, Walter began to make turns. He decided to stay on the traverse to the end of the Nose and then hang a hard left into the fall line of the Finger Chutes. There had been good coverage there yesterday and it had been snowing all night, today should be surreal.

The traverse emptied out briefly under the chair for about three turns. As Walter carved the perfect powder turn to enter the last Finger, the "Pinky" as it were, he heard a shout from above- from someone riding the chair. "Hey you!" it came, somewhat muffled by the snow and dimmed by the rush of air past his ears. "Hey you STOP!"

'Yea, right,' thought Walter. Cranking a sharp left turn, he felt the world drop out from under him in a soft white rushing uncertainty, as he dropped into the perfect line. The Finger Chute Walter had chosen was shaped like an hourglass laid slightly on its side. The top of the chute was reasonably shallow, then as it closed up it became dramatically steeper and steeper until it disappeared entirely from view with the vertical. All Walter could see for certain were the gnarly lichen-covered rocks that formed the walls of the chute. The rest was just white oblivion... the End of the World.

No matter, Walter knew this place by heart; he did not need to see. He could ski it with his eyes closed, but that would be no fun. Better to watch the walls slide by, anticipate the texture of the powder, make that special turn where the sculpted snow beckoned, feel it caress his soul, revel in the weightlessness, the sudden "G" forces, the next delightful release down the fall line, just to start it all over again. Turn, turn, turn... Only the combination of motion and control could create such a feeling of adrenaline, of well-being and belonging, high up on a mountaintop in the middle of a soothing blizzard.

Down into the narrows he slid, always pointing them down, down to where the chute became impossibly thin like the waist of a shapely lover. Down there, in the bosom of life and death, half a dozen turns demanded incredible daring and precision. Walter banged them off. Through the snowy mist he spotted the bottom of the hourglass and pointed his boards just... there!

Accelerating, he shot out of the Finger Chute at a crazy high velocity, and laid into some big sweeping giant-slalom turns, Victory Turns, everything disappearing in a plume of frozen rapture. In a dance of grace between a lonesome skier and Mother Nature's extremes, Walter sped to the bottom of the West Face. As the World began to flatten out, he stopped suddenly with a rooster tail of white, and looked back up, panting, at the way he had come. The snow he had just carved continued to follow him down in slumping cascades. Otherwise, nothing moved. Time to get back up there and "8" those turns, he thought. With a 'whoop' he fell back into the fall line and raced on.

Reaching the bottom of KT he was delighted to see Lori, cute little snow-bunny Lori, walking out towards the lift with her skis over her shoulder. She didn't recognize him in his blizzard suit at first- all humans were like strange powderhounds. He slid to a halt and wiped at the snot running down his nose.

"Hey Babe!" he said with enthusiasm. "Single!"

Lori was all grins and agreed there was little time to waste. She dropped her skis and clipped in. Her cute little fanny was poured into her powder suit; the day was indeed pregnant with promise. Things were looking up. Stepping into the maze with the other latecomers, Lori looked at Walter, "Well, where'd you go?" There were a dozen or so skiers ahead of them, awaiting their chair, slowly shuffling forward.

"The Fingers!" panted Walter, still spent with excitement and adrenaline. "Fresh tracks! I followed the bomb holes down the nose."

"Awesome day," agreed Lori. She was already covered with white flakes. Her ponytail and her smile were all that was visible of her young strong body.

Suddenly, there was a swish of snow next to him and Walter turned in time to see a skier lunging at him, and hear again the voice that had called from above, from way up on the traverse to the Chutes: "Hey YOU!" it said, and went for Walter's neck.

Not sure what was happening Walter's reaction was automatic: he pushed back at the snowy form. Completely outfitted in powder suits as they were, it was difficult to tell if the attacker was friend or foe. The actions did not speak of friendship, however, so Walter just put up a hand and shoved. It was an auto-response. The attacker leaned, off balance, and the maze ropes caught him behind his knees. He tried vainly to flail his arms and poles and regain his balance but Walter's push had been just enough, just too much. In slow motion he fell backwards, over the rope, and landed with an appalling thud in the hardpack of the lift-line. The wind rushed from his lungs with an undignified "uuggh" Thrashing about a bit and trying desperately to suck air, the attacker soon ripped off his face mask and goggles, as Walter and Lori made further progress down the line.

It was then, suddenly, when Walter understood that he was in a real horrible fix. The face that gaped out from under the mask, gasping for air in a most undignified manner and looking like some sort of fish out of water, was none other than Jimmy Potter himself- Squaw Valley mountain manager! And OH he was PISSED! But why? Without much further thought Walter and Lori scurried on to the KT chair and plunked themselves down, looking at each other in horror. "Uh oh," Walter wasn't sure who had uttered it, but he glanced over his shoulder as the chair sped off with them, to see Potter unclip from his bindings and scramble to his feet. His face was hot with anger, visible even as they rode away in the chair. Finally, suddenly, inevitably, Potter sucked a lung-full of wind, and was again articulate.

"STOP THAT CHAIR!" he bellowed weakly at the lift operator. "STOP THAT DAMN LIFT!"

Walter felt a horrible sinking sensation as the KT chair lurched to a halt and left him dangling in uncertainty. He wasn't sure why, but it looked as though he was in trouble. Big trouble. Lori wasn't smiling anymore either; she gave him a look as though he suddenly had the Black Plague. Potter himself had lunged at the panic button- the large red button about the size of a dinner plate on the lift shack wall, which in turn caused the KT chair to lurch to a stop. As the chair swung back-and-forth with spent momentum Potter, ski-less now, strode through the deep snow until he was below Walter. Some three feet of air separated Walter's skis from Potter's grasp, or he would certainly have pulled on them, he was that mad- a snarly dog with his prey treed just out of reach. Like a dervish, Potter hurled oaths at Walter. "You'll never ski Squaw again!" he declared. "You're a Northstar skier now! Your days at Squaw are OVER! You can go ski Sugar Bowl for all I care!" It was a nightmare curse, banished from Squaw Valley.

Walter's heart sunk. Sugar Bowl? Northstar? Like being sentenced to the bunny-hill. But if anyone had the authority to yank Walter's pass here at Squaw, to exile someone to some novice Hell, it was this demented spectacle below him. Potter had lost face. He was steamed. "Get down from th...." he began. Then, turning to the operator, "Ease off those brakes so the chair goes back!"

But it was unnecessary. With a weak grin at Lori, Walter pushed off the seat and plopped into the deep snow below. Now the adversaries were face-to-face.

"Alright, already," he offered. "What's the problem?"

"The Problem?" roared Potter. "The PROBLEM! WHAT'S THE PROBLEM he asks! How about skiing closed terrain, for one. How about assaulting a mountain employee, for another. I'm calling the Sheriff, that's the PROBLEM!"

"Closed?" questioned Walter, "What'd ya mean closed?" He ripped off his mask and goggles, revealing his identity. "I didn't assault anyone!" Again, Potter went ballistic.

"YOU!" he bawled. They knew each other all right- had been sharing the same woman- Julie of the ample breast and tiny waistline, the gorgeous smile and delightful fragrance. Potter claimed her as his own, yet she told Walter otherwise. Who cared? It was just a fling. There were women everywhere for the taking here at Squaw, they were easy come, easy go- one of the perks of skiing.

"YOU!" screamed Potter again. "I want your PASS!" He was referring to the laminated ID Walter wore around his neck, allowing him unrestricted access to the Squaw Valley lift system. It had cost him $475 for the winter (if purchased by August 1). It was a skier's Holy Grail, his Ticket to Ride— a status symbol. It was Walter's most cherished possession. It was what Potter had been grabbing at back there at the maze.

"Closed?" repeated Walter as Potter closed in. "Where? Whaddya mean CLOSED?"

"The West Face!" screamed Potter. "Not open yet!"

"But ahh... but I followed the bomb tracks. The bomb tracks were..."

"Not good enough. The sign up top clearly said CLOSED!"

"Sign? What sign?" If there had been a closed sign up there, it was buried under new snow. Maybe there was one, but Walter had blazed right by. Visibility was near-zero up top. If he'd seen a closed sign on the way to the West Face, he would have bailed for the Chute 75 instead and been quite happy.

"I WANT YOUR PASS!" exploded Potter. He lunged once again, aiming for the string around Walter's neck where the pass hung. There was nothing Walter could do to protect himself that would not just dig his hole deeper. He dropped a glove to the snow and unzipped his parka. Like a captured prisoner surrendering his weapon, Walter handed over the pass. It was April, the season was mostly over. But KT beckoned, as did Lori... Lori?

Walter glanced up to the chair where Lori looked aghast and just shrugged her shoulders. She turned away from Walter then, as though to separate herself from the misfit, the exile. Her golden ponytail was covered in snow. Walter didn't blame her, he felt about as welcome as a dead polecat in a flower shop. "Yer outta here!" roared Potter again. He had fully regained his wind, if not his dignity. He grabbed Walter by the arm and shoved him brusquely towards the Ski Patrol shack. Even now reinforcements were arriving, hustling over to see what the boss was all shook up about.

"Jesus," protested Walter. "You don't hafta..."

"SHUT UP!" said Potter. "Yer OUTTA here!"

The incident at the KT chair led to only a week of suspension for Walter. If he were found on Squaw Valley property during his exile, he would be arrested and punished for trespass. This was actually a lenient sentence—a reprieve of sorts. There were grounds for Squaw to banish an offender of this sort for life. Potter had been under a certain peer pressure from mutual friends, who couldn't believe that Jimmy would actually exile Walter, a fellow ski-bum after all, from the love of his life. But a week later Potter had capitulated, called Walter into his office, and laid down The Law. He told Walter that he had reconsidered his permanent expulsion from the slopes of Squaw Valley, but would settle for permanent probation. "If I catch you out-of-bounds or skiing closed terrain... If I catch you skiing too fast (huh?), if I have any complaints about you at all... I won't hesitate to call the authorities." By that time everything had changed however; Walter was no longer interested in skiing, something wonderful had changed it all.

During his banishment Walter had taken a hike up to Mt. Talac to ski the Cross, and then on to Lassen Peak. He had climbed them both and laid down his tracks with other backcountry types. They had all been impressed that Walter was in lift-chair exile, offering up tasty doobies at the news, assuring him that there was still Life-After-Lifts.

And then on the journey home, a wonderful thing happened. Walter was riding with Captain Kurt in his VW microbus. They puffed a reefer and rocked down the highway. Spring had returned to the Sierra and Walter was anxious to return to Squaw. It was all fun, this backcountry stuff, but the lift-serviced terrain was just too good. Instead of one run per day and then a lengthy hike back up, a guy could get a dozen runs in a morning and still be fresh.

But, "Check it out," said the Captain as they drove along. He pointed out the window. "Some glidehead just launched." There was a mountain out the window to starboard and Kurt was pointing at it, but Walter saw nothing of interest.

"Launched?" he asked.

"Yeah launched," said Kurt. "A hang glider. See him? He's just turning above those towers." There were towers atop the peak all right, but Walter still couldn't see anything. "Looks like he's hooked it," continued the Captain with a hoot.

"Where? Who? What?" asked Walter again, confused. "Hooked what?"

"A thermal," stated Kurt as he wheeled the bus over to the side of the road and applied the brakes. It was the first time Walter'd ever heard the word not describing underwear. Walter had never heard of a 'thermal' before, but it was about to change his life, to change everything. What was it... some kind of... Long John?

"I'll show you," and they jumped from the bus and looked towards the peak towering above. It was a pivotal moment in Walter's life, though he didn't understand quite yet. At first, Walter saw only empty sky. Whatever he was looking for, he was not expecting a tiny speck. But finally the wing turned just right and an aluminum tube glinted, reflecting sunlight. A flash appeared from the sky above the peak and suddenly Walter spotted what Kurt had already seen. It was a tiny dot all right, but how was this? How could it be? By all appearances, he's ABOVE THE PEAK?! How could that be? Ain't it just a HANG GLIDER?

The Captain was delighted. "He's crankin'!" he said with glee. "He's bankin'," he yelled. "HOOK IT!" he hollered. "Sky out!" and "WahOOO!" The glider was miles away, a tiny dot in the sky. There was no way the occupant could have heard the Captain's gleeful imperative of course, but Kurt was obviously excited, and the wing was obviously above the peak. In fact, it appeared to be climbing ever higher. Walter was speechless.

Heretofore, he had only seen hang gliders go down. That was what they did, he thought. But this! This was something... entirely different. "What are we waiting for," he inquired of Kurt. "Let's go on up there."

"You kiddin'?" said the Captain. "I don't have my glider."

"You've got one of those?" questioned Walter.

"Sure do," said Kurt. "I've got a Moyes Maxi. Fly it every chance I get."

"Does it do THAT?" asked Walter, pointing.

"Do what?" replied Kurt with a grin.

"Does it go... UP? Like that?" queried Walter making big circles with his hand. "Big circles like that?" The glider was making turn after turn and climbing. For Chrissake, it was climbing, and appeared to be headed towards a puff-ball cloud that had formed above the peak.

"Hell yes it goes up!" said Kurt, incensed. "That's what flying is all about."

"It is?" asked Walter dumbly. "Then let's go do it!" He had seen enough to know he wanted to see more, to see it all. To see it all from up there. He wanted to see it all and do it all UP THERE.

They looked back into the sky. The glider had climbed well above the peak and was gliding over the back, disappearing into the sky. Walter was stunned, dumbfounded. Where had he been, all these years? Skiing?

Skiing?

Next day at noon they were back at Peavine Mountain, outside of Reno, Nevada, and this time there was a long skinny bag tied securely atop the van. Walter had never been up the long washboard road to the peak. But even as a skier the vertical here impressed him, and the vista spread out below. He watched as the Captain off-loaded the bag, opened his wings and inserted battens in the sail.

The previous night he had been unable to rest, his slumbers filled with dreams about what he had seen, dreams that awakened him in a cold sweat, dreams of his feet leaving the mountain cliff as always, but this time... not coming down. Never again! For the first time since his banishment, he thought not about his exile from Squaw Valley, of his Shame and the futility of Life. He could think only of what he had seen in the distance, of what Cap'n Kurt had said:

"That's what flying is all about!"

When he had awaken yesterday, Walter had no idea that he would find himself unable to sleep that night, for a sensational burning desire to FLY. But that was all it took.

Soon, Kurt was all set-up, had completed a pre-flight inspection of his equipment and was ready to launch. He moved the glider to the edge of a natural slope ramp, had Walter hold the nose while he clipped in and gave himself a final hang-check, and then lifted and steadied the wing. Suddenly, he hollered, "CLEAR!" and when Walter scurried out of his way, he charged down the launch slope. His feet left the Earth with a puff of dust and he carved a graceful arc back into the sky. Moments later he began to climb in the thermal currents in front of launch. Walter had heard the word, now he was seeing it with his own eyes. Beholding it! Witnessing it! Standing atop a mountain and feeling it for the very first time... A thermal in his face... Out of the blue, it was obvious...

Thermal!

Thermal!

Thermal!

Immediately, Captain Kurt turned back towards launch and began to circle. Two circles later and he was over launch, directly above Walter's head. Casually, he flashed him the hippie high-sign. Walter could hear the wing slicing through the azure sky: wwwSSSSSHHHHHSSSwww A dozen more mesmerizing circles and Captain Kurt was beginning to get small. Walter lay down on the gravel atop the peak. This way he could look up, relax, and study the spectacle. A red-tail hawk glided in to the rising air with the strange flyer and the two danced, wingtip-to-wingtip, into the sky. The hawk screamed at the glidehead, "KREEE!"

Captain Kurt climbed, and climbed some more until he was just a tiny speck in the sky. Finally, he made another turn, became a tiny dot for a moment, and when Walter blinked he disappeared!

Again, Walter was stunned. What had he been doing all his life? SKIING! Trying to get air off cliffs and cornices? This...

this was air! THIS was AIR! THIS was BIG! This was BIG AIR! The day would change Walter's life forever. He would never, could never, be the same. Life had a new focus, a new flavor, and a new urgency.

Walter was going to fly.

Gordon Stitt bails off Slide Mountain

Fly-on-The-Wall or,
Slide Mountain Hubris

Extreme pucker factor gripped Walter as he watched Dougal turn downwind and blaze into the ski bowl for a landing. He made it look so... easy. Walter watched from above as Dougal lined up his landing and stuffed the bar at the hill. He was diving, almost straight down, at a mountainside. There is nothing about this in the hang gliding textbook, thought Walter, no guidance for this insanity. He could see Dougal's streaking shadow come flying up the slope to meet him just as the wing made an abrupt pitch-up and began skimming up the snow-covered slope at a high rate of speed. Just watching sent an involuntary chill along Walter's spine.

But he didn't dare blink now, and as he continued to circle over the Slide Mountain ski area parking lot he craned his neck to watch what happened next: it was as though Dougal simply dropped his feet out of the harness and began skiing as he flared... up the slope! Walter could plainly see, even from his moving point-of-view, that Dougal had made a perfect landing.

Without even stopping now, Dougal swung the wing about and started slipping and sliding and walking his way back down the snowy ski slope where he could carry the wing back to launch, and his truck. They were on the east slope of Slide Mountain, three thousand feet above Washoe Valley and sixteen hundred feet below the peak. It was a soarable day and several flyers rode the thermals that rolled up past launch, but Dougal was the first of the day to bail for the ski bowl.

Could he- Walter, do the same? Was he pilot enough, man enough, crazy enough? What was the word he had learned just the other day, something the Sky Gods allegedly abhorred... ah yes, *hubris*, that was it! Did he have the hubris? Did he have the hubris and the balls, to dive on in there like Dougal had done? Because that was what it was going to take, hubris and balls. It was said that the Sky Gods abhorred hubris, but...

Yes! By God, he could!

In fact, he NEEDED to; it was time to get to work, to get to his job. If he didn't make a move soon he would certainly be late. If he was lucky enough to climb over the mountain and land in the meadow, pack up quickly, and hitch a ride he would probably be late. If he sunk-out all the way to Washoe Valley below and had to hitch-hike up from there, then he was sure to be late. So...

Walter pointed the wing over to just the same spot as he'd seen Dougal begin his dive and he stuffed the bar. Blazed in! Doing EXACTLY as the book (How To Hang Glide) said: NEVER Past the point-of-no-return, too late to turn back now, his balls puckered up for better or for worse, Walter was headed in for a Fly-On-The-Wall, his first one ever.

Get the stretcher!
Dial nine one one!
Call the ambulance!
Here I come!
AAAHHHHAAAA!

Aviation had been born, by most accounts anyway, in 1904 when the Wright Brothers made their initial powered flights in a tiny airplane. In the subsequent eighty years of aviation history, certainly many people had crashed into mountains. In fact the Federal Aviation Administration, in all their wisdom, had even given this catastrophe a moniker, turning it into folly. They call it "controlled flight into terrain".

Little did they know. Controlled flight into terrain, indeed...

Usually, such a blunder resulted in tragedy and widespread wreckage. Search and rescue teams and volunteer aviators would be called out and the hunt begun, often lasting for days, weeks or months. In high alpine terrain like here in the Sierra Nevada the crash site might quickly be buried in fresh snow and never seen until spring, if at all. In the eighty-some odd years since flight had come to humanity, very few humans had landed on a mountainside and lived to tell about it and then walked away. It was the territory of birds alone. Few had even considered the idea. Yet, here goes Walter, wings level and nose stuffed to his knees, straining his arms to wring out all the airspeed, diving, diving. Watching the snow bowl looming up to swallow him.

"WAAAHHHHAAAA!"

According to the text of Hang Gliding 101, there are a few things one must never do while hang gliding. Among the top few sins one must never contemplate while hang gliding are:

1) flying too close to the hill, 2) flying downwind close to the hill and 3) flying close to stall, downwind, next to the hill. Well, Walter was about to attempt all three at once, just as he had watched Dougal do. After all, if he hoped to land on the hill, he would definitely need to do just that: fly downwind, fly close, and fly slow. But Dougal had explained the trick to him:

"Come blazing in so hot that there's just no chance to stall," he enthused. "Round-out big to fly up the hill. Then quickly, quicker than you ever have before, FLARE! HARD!"

It would be quite impossible to land going down the hill, as the wing's glideslope was shallower than the ski hill itself, you just can't get stopped trying to land going down a hill. Likewise, any attempt to land across the hill would lead to a tip dragging the ground and a maneuver known amongst flyers as a "ground loop", ouch!

When done properly, with a high airspeed on approach and a crisp flare up a steep slope like the Slide Mountain ski bowl, the ground comes up to meet your flare and a crash is averted. Nonetheless the "fly-on-the-wall" landing was, at Slide Mountain anyway, a "Locals Only" trick. Maybe "just plain nuts" was a better description, a move seldom contemplated by flyers in general: controlled flight into terrain.

It is a trick best practised on deep snow, for obvious reasons, and today there was a good ten feet of sloppy spring mashed-potato-type snow left over from winter, to cushion any newbie miscalculations; only a few rocks poked through and the ski lifts had been closed for weeks- there would be no skiers to worry about.

Well, Walter was a local. This was his second spring of flying at Slide on a regular basis. He had seen this craziness performed enough to believe in himself. It was time.

Two visiting pilots were setting up on launch, hurriedly stuffing battens and glancing up at the show overhead, as several colorful wings made graceful circles above. They were in a big hurry to join the fun. Their attention was diverted to the ski bowl when Dougal bailed: he let out a wild scream...

"WAHOOO!"

"Holy shit, is that guy all right?" The visitors were unfamiliar with the fly-on-the-wall landing. They had been flying for some years but never seen or even considered such a move. They dropped what they were doing and sprinted a short distance up the road to see the grim results. Instead, they saw Dougal happily carrying his WhiteHawk down the hill, slipping and sliding through the wet snow as he went.

"Shit!" declared the visitors. "Did you see that?"

"Crazy, man!"

Just then Walter gave a holler too. Or maybe a squeak better fit the description. A sound anyway, a feeble whimper of effort, resolve and/or panic slipped through Walter's lips and caught their attention. Maybe it was only just a pathetic grunt of effort, but the flyers stood transfixed as Walter followed Dougal's lead with a reckless near-vertical dive at the ground.

The wind, or rather his airspeed, was a roar in his ears. One thought suddenly emerged as he blazed towards disaster, one glimmer of Salvation that grew quickly and began to give him a bit of confidence now: snow.

Snow.

Snow!

Snow is all around me!

Snow will be my salvation!

Walter was a skier after all, had been throwing himself off cliffs since his early youthful delinquency. He had performed many face-plants in the snow. This particular snow was on the verge of melting, even though it was about ten feet deep. It was mashed potatoes, it was Cream o' Wheat.

Suddenly, Walter began to feel better about his situation. And suddenly was good. Suddenly, after all, was what this landing was all about: things were happening suddenly. Suddenly, Walter was approaching the slope, grunting, diving, blazing.

Suddenly, he flared up the hill.

Suddenly, the slope was flashing past.

Suddenly, he stuck out his feet and...

SUDDENLY, he was skiing. A splash of spud spray smacked Walter in the face and then suddenly...

HE WAS STOPPED!

"WaHOOO!" Walter had done it and it was GREAT! "WahOOO, I did it!" he bellowed.

Without the roaring airspeed there was a sudden welcome silence. The sweet mountain air was warm with springtime, redolent of the smell of mountain pines. His heart played a wild percussion while the songbirds chirped a pleasant melody. He plunked the wing down and wiped the snow off his face and the sweat off his brow. He dug up a handful of corn snow and slaked his thirst- his throat suddenly parched. "WahOOO!" he hollered again. He unclipped from the wing and stepped out from under; it was strange to be standing under the ski lift that he was so used to flying over. Adrenaline rushed through his brain as he looked back down the slope where Dougal had set down his wing, and watched as his friend gave him a two-fingered high sign salute. Except for his pulse and his breathing, the whole world was suddenly so... quiet.

"Awesome dude!" yelled Dougal.

Walter had just become a member of the "Locals Only" club: Fly-On-The-Wall at Slide Mountain, he had landed in the territory of birds. Life was great, and there was plenty of time to get to work.

That spring Walter and the Slide Mountain Boys made many ski-bowl uphill fly-on-the-wall landings in the snow. Gradually of course, the enormous snowfield became scattered snow patches. Then just an isolated few blotches, brown with dirt and weary of the sun. Soon there was but one scruffy patch all alone, masquerading as dust, with several sitzmarks from landings past. One afternoon Walter watched from above as Dougal and then his brother Terry make perfect landings on the last measly little bit of snow. When Walter blazed in he missed it by a mile, but landed ge ntly amid gravel and rocks anyway.

Summer had come for the Slide Mountain boys.

Slide Mt. ski bowl landing

Land here

Launch here

A Gringo Makes The Earth Quake or, Bad Day At Puerto Peñasco

The tallest structure on Cholla Beach lay in ruins upon the sand. The tallest structure in all of Rocky Point, Mexico perhaps, an antenna serving as the primary communications link for a rickety palapa shack selling maríscos and cervesa, and which even now should be receiving a Saturday afternoon football game from up north in 'Gringolandia', had been suddenly ripped off the roof and sent crashing to the beach.

Walter and Dan approached the scene as casually as possible, just two innocent gringos out for a pleasant seaside stroll. The owner of the seafood shack strode woefully back and forth on the sand, clutching at his sombrero and muttering imprecations towards the Heavens. Periodically, he prostrated himself in the sand and crossed himself, genuflecting as is the Catholic way. His señora, meanwhile, sat Indian-style in the sand and clutched her children to her breast. She too exhorted her God, but with a strong and mournful wail, one loud enough to be heard well down the beach, and which was also causing three of her four children to join in. They all moaned loudly as she rocked back and forth on the sand.

Walter, being the linguist of the two, approached purposefully and asked the question: "Que paso, señor?" he inquired. *What happened, sir?*

The señor paused long enough to face the gringos. "Terremoto, terremoto!" he exclaimed. *Earthquake, earthquake!* "No lo sentiste?" he inquired. *Didn't you feel it?* "TERREMOTO!" He clutched Walter by the shirt and pulled the big gringo towards himself with surprising strength. Walter could smell his BO and foul breath. He reminded himself never to return here for Cholla Bay ostiónes. "Terremoto!" cried the old señor again. He held his hands to his head now, and returned to his Heavenly entreaties.

Brad's really done it this time," said Dan as they surveyed the damage while moving on.

"Leave it to Brad," said Walter. "The only gringo I know who can cause an earthquake."

"Is that what the ol' guy was saying?" laughed Dan.

"He was pretty shook up, so to speak. Appears God sent an earthquake to him, personally." Another gringo, a biker type, leaning against the bar at Maríscos Cholla Bay. He sucked at a beer and shook his head at the gringos.

"Damndest thing I ever did see!" he said.

"Uh... what's that?" asked Walter innocently.

"Man I was just leaning here on the bar drinkin' this beer and watchin' the Steelers kick ass on the Broncos. All of a sudden this place starts a shakin' like I never!" The biker shook his head. "Friggin' place nearly came off the sand. Then the antenna crashed over there. Looked like someone THREW it there fer Chrissake. Shit HOWDY!" he said. "I never!"

Walter shook his head in agreement. "Strange indeed," he agreed.

"Shoot!" said the biker. "You tellin' me?"

Departing the shack, the two flyers continued up the beach in search of the string, a piece of one-sixteenth-inch Kevlar towline specifically, about three thousand feet long. It had passed through here about ten minutes ago, and caused a good deal of damage along the way, including the downing of the antenna. It had to be found, or the weekend would be lost.

"Nobody will believe me when I say I was there the day that Brad caused an earthquake." remarked Dan.

"Only those of us who know him will believe," replied Walter sagely. "But fer cryin' out loud, what was he thinkin'?"

Brad crabbed his glider into the wind and hauled the towline out over the waves lapping the shore at Cholla Bay. This was behavior that would be frowned upon if done by any other pilot on a tow. But it was Brad's string after all. It was his tow truck and tow rig too for that matter. If he wanted to risk a flight in that direction, then no one could stop him.

But there were certainly better places to drop a towline. Just down wind of the tow road for example, where the glider drifted naturally due to the onshore breeze, was about ten square miles of barren saline scrub flats and scorched earth where there were no humans and nothing grew more than a foot tall. It was the natural place, the obvious place to drop a towline, where nothing could entangle the retrieval and no one might be endangered by thousand-pound string. This stuff was strong enough to haul in a sailfish, which was its standard purpose. Wrap it around someone's neck and pull it hard enough, and it could cause a clean decapitation.

But Brad had spotted a couple of gringa chicks sunning themselves on the beach in front of the row of motorhomes and campers, like fragrant greasy iguanas. They were clad in skimpy string bikinis and they glistened with suntan oil. Brad claimed to know them from somewhere, said they were hosebags looking for some hot gringos. The sight of bulging mons Venus and décolletage, the pheromone smell of fresh female flesh, was just too tempting for Brad. So he hauled the towline out over the beach where he could make a spectacle of himself and impress the girls with his flying skills, the daring aviator.

Hey there girls!

Brad had a nice tow going, he pulled about three thousand feet of line off the payout winch while climbing out to altitude. But then he dropped the line, not over the desert scrub where it belonged, where everyone else had been dropping it, but out over the waves, where it lofted down on the gentle sea breeze to drape over the myriad vehicles pulled up to the beach. Partying gringos, motorhomes, campers, trailers, coolers, umbrellas, quads, 4X4s, three-wheelers and dirt bikes were all lined up on the beach. A couple of burros as well. It was not a wise decision to drop such a mess on such a mess. But that's exactly what Brad did. Dan and Walter watched the line fall like some demented and very skinny, almost invisible snake, falling, falling, falling from the sky. It fell and fell and wrapped itself around a dozen or more wagons and finally lay twisted over a quarter mile of beach.

"Oh shit!" exclaimed Walter.

"Chingada Brad!" agreed Dan. "If one of us'd done that we'd never hear the end of it." The tow truck had stopped, conveniently, in front of a beachside cervesaria and soon Dan leaned against the bar sucking up a chilly cervesa. The day was hot and he was working up a thirst. He watched as Walter grabbed the towline and began walking it up the beach to straighten it out for rewind.

As Walter walked, he could see the coils of rope on his one side and the straightened-out rope on his other. It was beginning to look like a long dusty chore. Then suddenly, Walter noticed the tangled towline rapidly being uncoiled in front of his eyes, as though someone, or something, were yanking on it very hard! The coils were disappearing quickly and from which direction, he was unsure. The line was impossibly thin for thousand-pound test, and the same tan color as the sand at his feet. If the coils managed to wrap around his foot and continued to spin away at this velocity, they could easily dismember him in a flash. He did a dance around the coils and jumped clear just in time: the last coil snapped tight and the line disappeared from sight.

Now Walter was pissed. He looked down the beach to where Dan stood next to the truck. Was he rewinding the rope, or what? *Thanks a whole bunch, amigo, you just nearly amputated my leg*, he thought.

But Dan too was acting strange; Walter could see he was brandishing a knife and hacking wildly behind the truck. He slashed several times at what looked to Walter, standing some hundred yards away, as thin air. Finally he stopped and looked up the beach to Walter and shrugged his shoulders. "What the FUCK?!" he hollered angrily.

Walter walked back to the truck and asked his amigo, "What the Hell you do that for?"

"Do what?" said Dan, astonished. He stood looking around as though at some mystery. "I cut the fucking line 'cause fucking brake pressure wouldn't fucking stop it! The disk started to smoke and the line was still paying out and I thought if I didn't fucking cut it, it would soon reach the end of the spool and we'd fucking lose it ALL! Whadda you mean why the Hell did I do that?" He was putting the knife back in its holster.

"You mean the line was paying OUT?" asked Walter.

"Yes the line was paying OUT, you think I'd cut it if it was on rewind?"

"Well..." Walter considered his amigo for a moment. He had thought that Dan was rewinding the rope, which was why it uncoiled so fast. The idea that it had paid-out had serious implications. "Which way did it go?" he asked.

"Beats the Hell outta me," exclaimed Dan in disgust. "It went out is all I know. Must have gone up the beach," he pointed. They both looked in that direction but saw only Brad, now lugging his glider across the sand towards them. Moments before, he had been doing graceful wingovers above the Sea of Cortez and Cholla Bay. Now he huffed and puffed under the weight of his Axis 15 and grinned from ear to ear.

"Aw Jesus H!" said Dan. They stood there as Brad approached, full of excitement and enthusiasm.

"Hey amigos!" he called. He set down the glider to catch his breath. "Let's do that again!"

"You just lost the rope Brad!"

But Brad seemed not to hear. He picked up the wing and continued on. "That was a dynamite tow. Let's do it again."

He was closer now and so Dan tried again: "Brad, read my lips goddamn it! You just lost our towline!" This was bad news indeed. It was only Thursday morning, the long Thanksgiving weekend was just beginning and all would be lost without a towline. There was nowhere to foot-launch at Rocky Point; the towline was their only link to the sky. Without it they were just a bunch of turkeys sitting around on the ground with colorful wings.

"Whatja mean... lost... the towrope?" huffed Brad. He hustled up to the pickup and hoisted the glider up on the tow platform for some more fun.

"Oh fer Chrissake Brad!" said Walter. "I don't know what you did but that damn rope nearly severed my left testicle, and then Dan had to cut it!"

"He cut the line?" asked Brad with dismay. This was expensive line: Kevlar, one-sixteenth-inch, thousand-pound-test, sells for about $11 per hundred feet. "You cut the line?" Brad asked again.

"Yes I cut the line!" hollered Dan. "I tried full brake pressure and then the brakes began to smoke but still the fuckin' line was paying out faster than I've ever seen it go. I think you'd a cut the damn thing too!" Dan was obviously agitated. Roughly $330 of line was missing.

Now the three gringos gathered around the truck and inspected the scene. Maybe a thousand feet of Kevlar remained on the spool, with a frazzled end where Dan's knife had done its work. There was enough to get a glider off the ground, but hardly enough to reach the thin cloud layer through which they'd been towing all morning. Certainly there was not enough rope for a successful weekend of towing.

"Shit!" bemoaned Walter. "What the Hell we gonna do now?"

"I guess we gotta find the rope," said Brad with a resolve only he felt. He looked each way along the beach. "Couldn't be too hard."

"Oh yea right," said Dan sarcastically. "Find the fuckin' rope!" He shook his head and walked back to lean on the bar and order up another beer. "Good fuckin' luck!" he hollared.

"It couldn't have gone too far," observed Brad. His determination and optimism came perhaps, from the fact that he, personally, had bought the line; he had the most to lose.

"How the Hell we gonna find a towline?" wondered Walter. "You can't even see it in this sand."

"Somebody must have it," observed Brad. "Wrapped around their car or something."

"Well, YOU look for it then," said Dan. "I'm staying right here to quench my thirst. God dam gringo!" Dan was pissed. He'd driven down for a weekend of partying and towing and now it appeared that the towing was out. He hadn't even had one tow. Thank God there was still beer and tequila.

"I'm goin' down the beach," muttered Brad. "Must be there somewhere." He jumped in the truck and popped the clutch. Two small boys on rusty old bicycles caught his eye and he stepped on the brake, stood out of the truck. "¡Oye amigos!" he called. *Hey friends!* The kids looked askance at the gringo; he had a loco look in his eye. Brad strode over to them with a bit of towline in his hand. "Hey Walter," he called. "How do you say 'reward'?"

"Recompensa," said Walter.

"¿Recompensa?" confirmed Brad. He turned back to the two chavos, and held out a bit of the towline for inspection. It was show-and-tell time on Cholla beach. "¡Recompensa!" he said. The children looked skeptically at the gringo and between themselves. "Walter! Help me!" insisted Brad. Walter strode over to help. "Explain to them that I'll give them a reward for the rest of this line," insisted Brad.

"Do you kids speak English?" asked Walter. Silently, they both nodded yes. "You tell 'em," said Walter.

"You lost some rope?" said one child. He spoke with only a slight Mexican accent.

"Yes," said Brad. "About a kilometer." The children spoke briefly to each other in Español, and turned back to Brad.

"Does this mean you won't be flying the kites?" asked one.

"¡Sí!" said Brad. "At least until we find it. It's gotta be around here somewhere. You kids find it and I'll give you a nice reward." He walked back to the truck. "You coming?" he asked Walter. "Or you just gonna stand there?"

Brad and Walter drove slowly along the beach, observing a path of chaos and destruction telling them they were heading in the right direction. Lawn chairs lay scattered about and a plastic table with umbrella was upside down in the back of a pickup. A couple of fancy dirt bikes lay one on the other in the sand and someone's clothesline was draped on the ground. A satellite dish was hanging over the roof of a camper. Someone yelled as they drove by. "...rope... it was a dammed rope I swear! A... a piece of STRING! I saw it for a moment and then... then all Hell broke loose!"

The gringos concluded that some unsuspecting soul must have been driving down Cholla beach when the towline fell on their vehicle and they didn't realize it, it was quite invisible after all. They had then dragged the line along, draped as it was over the rest of the campers.

"Must have something to do with them damned hang gliders," came another voice.

"Nothing is ever safe with them around!"

Brad and Walter looked at each other. This was getting ugly. "Let's go the other direction," suggested Walter. "I don't like the looks of this." There was a child crying hysterically in one of the campers somewhere, and other shouts too. If these people caught on that they'd been victims of Brad's carelessness, it might get worse. Walter had a vision of Brad behind Mexican bars, in the local *carcel*. Maybe that was where he belonged anyway. At least that way, if they ever did find the towline, Brad would be where he could cause no more problems.

"Nahh!" said Brad, returning to the search. "Gotta be out there somewhere. I think we're headed in the right direction."

"So you go look," replied Walter. "Somebody might be dead out there too! Missin' their left testicle, or maybe their head!" He opened the door handle and put out a foot.

"OK, OK!" agreed Brad, reluctantly. "Let's go the other direction first. Make sure it's not up there. Somewhere, somebody has that rope. They're no doubt wondering where it came from."

"Yea... it fell from the sky," returned Walter. "The Rope-From-Heaven. You go find it, I'm staying here with Dan." Brad was dismayed, his amigos had forsaken him. He drove slowly up the beach searching for his towline.

Dan and Walter quenched their thirst with a couple of cold cervesas. There would be no more flying today- maybe not all weekend. If such was the case, they agreed to leave Mexico pronto and drive back to Arizona where they could at least huck themselves off a cliff, and get some badly-needed airtime. Thirst quenched, they walked on down the beach for some delicious oysters. That was when they discovered that an earthquake had struck Maríscos Cholla Bay. The Gods had sent a terremoto to a hard-working Mexican family and their humble seafood stand. The Gods were a cruel and indifferent bunch.

After that brief encounter, the two gringos continued up the beach as though they had no insight into the disaster. But it was all too obvious they were on the right track. "Those poor folks are really distressed," observed Dan.

"They probably never saw that rope, just felt the effect," replied Walter. "Musta been wrapped around that place or something. Musta really shook it to bring down that antenna." They could see the pole and receiver smashed in the sand. It actually lay some meters away from the palapa, separated from the building as though it really had been tossed there.

"Oh, shit!" said Dan. "I hope they don't figure out who caused this. If we ever find that rope we'll have to stand that antenna back up and tie it off."

"Look up ahead," said Walter as he pointed up the beach. The two small boys to whom Brad had offered the reward were pedaling towards them on their bikes. One of them clenched a paper bag in his hand. They made a beeline for the gringos.

"¡Hola amigos!"

"Hola señores," said the bigger of the two. "Where is the other gringo?"

"Did you find the rope?" asked Walter. The children looked at each other as though seeking each other's approval, then nodded at the two gringos.

"¡Bueno!" said Walter holding out his hand. "Da me lo," he demanded. *Give it to me.*

"We get a recompensa señor," said one child. "Remember?" They were holding the goods, but they weren't about to surrender them without fair compensation. No fools these little chavos.

"OK," said Walter. "¡Vamanos!" Together, they started down the beach to find Brad.

The kids had indeed found the towrope. It was wadded up in a ball about the size of a casaba melon and stuffed into the brown paper grocery bag, three or four thousand feet of it in a tangled mess. Brad was gleeful, he paid the kids twenty pesos each and they went happily on their way. Before they left, they agreed that, for another twenty pesos, they would return at moonrise to help with the untangling. That would be a monumental chore, especially if Brad had any hope of completing the job by sunrise and salvaging the flying trip. There was a full moon scheduled for tonight, however. If the gringos were to succeed, they would need to get some dinner and replenish their beverages. It was agreed to dine at La Cantina and then return to begin the daunting task.

Walter and Dan arrived at dinner first, and ordered up a pitcher of margaritas on-the-rocks. It would be a long night. They pounded a couple of the refreshing sweet-and-sour Tequila beverages and enjoyed the sunset. A jukebox wailed a Mexican polka:

¡Renalda, Renalda, quitate tu minifalda!
¡Renalda, Renalda, take off your mini-skirt!

Brad was late when Dan spotted his truck bouncing down the rutted Peñasco street, in a cloud of dust. The gringos had already ordered another pitcher of margaritas 'rocas' and dinner, as well. "What the Hell is he up to, now?" he pondered. Walter followed Dan's gaze to see Brad, standing in the back of his own pickup truck while another gringo flyer did the driving. Brad was gripping the glider rack with one hand and an enormous gaudy sombrero with the other. Perched atop his head and flopping in the wind, it looked to have about a six-foot wingspan. A fabulous Mexican creation, it was festooned with silver braiding and tassels, tiny reflector mirrors that dangled all about, and large lettering on the brim which declared: ¡VIVA MEXICO!

The truck lurched to a stop in front of La Cantina and the ocean breeze washed the dust into the dining room. Brad jumped out, one hand still holding the sombrero atop his head. "¡Amigos!" he grinned.

"What the Hell...?" started Dan. Brad joined them at the table and looked out from under his new headgear, which was quite outrageous. It was even gaudier on closer inspection, it had a towering crown and, as hats go, it must have weighed a great deal. It was made of some wild purple fabric with elaborate gold piping and looked as though it was made to last. Not yer basic cheap sombrero. "What the Hell you gonna do with THAT?" asked Dan.

"THIS?" said Brad. "This?" He pointed to the sombrero sitting on his head as if there were some doubt and gave a look like he was surprised by the query. "This is our new recovery system," he explained matter-of-factly.

As a matter of fact, the day's misadventure with the rope was in large part the result of Brad having left his towline recovery system at home. With a small parachute attached to the end of the towline, it could be 'flown' back on to the spool and never touch the ground, at least in theory anyway. If Brad had released the towline over the beach with a small drag 'chute deployed on his end, the line might have floated downwind with the breeze and never caused such havoc. The practice still had a few bugs but without the recovery system, the kind of troubles they'd experienced today, although usually without such disastrous results, were likely to happen. But as usual Dan and Walter did not follow Brad's logic.

"Recovery system?" they asked in unison.

"Yeah," said Brad. "Recovery system." He happily sucked at a margarita while the other gringos remained unenlightened.

"Recovery system," repeated Dan. "What the Hell are you talking about recovery system?"

"We need a recovery system, right?" Brad pointed out. "Now we've got one."

"Well I DON'T KNOW," said Dan. "It looks more like a silly hat to me. The way YOU fly, we'll need a miracle. Why the Hell did you drop the line over the campers, anyway?" he demanded. But the words went in one ear and out the other. Brad was lost in thought.

"Should be a good night to untangle string," he noted pointing at the sky. "Full moon. Tequila."

"Roll out!" ordered Walter. Dan eased off the clutch. "Speed!" demanded Walter. The truck accelerated to flight speed. "Release!" It would be Walter's final command, and Brad released the wing. The glider popped off the truck and pitched towards the sky, bringing Walter along with it. The towheads were back in business.

After spending most of the night trying, they had eventually succeeded in untangling the towrope and getting it wound back on the spool where it belonged, getting fairly snockered in their effort. The next morning had dawned clear with light winds, and now Walter pushed the nose up and sped for the cloud layer that had formed again over Cholla beach. "Wahooo!" he hollered.

At seventeen hundred feet, he popped into the thin layer of clouds. Meanwhile, back on the ground, Dan monitored the airspeed on the truck. With the airspeed indicator mounted on the glider rack, he could accelerate or decelerate, keeping Walter's speed atop the string more or less constant. Brad, standing in the back of the truck, monitored line tension and stood ready to terminate the tow, should anything go amiss. Walter flew happily along and pierced the cloudbank, popping through the top and breaking into bright sunlight; the cloudbank was only a hundred feet thick or so. Looking about, Walter could admire the Sea of Cortez in one direction and the Sonora Desert in the other. Looking straight down however, Walter saw the thin Kevlar towline disappearing into the cloud below. Otherwise, nothing!

This is so awesome, he thought, *just flying along up here on the end of a string. Incredible!* Looking off his larboard wing Walter was delighted to see a pelican flying along with him; the giant bird was laboring along in a stately manner, but obviously expending lots of energy. The flying gringo could almost hear the bird panting, and he wondered what business the pelican had up here above the clouds. For Walter, the experience was nearly effortless.

In the truck, now about eighteen hundred feet below, Brad grabbed for his giant purple sombrero. He had fastened one end of a three-foot section of towline to the crown of the gaudy headgear, and a 'quick link' to the other. Now, he reached up to the towline, which stood up in an unlikely arc towards the sky, and hooked this link to the line. He tossed the sombrero into the airstream and stood back to admire his work.

The sombrero sailed skyward, doing a loco dance towards the Heavens. It must have looked very bizarre indeed to a bystander; it collapsed its wings from the drag of the rushing airspeed and slowed its climb up the string for a moment, and then the wings spread again as the drag decreased and the airflow would grab it again and send it screaming back skyward, where it would collapse upon itself yet again to repeat the cycle. Each cycle, the demented hat would gain about a hundred feet, climbing the invisible line. Any innocent bystander down below, would have to think... *hallucination!* Sombreros just don't behave like that.

Up above the clouds, Walter was pondering when to release himself from the towline. He could not see the end of the tow road through the clouds, but was familiar enough with Cholla Beach to guess its location. Another thirty seconds or so and he would have to release, when the beach tow road ended and the tow truck came to a stop. Meanwhile, he just reveled in his location, far above a cloudbank over the Sea of Cortez, cruising along with a bird and being held aloft by a string... It seemed quite impossible.

Suddenly, Brad's loco sombrero punched through the cloud, climbing rapidly at Walter like a sombrero should not. It collapsed and hung suspended for a moment, then sprung back and resumed its bizarre ascent. It startled Walter into inaction, he froze atop his perch.

What the chingada?

Brad's sombrero?

Brad's recovery system!

What if it hits me?

Mierda!

These and other disturbing thoughts possessed the gringo as he reached for the release to free himself from the string, but too late! The sombrero came to the knot stop Brad had fashioned into the towline, and just kept going. The knot ripped the crown from the hat and it smacked Walter in the face, then slid past him and disappeared somewhere to stern. Walter popped the release anyway, and turned a one-eighty, soon enough to glimpse the crazy sombrero tumbling towards the clouds below, down where sombreros rightfully reside. The sombrero punched into the cloud and disappeared from whence it came.

It was just another Brad insanity, but the loco gringos were back in business in the sky above Cholla Bay.

Ponderosa Safety Meeting or, Rescue in the High Sierra

Rowdy Roy wrings it out.

"**S**AFETY MEETING!" came the call. It was the Glide Mountain Rally Cry, and it stopped Dougal in his tracks. Dougal, as it happened, was riding past the Safety Wagon on his skateboard- doing a handstand. Hearing the Rally Cry, he gave his powerful arms a quick pump and sprung lightly to his feet, still holding the board with one hand, a silly grin on his face. His dismount had landed him conveniently next to his brother Terry's pickup, from where the Rally Cry had originated.

"Safety meeting!"

Clearly, brother Terry was already getting safe, puffing on the Big Fat One, the Safety Materials, so Dougal reiterated for benefit of the gathering:"SAFETY!" he hollered...

"SAFETY MEETING!"

It was the summer of 1981 and Walter was just glad these guys would have him, would accept him among them, would consider him capable of "hanging", both figuratively and quite literally, and would even pass him the joint if he but reached out a hand. Newbie that he was- he still wanted to be "safe".

"SAFETYYYY!" the call went echoing on down the set-up area, was picked-up and passed-on, inviting all glideheads to partake, yet hopefully leaving the innocent tourists, the "Wuffos" quite ignorant. It just wouldn't do to have some Groundogon show up at the Washoe County Sheriffs' substation down in Steamboat with a report of stoned Glideheads hucking themselves off the cliff at Glide Mountain. This was Nevada after all, where the pot laws were quite draconian... Nothing good could come of that, and so "SAFETY MEETING!" had become the call. It was a primitive yet effective need-to-know invitation to get high. And getting high was what this gathering on the side of a mountain was all about after all. "SAFETY MEETING!" came the Rally Cry again. Meanwhile, the OUTLAWS ripped off a fabulous tune, Green Grass and High Tides Forever!

Soon a small crowd had gathered at Terry's truck- the Safety Wagon. A billowing cloud of sweet smoke roiled out the windows and doors, was caught by the thermal updraft as it flowed up the launch, and disappeared high into the Wild Blue Yonder. "Hack, hack, gack!" came the commentary- these boys were getting safe.

But by the time the Safety Meeting had concluded another cry went up, a more desperate forewarning: "IT'S SWITCHING DOWN!" and then "GRAB YER GLIDERS!" The Safety Meeting had been quite successful, but this day there was to be no party in the sky above Glide Mountain. Nope, the Wind Gods were taking over and shutting down the fun. Now the flyers were scrambling, nasty ol' Mr. Southwesterly was moving across Lake Tahoe and spilling his guts over the top of Glide Mountain, then roaring downhill towards Washoe Valley and the Great Basin beyond. One and all the Glideheads began frantically pulling ribs, folding wings and zipping bags. The hang gliding on this beautiful day, at least at Glide Mountain, was over before had it begun.

It was otherwise a beautiful summer day in Tahoe however, so all was not lost. There were even some flying sites on the Tahoe side of the mountain where this same wayward wind would be blowing up, but Walter had looked them over and come to the conclusion that they were way more advanced than his newbie skills. Maybe some day, some year... The party on launch slowly broke up as everyone loaded up their wings for another place, another day.

"You gonna jump?" asked a stupid Wuffo a recent arrival. "You gonna jump?" By this time the southwesterly was howling down the mountain at a ferocious rate, a very impossible situation for hang gliding. But of course the Wuffo didn't know that, nor could he be faulted for such a dumb question. He was clueless. He was a Wuffo.

"Maybe later," replied Walter. "Maybe we'll jump later. Why don't you all come back this evening?" It was really a rotten trick to play on a Wuffo- the ol' Prevailing Wind certainly had no notion of slacking off this evening, probably not until somewhere around midnight would the wind abate at all- there would be no jumping today at Glide Mountain, no how. But, though disappointed with the first news, the Wuffo seemed buoyed by the latter, and went off grinning to explain to his little Wuffo family... "They say come back this evening, come back this evening."

Walter smiled. "Tell the Wuffos what they want to hear," was a good creed. He tied the glider securely atop his van and headed over the pass to Lake Tahoe...

Driving through Incline Village, coming up on the Ponderosa Ranch is when the incident really began. Walter was surprised to see a roadblock on the highway, and a fire truck maneuvering a ladder towards the side of the road. There was no fire though; at least Walter could see no smoke. It appeared as though the fire truck was inching the ladder towards a tall Ponderosa pine tree, but it fell short of even the lowest branches due to a rather deep ditch it spanned, which limited the ladder's reach. Walter had pulled off to the side of the road to watch the show when suddenly a voice came over loud-and-clear from a bullhorn:

"HEY YOU! STOP RIGHT THERE! YOU ARE VIOLATING A COUNTY ORDINANCE!"

For a moment Walter was confused, and thought the directive was for him. But suddenly he saw two characters who made him stop in wonder. At the same moment when Walter saw the Captain of the fire crew holding the bullhorn and pointing an accusatory finger across the street, he also saw Dougal, his flying buddy Dougal, whom he'd last seen at the Glide Mountain Safety Meeting, and who was now sprinting as fast as he could fly, across the street. Incongruously, Dougal was draped with climbing gear, a lengthy coil of perlon rope over his shoulder, his bag-o-chalk swinging from his hip and emitting tiny puffs of dust as he sprinted, and he was shod in his fancy climbing shoes. As Walter watched dumbfounded, Dougal hurtled the barriers like Edwin Moses taking the hurdles, sprung like Spiderman for big pine tree, and grabbed on to the thick bark about twenty feet below the bottom-most branch. From there he scrambled up the trunk like a squirrel on a mission. Barely gaining the first branch with a gymnastic move, Dougal hung there one-handed for a moment and then hollered back down at the rescue squad:

"SCREW YOU GUYS- THAT'S MY BUDDY ROY UP THERE!"

Now Walter was really confused. Roy was up there? Where? Walter popped the door handle and slid one foot out to the ground. He craned his neck up towards the sky and gazed up at the treetops. These particular Ponderosa pines were indeed tall, as they should be, actually within the Ponderosa Ranch parking lot as they were. Glancing back down to the lower reaches of this particular Ponderosa where even now Dougal was scampering up the tree trunk, gaining finger and toe holds in the rough bark. Walter gazed up the trunk to the very top of that stately tree where he suddenly spotted... a glider! Just a scrap of brightly colored Dacron sailcloth was all that was quite visible, but there was little doubt that a glider was caught in the top of that big ol' Ponderosa pine.

Holy shit!

"GET DOWN FROM THAT TREE BY ORDER OF THE INCLINE VILLAGE POLICE!" came the command. "GET DOWN!" But Dougal didn't even seem to hear. Finally throwing a leg over the bottom branch, he scrambled up from limb to limb and called out a command of his own:

"HANG ON ROY! I'M A COMIN'!"

Atop the towering Ponderosa pine, which was swaying in the Sierra wind, and which was firmly planted in the soil of the Ponderosa Ranch parking lot itself, was the owner of the Ponderosa Ranch himself- "Rowdy" Roy Sanderson, glidehead cowboy extraordinaire. Rowdy Roy had not been at the Glide Mountain Safety Meeting that morning, or in evidence at all atop Glide that day, but he had apparently chosen to fly the Tahoe side of the hill and found himself pinned against the mountain when the wind picked up, which had not allowed him to fly the entire distance out to a safe landing on the beach at Tahoe as planned. So he had attempted to land instead in the Ponderosa parking lot, which he could theoretically get away with and no one would mind since, well... since he owned the place.

But the Sky Gods had other ideas for Roy- they gave him a big shove disguised as a turbulent gust of wind, and deposited him about two hundred feet above the ground in the lofty crown of a Ponderosa pine. Even now, as Walter watched in horror, the wind snatched at Roy and his wing and gave them both a good shake. Roy was a strong lad however- built along the lines of a Hoss, and so he gave that treetop a big ol' bear hug, and he hung on...

"HANG ON ROY!"

"I'M HANGING!" came the reply from the piney heights.

Scampering upward like a colorful monkey, swinging recklessly from limb to limb, Dougal quickly reached the upper-most branches of that big ol' tree and found Roy, his arms in a bear hug around the trunk, his legs in a scissor lock on a nearby branch.

Roy was a strapping sort- he looked like he could hold on all day. But Dougal swung into action with his climbing rope and soon had Roy and his glider secured- tied safely off to that Ponderosa. With that, Roy was able to slide out of his harness and sit casually on an elevated perch, taking a bit of a breather. Together, the glideheads lowered the wing with Dougal's rope down to the waiting rescue squad, whose numbers had grown significantly over the past few minutes.

With that chore accomplished it was time to climb down from the heights and face the music. But... it was a beautiful Tahoe day after all, the view was quite un-obstructed, and the breeze would carry away any incriminating evidence. There was perhaps no safer place in all of Nevada to get safe.

"You got any safety materials?" inquired Roy.

Dougal fished around in his gear for a moment, came up with a big fatty, and wagged it under his nose with a mischievous grin.

"Safety meeting?" he offered.

"SHEET!" or,
Communication Breakdown, Mexico Style

Walter took a comfortable seat at the bar on the marina in lovely Plaza las Glorias. While a gentle breeze cooled the wharf, and the guests relaxed over cervesas and camarónes, he enjoyed the tranquility of the Mexico sunset- 'atardecer'. The happy hour crowd inside the bar was quite vocal and very happy, but out here on the terraza all was peacefully festive. A pelican floated over the scene, banked suddenly and flared to a landing on a nearby piling. He squawked once, folded his wings, and stared vacantly at the gringo. Walter admired the bird's flying skills; he was looking forward to tomorrow's flight.

Suddenly one of the diners called out to Walter. The señor sat several tables away from the gringo and had to speak up to be heard over the music and revelry: "Desculpe señor," he leaned as he called, "usted habla Ingles?" *Do you speak English?*

Walter sat forward in his chair. It was an unusual question, usually he was asked just the reverse- *'Do you speak Spanish?'* After a moment's consideration he realized that the reply could be much the same as always and so, "Un poquito," he answered. *A little.*

"Bueno," replied the señor. And then, "Que es la diferencia de 'cheque' y 'hoja'?" he inquired. *What's the difference between the words 'check' and 'sheet'?* The señor was dining with his two young sons and apparently teaching them a little English lesson. Quite willingly Walter attempted to explain:

"Un 'cheque' puede ser cuenta de restaurant," he said... *A check could be the bill from a restaurant.* "Tambien 'cheque' es de acuento del banco." *It might also be from your bank account.* The señor nodded expectantly, awaiting more information...

So far so good, Walter continued: "'Hoja' es sheet," said the gringo, feeling very worldly. But the señor appeared suddenly shocked, surprised.

"Mánde?" he asked pointedly. *What?*

"Sheet," said Walter again helpfully. "'Hoja' es sheet." This news was met by an unexpected scowl from the señor and some of the other diners too, who turned to look at the gringo with astonished disgust written on their faces. Walter grinned back at them, pleased to be of help. One of Walter's true joys in life was speaking Español.

The señor turned from Walter and mumbled something to his sons. They, in turn, looked from the gringo to their father as if confused. They looked again at Walter who repeated his wisdom, only louder this time, to clarify the situation, "Sheet," he declared. "SHEET!"

The señor scowled openly at Walter, other patrons looked at the gringo as though he was on fire. Confused now, he reaffirmed the words- "'Cheque' is check y 'oja' is SHEET!" he called over the marina. There were more scowls then, accompanied by many frowns. The diner nearest Walter gave him a stern look and turned away.

"Que feo el gringo," he said to no one, to everyone. *What an ugly gringo.*

It was Walter's turn to wonder now... Ugly? He was just trying to be helpful! What was the problemo? Cheque, he thought... sheet...

Sheet?

Oh no!

Suddenly Walter realized his mistake, felt about two feet tall. SHEET! Of course!

There are no short vowels in Español. The Latino tongue just cannot say 'shit', with a short vowel. It is trained for long vowels only. Any attempt to say this lowly four-letter invective would invariably result in 'sheet'. Walter had been calling one of the gross English swear words that ALL Mexicans, probably people the World over would recognize. SHEET! SHIT! In polite company! Oh no!

"Ah, señor," he stuttered, and changed his approach. "¡Hoja es un pieza de papel!" *Sheet is a piece of paper!*

But by now the señor had redirected his attention to his children. He pointed at their plates and told them to eat- pay no attention to the rude gringo. Walter considered how he might possibly repair the damage that had been done to his image, the image of all gringos really; just another ugly American, yelling curses over a polite Mexican repast.

"¡Pieza!" he spoke loudly, for all to hear. "¡Hoja es pieza!" *A sheet is a piece!* But it was too little too late, brought only more scowls and frowns, the damage had been done. Walter turned to the bartender for help, a Mexican who spoke perfect English without trace of an accent. HE must have known what Walter wanted to say.

"¡Explícale por favor!" he implored. *Explain to them!*

But the bartender deferred. He grinned at Walter and shrugged his shoulders, he was too busy to get involved. He held up his hands in universal Mexican sign language that declared: "I accept no responsibility for events past, present or future." He picked Walter's cheque up from the bar and offered it to him as though to suggest he should get out now, before more damage was done. Better luck next time amigo.

Walter looked over the delightful scene, feeling the warm burn of embarrassment. How could he ever explain his good intentions? He dug into his pocket and came up with some pesos. Leaving a tip behind with his half-empty beer bottle, he offered a lame apology to the bartender, who grinned some more at the gringo and said, "No se preocupe, señor." *Don't you worry, sir!* He scooped up the tip and turned his back on the gringo. Walter could see him still chuckling, as he turned sheepishly from the bar and strode out. He could still feel the anger from the patrons as he walked through them and out on the wharf. Even the pelican suddenly spread his wings and took off with a squawk.

Time to find another bar he decided. Better luck next time gringo.

A Taste of Valle de Bravo or, Flyers' Paradise

I have just returned from my annual flying pilgrimage to Valle de Bravo, a lovely mountain village in the Mexican highlands, in the Mexican State of Mexico.

It was an awesome trip from the moment Gordy and I stepped off the bus. We walked out of the depot gates looking for a taxi. I look one way, and I look the other. There were some cabbies lounging in their cars waiting for fares. One of them yells, "¡Oye, Kalimán!" (Kalimán is my alter ego which I enjoy in Mexico, when I wear my stupid turban). Sure enough, it was Chocho, who had been my driver some years ago in the Ford-From-Hell. It was as though he had been awaiting my return all these years. We quickly loaded our gear in Chocho's taxi, and off we went.

I am crazy about Valle de Bravo, the whole experience, which is much greater that the sum of its parts. I was a tour guide for hang glider pilots in Valle for a number of years, I like to think I was the very first such gringo. I would drive south each November with a stack of wings from Pacific Airwave, and spend the winter roaming Mexico and Guatemala. Valle was a favorite destination. I enjoy bringing pilots to Valle, to see the look of wonder on their faces, not only from the bitchin' flying, but at the village, the people, the food, the drink. If I were to title what follows here, it would have to be something like; A Taste Of Valle de Bravo, Flyer's Paradise, and subtitled: Land of Sights, Sounds and Smells.

On Day One, I flew over the pass to Buena Vista. When I landed a crowd of kids gathered as always. I was feeling very pleased with myself for having made it that far, and I told them that I had landed in this same field some years back and that a mangy dog had run out and bit me right on the ass (true). One kid seemed to find this hysterically funny. He rolled around in the dirt and held his belly as he laughed. "What's so chingada funny about THAT?" I asked.

"Era mi perro," he replied. *That was my perro.*

"So… what ever happened to that chingada perro?" I inquired.

"Se morio." *He died.*

"Let that be a lesson," I told him: "Don't Go Around Biting Gringos!"

There were many notable moments. I flew sixteen of seventeen days and only pianoed once. The day I didn't fly was a day on the Volcan de Toluca Xinantécatl, launching at 13,200 feet above sea level. Only El Gallo got off before conditions deteriorated, but he skyed-out and took some wild shots from above the crater, looking down at the twin lakes therein; Laguna Del Sol and Laguna Del Luna. Then he got lost in the clouds and landed way out, near a lovely high-mountain village called Temascaltepec.

Xinantécatl *Photo by Jim Afinowich*

Happily, El Gallo speaks Español well enough so that he was able to get a ride to the local gasolinera, where we found him drinking cervesa. He has his own adventures to recount.

The Mexicans do not use the term 'sled ride' to describe a flight with no lift as we gringos do, perhaps because there are so few sleds in Mexico. No, they have coined a term that is much more descriptive, much more fun, much more poetic, in my view: piano. This term may originate elsewhere in Latin America, for all I know. You see, it is said that at El Peñon del Diablo, there is just so much lift about three-hundred yards left of launch, that you must fly like a piano, a large, heavy, completely un-aerodynamic object, to end up in the fields down below. The Piano, in this case, is a pronoun that describes the field below.

And this is also the only time I have ever heard the noun piano, used as a verb.

"Que paso con Jorge?" *What happened to Jorge?*

"¡Se pianó!" comes the answer: *He pianoed*, verb- to fly like a large, heavy object.

I only flew like a piano once this year. The rest of the time I flew like a full-race Halcon. But even the piano experience was gratifying. It gave me an opportunity to visit the kids down there, whom I had not seen in a year, and who are ALWAYS hoping that someone will fly like a piano. They must get pretty tired of everyone skying-out, and turning into tiny specks in the sky, before disappearing completely.

On the afternoon when I pianoed, I took off my headgear, and the cry went up: "Oly, Oly... OLY!" Along came Israel, who had grown considerably in my absence, like all the rest of them. He asked where was my señorita Patricia? He asks that same question every year. I informed him, like every year, that Patricia was no longer my señorita, that she has a new gringo, and that she lives far away. The look of total gloom this news brought to Israel's face was mirrored in my own. But it only lasted a second. Israel threw off his sorrow and commenced to very efficiently organize the break-down of my Wills Wing Falcon. That chore completed nicely, ten niños all shouldered the wing and carried it towards the road.

El Peñon del Diablo, seen from casa Israel.

Some years back, one of the local pilots had informed first my friend Derrick and then myself, that we were "muy cabrón". This is a "Mexicanismo" that seems hard to figure out, for this gringo. A cabro is a goat. A cabrón, then, must be a goater. This word, when said with a smile between amigos, means one thing, yet when said with a scowl to an enamigo, means quite another. Fighting words.

Looking this word up in the dictionary, I find this: cabrón m. buck, he-goat; (fig) acquiescing cuckold

Since Derrick and I were both single gringos in the rut, and we were quite acquiescing for any and all forms of sex, we found this quite entertaining. Well, it seems this pilot had tired of paying my fee for a ride to launch. She felt that I should offer this service for free as a means of showing my appreciation to my amigos, or some such female logic I guess. I should just absorb all the expense myself. She gave me a good tongue-lashing right there, in the back of my truck. When I offered to off-load her wing from the Ford right there, and let her carry it to launch herself, it was then she called me "Muy cabrón!"

Derrick and I lived in a nice old casa with a beautiful lake view. That day when I returned from flying, Derrick and I relaxed on the terraza and I told him what she had said. Over a chilly Bohemia, Derrick and I christened our house 'Casa

Cabrónes'. We toasted to it. To this day, I try to continue the tradition.

Radio broadcast: "Donde estas, cabrón?" *Where are you, goater?*

"Estoy en la Casa Cabrónes, cabrón." *I am in Casa Goater, goater.*

Now, Flaco is king at Casa Cabrónes, and I spent my stay in my old room. ¡Viva Casa Cabrónes!

Speaking of Casa Cabrónes, I have mixed emotions about this place. It is a rather old stone house that requires intense daily upkeep. Dust is the big culprit. The floor needs a daily scrubbing, especially with all the comings and goings of a bunch of gringos who are constantly loading and unloading a stack of wings. When the maid washes off the dust, the floor tiles become treacherously slippery until the water evaporates. Meanwhile, you'll wanna wear yer helmet. She uses Pinesol, a powerful astringent, the smell of which causes my eyes to water and makes me gag.

View from Casa Cabrónes towards El Peñon

Also, it is a very noisy casa, and rings like a tuning fork at every sound within. Then there is a rooster or two outside my bedroom window and a tópe (speedbump) down in the street below. The rooster crows with pride and satisfaction each time he bangs off a piece of one of his legions of hens, and the speed bump causes constant rumblings as legions of logging/beer/coconut/cement trucks first down-shift to slow, then bang over the bump, and finally roar off gathering speed. All day and all night.

Yet, I am very fond of Casa Cabrónes too, and I look forward to my annual visit. I feel at home there. Maybe it's the address that pleases me. You see, Casa Cabrónes is located at the intersection of two impossibly steep and narrow calles called Monte Allegre and Atardecer. (Happy Mountain and Sunset Streets) More exclusive digs abound in Valle and the surrounding hills, but few have such a pleasant address.

Mexico has a radio and soap-opera hero named Kalimán, who wears a gold turban, with a saphiro on the forehead. Kalimán has a young sidekick named Solin who is always getting in a fix. Like Batman and Robin, they have been fighting the forces of evil for many years. How do I know this? Why is it important? Well... by chance, I too began wearing a gold turban, complete with a red stone, just a cheap piece of costume jewelry that I bought for Halloween some years back. But when I wore this headgear in Mexico the kids would shout, "¡Kalimán Kalimán!" The boldest of them would run up behind and tag me. Slowly— I am a slow learner- I divined the meaning of this greeting, and finally came upon a comic book about Kalimán, El Hombre Increíble.

Eventually, I developed a song and dance routine using this knowledge. I was one of the few gringos who knew this bit of Mexican trivia. I was determined to make the most of it.

Many of the villages where you land around Valle are very back-country. The people are extremely poor and backwards; they spend their time struggling to eek a living from the land. You drop in looking like something they've never seen before, you might decide to make the best of it, especially if, like me, you can't run very fast. I landed somewhere in the backcountry, amongst a rough-looking crowd of campesinos, and asked the nearest child: "Como se llama este lugar?" *How do you call this place?*

The niño replies: "Jesus Del Monte" *Jesus of the Mount.*

"Jesus del Monte?" I ask, puzzled. *This place is called Jesus of the Mount?*

I reached into my gearbag, and put on my turban. I sang them a few bars of *¡Oh, Mexico!* I grabbed three nearby rocks and juggled for them. Then I radioed our driver, hoping he could hear me over hill-and-dale: "¿Solin, Solin, me escuchas, Solin? ¡Estoy bajo en Jesus Del Monte, Jesus Del Monte! ¿Me escuchas Solin?" *Hey Solin, I'm down in Jesus of the Mount! You hear me Solin?"*

Of course, there is no Solin. And I of course, am not Kalimán. But the kids look at each other with pride and happiness. Hope springs eternal, they say. It was the day Kalimán, El Hombre Increíble, came spiraling out of the Heavens and descended on Jesus Del Monte.

Kalimán, Hombre Increíble and his amigito Solin

Soon I was offered a ride to the nearest pavement in a 'caro', which was not a car at all, as I had thought. No, this 'caro' was a 2-ton gate bed Hudson dually with a Perkins diesel. Throwing open the rear doors, my Falcon 195 fit diagonally inside the bed with inches to spare. The driver swung the gate doors closed, threw the locking-pin, and we rumbled out of the Mount in low gear. The truck was painted up fire-engine-red with ivory stripes, and draped with fragrant red and white carnations and orchids- hundreds of fresh flowers. There were shrouds that ran from atop the gate bed to the hood ornament and they, too, were heavy with flowers.

I inquire about the festive decorations and am told simply, "Va ver boda." *There will be a wedding*, an answer that just leaves me with more questions. The caro itself had its name painted on the cowcatcher bumper: Dios Me Mando it reads; *God Has Sent Me*. It was an appropriate ride for a luminary such as Kalimán, and the driver's name was appropriate, too: Salvador.

At the highway, we found a little village called Los Zaucos, and a delightful restaurante/cervesaria called Las Tres Virgenes *The Three Virgins*. I invited Salvador in for refreshment; it seemed entirely appropriate that I share a repast with a savior and three virgins. We sat roadside in Los Zaucos, sipping our chilled cervesas and waited for the retrieve, attended by a lovely señorita. I am curious to know if she be one of the noted 'tres virgenes' from hereabouts, but I'm not quite sure how to tactfully pose this question.

Suddenly, Salvador holds out his arms like he's flying. He explains that he stood watching me soaring the ridge above his shack, back and forth, gracefully, effortlessly. He says it must be special to fly like we do. I could only agree.

Meanwhile, an enormous sow pig is rooting around out back, awaiting her fate I suppose. She is joined by a pair of ferociously territorial turkey hens that you don't want to get anywhere near. There are dogs and cats lying around of course, some cattle and oxen grazing peacefully nearby. Along came a kid on a burro, with a baby burro following closely behind. I was wearing my turban, so I grabbed the radio and pretended to key it and said to the sky:

"¿Solin me escuhas, Solin me eschuas?"

The kid's eyes get very big. He gazes upward looking for Solin, lost in the blue sky and puffy cumulus. A dust devil ripped through adjacent fields, but no one noticed except me. "Siempre anda perdido, mi amigo Solin." I explain to the child. *My friend Solin is always getting lost.*

Let me now explain about Flaco and Beto: Jeff Hunt is a long drink of water, a Tall Texan. We call him Flaco (skinny), for obvious reasons. Flaco and his Mexican associate Alex Olazabal have filled the void in flying tours in Valle de Bravo since my departure from the scene a few years ago. They are exclusively hang glider pilots by the way, committed to blades. I often said that if anyone could do that job better, or cheaper, than I did back with Safari Sky Tours, they could sign me up. Now I think they are doing both and I am happy for them. They have more gliders and spares than I ever had, they have two trucks where I had one, and they have some nice digs, they have even taken over Casa Cabrónes. I have promised to help them spread the news about their tours and about the bitchin' flyin' over Valle.

Flaco's driver's name is Umberto; Beto for short. Beto is about twenty years old and very, very cool. Reflector shades, backwards ball cap, muscle shirt, baggy pantalones, a slouch, and an attitude. The cap is embroidered with the silhouettes of two shapely females, genuflecting. Here he comes now driving Flaco's Chevy Suburban.

Beto has fancied-up Flaco's truck in the past few days. He found an awesome cow skull with a nice set of longhorns. He zip-tied it to the Suburban's grill and filled the eyeholes with a set of running lights he found at a nearby refraccionéria. These lights he is able to activate with a toggle switch. To complete his modifications, Beto bought a musical klaxon;

now, at the touch of a lever, the truck would issue a loud and very reasonable facsimile of a bull in rut.

As Beto pulls into the Three Virgins Place of Eat and Drink he lays on the horn: "MoooOOOm!" And again: "MMMOOOOO!"

One of the skinny heifers grazing next to the posada perks up her head and looks about. She spots Beto and the horny Suburban just as Beto gives another strident toot:

"mmMMOOOO!"

The heifer can't believe her good luck. She perks right up and sticks up her tail and prances along the fence, looking like a teenage Farside Cow in Love. Her giant floppy ears stand up, her bony tail points at the sky, and she bats the flies away from her eyelids. She prances over to the fence, answers the call with one of her own, and looks for a way over. She has fixated on the Suburban.

But Beto has other ideas. He parks the vehicle and saunters around the truck and slouches against it, keeping guard. ¡*Pinche vaca! Don't you DARE!*

The weather and climate in Valle is worth mentioning. Valle is not at all what most gringos think of when they imagine Mexico- hot and humid, coconut groves and beaches. Valle de Bravo lies on the edge of the central Mexican highlands, at 5,500' above sea level. The climate is one of rolling mountains, tall pine tree forests, and fields of corn. The days are just hot enough to be uncomfortable for a few hours in the afternoon. At night, grab a sweater or a jacket, because it cools off nicely.

Several times this year, I heard one or another of my amigos say something like: "This is the most perfect summer day (or night) you could ever imagine in Tahoe." In the morning, the sky is usually without a cloud. By 9 or 10AM there are vague mists of thermals appearing over Cerro Gordo, soon topped with wispy cumulus. By the time we head for launch, these are usually well-defined clouds with flat bottoms. Taking the turn on the highway to launch where the imposing volcano first comes into view in the distance, we are treated to a good view of cloud base, where we get a chance to gauge the cloud heights. Is it above the volcano peak, or below?

The peak atop the crater reaches to fifteen thousand feet and more. The Spaniards called this imposing geograpy the Nevado de Toluca— *Snows of Toluca*. Before them, the Aztecs called it Xinantécatl. Some days, the cap clouds and cumulus over the Nevado looks to be around twenty thousand feet.

Zinantecatl- pucker factor extreme

There are just two seasons in tropical Mexico- wet and dry. The dry season begins around Thanksgiving and runs through Easter. By the time we got there in February, it was dry all right. In fact, after three weeks there, I began to feel like a very dried-out prune. My eyes were sunburned and raspy, my eyelids felt like sandpaper. My nose was blistered on the inside as well as the outside, despite using zinc oxide, and my throat was parched constantly. My skin was peeling in flakes large and small and I was in need of constant refreshment, yet I never felt refreshed. I made an effort to avoid the cervesa, which I have always enjoyed, in an effort to stay hydrated. Valle was high and dry, indeed.

I landed one day in an impossibly small field on the far side of the lake, which was surrounded by a chain-link fence. There were other larger fields available, but none as close to the boat dock- I would not have to drag my glider and all my gear so far. I collected style-points for greasing my landing, and took a boat home drinking caguamas...

That day, Rooster and Flaco and I flew from launch to El Peñon del Diablo, to Los Tres Reyes, to El Divisadero, a favorite triangle. When I left the Divisadero to head home, I was skyed out for sure, around twelve thousand five hundred feet. But there seemed little chance I could fly that Falcon, a very slow boat after all, all the way across the lake to somewhere reasonable to land beyond Valle. The LZ on the shore of the lake in town was under six feet of water so it was not an option, and the landowner at the next available field at Casas Viejas has informed the flyers that we are not welcome there anymore. So, I'd have to land out in some unfamiliar field somewhere, or get all the way to the Tanké de Gas— a Helluva long glide in a Falcon.

Rather than such a long and dicey glide, I started appraising instead the fields on the near side of the lake, across the lake from Valle, a few of which I've landed in before. I circled down and became aware that there was absolutely no wind sign anywhere. If there was no wind, then why not land lakeside, right next to the boat dock, a place I learned only later is called El Zarillo. It would sure simplify things for a busted-up gringo like myself, and was certain to offer style-points too. The lakeside LZ became Plan 'B'.

I circled down and circled down and looked for windsign and looked for windsign. If there were any wind at all, I wouldn't want to land lakeside. There would certainly be a lee-side rotor and maybe lee-side thermals, and the fields there were just too small for dirty, rowdy air.

But then, the lakeside also had a giant cornfield, harvested and sloping nicely uphill. Mentally, I replaced the familiar fields LZ with the cornfield LZ and kept the style points LZ as an option. I circled down and down and was drawn readily into the tiny dockside field. It was surrounded by chain-link, a 'V' shaped fence with a narrow entry, and was slightly uphill on final. From above it looked like a wedge of brown cheese that someone had bitten the tip off. I turned final and dove in *A Dogged Victim of Inexorable Fate*. (*This colorful phrase borrowed from Dan Jenkins)

Coincidentally, there was a burro staked out at the threshold of this final approach. The burro was not happy with the gringo's blazing entry into his field, but the gringo was. I dove it on down until I was just about eyeball to eyeball with the terrified critter, then blazed overhead about as flapping-fast as that Falcon would go... Flashing past I got a good look in the eye of the beast, and I saw... terror. Terror from the sky! Then I cleared the fence and greased the landing. The donkey commenced to bray and eeee-haw in protest. Ten minutes later, El Gallo turns final in a blazing Fusion. Half hour later Flaco flashes past in the Laminar ST. It was a tough day to be a donkey in El Zarillo.

El Gallo and Flaco actually landed in the field next to mine. It was marginally larger and was not surrounded by chain link. But it had one problem- a wooden fence post had been stuck in the ground right where a glider should be entering ground-effect. It was only when I'd been on base leg that I had spotted this obstacle, and had adjusted my final for the chain link field.

Rooster is overhead now, slowly circling down, checking things out from above. He keys his mic;.

El Gallo: "How about that field to the left of your field? It looks cleaner..."

Kalimán: "Which way is left?"

El Gallo: "The one next to your field."

Kalimán: "I just bought this here chilly cervesa, and I'm walking out there right now. Tell me if I have the right field, uh... the LEFT field."

Gallo: "Yeah, that's the one. How's it look? How high is that tree off to the side?"

Kalimán: "That's no tree. It's just a bush. About head-high."

Gallo: "Are there any other obstacles?" It WAS tight after all.

Kalimán: "Just this here wooden fence post I'm standing next to. It's loose, though. Let me see if I can pull it out." I shake the post and try half-heartedly to get it out. The local kids who appear at every landing in Mexico notice my efforts and gather around. I ask them whose fence post this is? They shrug shoulders and look at each other. With my turban atop my head, I command them to remove the post. They flop down in the dirt and begin to wrestle the fence post.

Kalimán: "Just stay there for a while, Rooster. I've got the kids working on it."

Gallo: "Stay here? Stay here? Whatyamean STAY HERE?"

Kalimán: "Yes, stay there. The post is very wobbly. There's a dozen kids. You will owe them all a soda pop." Rooster flattens out his turns and the kids struggle on with grunts and glee. I tell them: "Andale! Here comes Solin!" They redouble their efforts and the post springs free at last. It pops one of them in the face and he retreats in tears, with a bloody nose.

Kalimán: "There you go Rooster. Now you have a clean approach."

Later, we hired a boat back to Valle, the rest of the crew awaited us at the dock in town. We had instructed them to bring cold cervesa down to the dock, and were welcomed there like returning conquistadors. My old buddy Juan Clevenger was there. A flying fan, Clev had just come down to Mexico as an observer and photographer, and to offer up support, witticisms and astute observations. I was so glad to have him there. He took many photos too.

But El Peñon is really the star of the show. El Peñon del Diablo- The Rock of the Devil, a volcanic lava dome that protrudes from an extinct crater and dominates the view from launch. You don't actually launch from the rock itself, which is much too precipitous for any motor vehicle to scale. The top of the rock is almost a thousand feet higher than the launch, which in turn is atop a good dirt road at 7,500' MSL.

I have no explanation for why this launch has such an impressive and consistent thermal, but I have ridden this one out of there countless times. El Peñon is the kind of place where, when you arrive on launch with a truckload of gringos and a few locals, the gringos all head for launch and kick dirt, just like they are accustomed to back home. They are convinced that they will likely get skunked, just as they do back home. Meanwhile, over in the trees the locals are dragging down the sailcloth, unzipping the bags, and stuffing the battens. They KNOW they will fly. They knew that when they woke up in the mañana. Hell, they knew it last Christmas.

I am reminded of my amigo Pablo Voight standing on launch one day, it might have been his twentieth day on launch at the Peñon over the years, I don't recall. But he stood there as I walked up and he threw out his arms. "Is this place ALWAYS like this?" he inquired. "Don't you EVER get a day off?"

When I tell the gringos that I have been to launch here at least two hundred times, and I've NEVER seen it unlaunchable, I can see the look in their eyes: he's trying to sell us something.

Peñon, and all its variations, are a kind of theme in Valle, and it means "big rock, or boulder" in Spanish. Gringos frequently mistake it for piñon, which is a pine tree. Peñon is from the root 'piedra' which is Español for rock or stone. There are several extinct lava domes that jut into the sky near Valle. The topography is quite varied. Behind launch, for example, there stand two of these domes called Las Peñitas, *Little Big Rocks*. In the distance while flying above launch, you notice three more lava domes standing sentinel over in the neighboring state of Michoacan, these are called Los Tres Reyes, *The Three Kings*. In Valle proper, there is yet another volcanic formation called La Peña, *The Boulder*. And then there is the Big Daddy of them all, one mile out front from launch, El Peñon del Diablo. *The Rock of Angels*. El Peñon del Chingon!

El Peñon is the kind of place where you just make circles. Though there is a ridge here, it is not soarable as such. You try ridge soaring here, you just stink out. Uh uhh, nope... you gotta love circles to have any success here.

We peeled outta there, all right, and we made plenty of circles. I checked my progress one day when I hit the chronometer on my flight deck just after launching: take off and clear the trees, turn left and count to ten. Turn away from the hill and PUSH OUT! In six minutes I was at thirteen thousand six hundred feet above sea level. Six thousand feet- count 'em, six grand in six minutes. During that climb, I glimpsed nineteen hundred feet-per-minute climb for a moment, witnessed by my Alibi variometer, which doesn't lie, and was making tones I had never heard before.

WEEDEEDEEGAAKKKWEEDEEDEE!

I never even got to put on my gloves on the ride up. I was way too busy, and way too gripped. It was an awesome thermal.

This year, I got to see some of my ol' Tahoe buddies climb outta there like that. We were gaggling out, slicin' and dicin', and the radios were all too quiet. I keyed the mic and broadcast, "I think I speak for us all when I say: Yahoooo!"

Joel, Gordy and El Gallo all keyed at once in response. I didn't catch any of it- they were all steppin' on each other of course. But the spirit was clear. And... it was February.

You get up in the house thermal at launch, and you have a number of options. One of the most thrilling is to head straight for El Peñon itself and fly directly over it. For some reason, the rock is not the consistent thermal generator that one might think by the looks of it. But it never fails to provide extreme pucker-factor, and I for one am always terrified to fly over Rock of the Devil. There are plenty of other thermals sources however, and one of them is beyond the Peñon at The Wall. This is the route to take if you have set sail for Tres Reyes and the Divisadero.

But if you wanna head for the really high country, and if you're flying a slow boat like the Falcon as I did on this trip, then you have no time to waste going the wrong way. Instead, you head over the back and ignore the rocks behind at Las Peñitas, gliding for a wooded ridge called the Zacamecáte, a consistent house thermal. If you get high here, you dive for the pass at Los Zaucos. If you get high there, you are in great shape to start up the pass. As you dive in, the ground comes up to meet you with ever-higher valleys and you are never high for long. Happily, each valley usually has a higher cloud base, and each corresponding thermal takes you a little higher in turn.

At last you come to the pass where the highway crests ten thousand feet. This pass is the lower end of one of the arms reaching down from the volcano looming to the south. A tower of volcanic ridgeline is your last obstacle and last thermal generator. If you can hook the lift here to say, twelve or thirteen grand, you are on Easy Street for a long glide to Buena Vista.

Finally, you might drift on tailwind into the valley of Toluca, at nine thousand feet MSL a very high place. Cloudbase here may rise to eighteen or even twenty thousand feet. You can get seriously high in the Toluca valley. Quetzacoalt himself would be shaking at the knees. We gringos just drool on our chins. And the drool freezes...

There is an incredible amount of commerce in Valle de Bravo, and a walk down the street is always interesting. All the locals are selling stuff to each other, all manner of stuff. Besides the panadería, the tortillaría, the carnicería, the refraccionéria, the ferretería and the tacoría, the pulquería... Here's the guy who sells washing machines and televisions, the roparía, the veterinária, the perfumería, the farmacía, the one-hour foto, the list goes on and on, all tiny retail shops. Then, there is an incredible amount of food available, from tacos on the street where dogs clean up the scraps, to gourmet food in exclusive surrounds.

We dined once a week at Los Veleros, owned by our host's family. The food is great, nicely presented, and the site is one of the first haciendas in Valle de Bravo. The señora explained to us how the posts and lentils had come to be so delicately carved with an intricate design of grapevines throughout the building. During the re-model, she recalled, they had found an artist in Michoacan who would do the work cheaply. All he really required was a bottle of tequila during the day, and a cot at night. A deal was struck and the carpintéro spent months carving, carving, carving, throughout the building. A sort of Mexican Miguelangelo with a chisel, a mall and a hangover. The results are quite stunning.

On the other end of the dining spectrum, we were walking the square one night and bumped into Diego, who was chewing from a small bag of papitas— roasted pumpkin seeds. He said his greetings, offered me a few seeds, and went on his way. The seeds were incredibly good, and still warm from the fire, I had never tasted anything quite so savory. So when we noticed a gnarled and extremely tiny old crone roasting pumpkin seeds in the street, we stepped right up and negotiated a bag each. These seeds were hot from the fire and melted in your mouth. They were slightly salty, but with a delicate and satisfying roasted flavor that is quite indescribable. I was so impressed with papitas, that I bought an extra bag to stick in my harness, but by the next day they had lost their essence and were just pumpkin seeds. Papitas: get 'em while they're hot.

Food, food and more food. Most of my gringos would eat and eat and eat until they were stuffed. We would start with totopos (chips) and Pico De Gallo, fresh salsa- translates literally to "Bite or Beak of the Rooster". Then they brought fresh bolillos (buns) with paté and butter. For appetizers we often ordered queso fundido (cheese fondue) with fresh hongos (mushrooms) or sharp salchicha (sausage). A green salad or spinach salad was next, or maybe an enormous ripe Hass aguacate (avocado), stuffed with tuna or tiny shrimps, or maybe simply au naturál.

Entrees were often very stylish. At La Michoacana, for example, I noticed codornice (quail) and conejo (bunny). Most often I would opt for a filet mignon Roquefort or a brochéta de camarónes (skewer of shrimp). Another favorite is the filete huachinango relleno, a filet of red snapper stuffed with shrimp, calamari, cheeses, herbs and spices, the whole mess topped with Hollandaise sauce. This is Mexican cuisine at its finest.

Out on the street we find tacos al carbon. These are made as a loaf on a skewer, alternating layers of beef and onion, beef and onion, are stacked atop a skewer. When the loaf is about as big as your head, they top the whole thing with a fresh and juicy pineapple. This skewer is then placed vertically on a simple rotisserie next to a glowing hot electric element. As it roasts throughout the evening, the roasted pineapple juice drips down on the roasted meat and onions, basting the loaf with a delightful fresh pineapple flavor. When you order tacos al carbon, the chef slices into the loaf so that a portion of the pineapple, the beef, and the onion, fall into the tortilla waiting in his hand. You are then offered fresh onion, cilantro and lime, and an assortment of salsas, red and green. The first time I encountered these delights in Valle de Bravo I was quite hungry, and I put away two dozen.

Best of all, they think nothing of the fact that you have brought along a quart of cervesa, called a caguama, to wash it all down, right there on the street.   It's difficult for me to decide what's the best part of dining in Valle. Would it be the gourmet delights of Los Veleros, La Michoacana, or La Batucada? Or how about the economy of eating standing up with the blue-collar crowd on the street, quaffing beer?

We'll start with an 'esquite', an item sold over a small wood brazier. First, a plastic cup is slathered inside with a portion of mayonnaise. The lady uses a small wooden stick and a flourish to accomplish this. Then, the cup is filled with a scoop of piping-hot corn, fresh off the cob. Next, she tops the creation with another dab of mayonnaise, a sprinkle of red pepper and of course, a squeeze of lime. Price: two pesos- 20 cents.

Next we move on to the crazy old man who makes fantastic shrimp cocktails on his front terrace. When he asks you if you want picante (spicy), I suggest you decline, at least the first time. You may beg for mercy if you don't. Otherwise, they may be the most satisfying shrimp cocktail you've ever had, topped with a few slices of ripe avocado. Price: forty pesos- $4.

Moving on to the taco stands (careful not to bash yer head on the awnings, a likely experience if you are above standard Mexican height), for some tacos al carbon, described above, or other variations like tacos adobado. If that's not enough to fill you up, we move on to the Nevería- ice cream and Popsicles, where all the items are made fresh and use natural fresh ingredients.   There is watermelon in the watermelon popsicle, papaya in the papaya popsicle, nuts in the nut popsicle. If you're not careful, you might get drunk on the tequila ice cream.

Or… you may encounter the comóte cart, if you are lucky enough to encounter it somewhere being pushed laboriously along the cobbled streets. A comóte is a sweet potato. The comóte cart is a cumbersome contraption, a mobile potato oven standing about the size of your average deep freeze, with a wood fire in one end and a smokestack sticking up from the other. At the business end, a fire is being fed wood scraps and basura and anything else that will burn, by the same gang of kids who push it slowly along the street. The heat from this fire is routed within and slowly roasts the sweet potatoes, adding a delicious flavor. When you make your purchase, the kid scoops one out of the oven and quickly slices it open, handing it to you on a flimsy paper plate. You are invited to smother your treasure with a selection of toppings: butter, brown sugar, strawberry jam, miel de maple, crema amarga. As you enjoy this treat, the comóte cart lumbers slowly, painfully, off down the street, being pushed, wrestled, stoked and cajoled along by the niños.

But the comóte cart is more than just a sight, a smell and a taste of Mexico; it is a sound as well, for there is a small whistle in the smokestack of the comóte cart, which is powered by steam. When water is poured down the stack it turns to vapor in the heat, and builds pressure until it vents back out through this whistle, which sounds something like an old locomotive, starting out as a low moan, building to a shrill and strident chirp, and then fading out again as a low moan that echoes off the hillsides. The comóte cart has announced its status and location, for the whole village to hear. A sight, a smell, a taste and a sound of Ol' Mexico.

There are plenty more sounds in Mexico, that are part of the culture: the trash truck comes by twice weekly, the driver navigating the impossibly steep and narrow streets with aplomb. His helpers carry a whistle around their necks. They blow the whistle- you'd better be ready with trash in hand: they don't loiter. El Lechero (The Milkman) drives the neighborhoods in a battered pickup, which reeks of rotten spilled milk. He honks his horn and the señoras come out to meet him. He dispenses fresh milk from large cans, scooping with a giant ladle. This milk is neither pasteurized nor homogenized- that process is left to you. If you let this milk stand in your refrigerator, it will separate.

There is an expression in Mexico: 'El Lechero', as in "Quien es El Lechero?" *Who is the milkman?*

If, for example, you have a brother, but the two of you do not resemble each other, you may be asked this question: "Quien es El Lechero?" This is to say: obviously, your mother has become a little too familiar with the milkman. Which of you is the result?

Another sound- the tinkle of a small bell; a señor on his rickety old bicycle will arrive at your doorstep and ring his bell. You open the door to discover that he is offering a service: for a few pesos he will put an edge on your kitchen knives, or your machete for that matter, that will slice those vine ripe tomatoes, no problema. It is quickly agreed... As you turn to the kitchen for the knives, the knifeman releases a quick-lock on the stem of his bicycle seat and turns it around backwards. Next, he drops a large kickstand, raising the rear wheel completely off the ground an inch or so, and drops a grindstone on the tire. From this position he can then pedal the bike while sitting backwards upon it and turn the grindstone. The guy is very good, and probably has had his way with a few señoras too, I'm only speculating.

But I figure that when I get too damn old and broken up to fly trikes and hang gliders anymore, I'd like to retire to a life as a part-time knifeman in Valle de Bravo. I may have to apprentice for a while, first.

Other sounds abound. Everywhere, dogs bark and copulate. Roosters crow and copulate. Burros bray and copulate. If you are a lucky gringo, you may get to bray and copulate too. The female Mexican, the señorita, makes a very satisfying sound as she copulates, but that is another story best told in a later episode.

Oh, we flew too, every day, as mentioned above. There I was, halfway up the pass and sinking out near Los Zaucos. No worry; there is a most inviting looking grassy field in easy glide. It slopes gently down at the threshold, then gently up for touchdown. It looks like the most perfect place to roll in on my big training wheels, I decide that if I must land there, I will not even get out of my harness boot.

I circle carefully, hoping for another thermal. In the field next door there is a campesino tilling the soil behind a brace of oxen, toiling. The earth is knee-deep in volcanic ash, which floats above the plow, and creates the finest windsign that any glidehead could ever hope for. The dust blows right up the field, inviting me in.

I pass my shadow in front of the oxen. The farmer notices and takes a moment's respite to look skyward. He wipes his fevered brow, shields his eyes from the tropical sun with his sombrero, and watches as I fly the downwind leg, turn base and dive in for final, clearing the last few pines. When I touch down, he ducks under the reins and leaves the oxen where they stand and comes to visit the gringo. He smiles and waves his sweat-stained sombrero at the sky. He is nearly toothless.

His Spanish is too arcane, or his accent is too thick, or something. In any event, we can only converse with the basics: "¡Buenos tardes, señor!"

He nods in return, "Buenos tardes, guero." *Blondie*

"¡Vengo en paz!" I offer. *I come in peace.* He nods again and flashes a happy grin. His work clothes are incredibly tattered and sweat stained- rags really. There is no crown to his sombrero, only the brim remains. His shoes have but one lace between them, and he has no socks. Nonetheless, he points to his distant shack and offers me some hospitality, such as it is. "Bebida" he says. *Drink.* I beg off, saying that my ride will be along shortly and I must bag the papalote (kite). When Beto arrives with the truck, we give the old guy a cervesa and I offer him my calcetinas (socks). Though they are in serious need of a launder, he doesn't seem to notice, accepts then gladly. "Cien por ciento algodon," I offer. *One hundred percent cotton.* He admires my boots, recently purchased at Walmart, but I do not part with them. I wish now, as I write this, that I had. But those boots had more flying to do.

Beto and I tie on the wing. I shake hands with my campesino and he asks me when I will return. He suggests I come back mañana. He loves to watch. "¡Suave!" he says. *Graceful!* As we drive off, the old guy is still standing there, he waves a farewell. The oxen have not moved an inch.

This year I was really happy that my old buddy Joel showed up. I have been trying to get Joel down here for ten years, ever since his first visit. Back then, Joel was hauling around his own glider, and he had a great time traveling here and there. Since then, I couldn't get him down to ol' Mexico. He said one time, that he was not comfortable flying other people's gliders into unfamiliar fields. He'd only said it once, but I know that's what he was feeling all these years. Maybe it took the presence of our old friend Clev, who just wanted to come down and watch the action. Anyway, Joel came too.

But he was disappointed with his flying for some days. Joel is conservative anyway, and I think most any glidehead will admit that flying XC up this pass is an extreme sport, rather go-for-it. Joel would get up just fine in the house thermal- he never pianoed, even once. But the first fields over the back were like a magnet for him. He even flew back there from beyond, backtracking a time or two, while many others carried on. Even I, in the Falcon, was getting farther than Joel.

Then one day he set out with more determination. He sailed up the pass most of the way, landing above San Francisco Oxotitlán, at a village called Mesón Viéjo. I was happy for Joel. That was the same day I flew to Buena Vista and looked down on Joel's glider, sitting in a field surrounded by peasants. Joel was beaming when he arrived with Beto to pick me up in Buena Vista, and while we consumed a lunch of fresh trout with the fishmonger's daughter, he was philosophical:

"You just gotta point the nose and DIVE!" he kept saying. "Go for it!"

Later, relaxing on the terraza with an icy Cervesa Victoria, Joel kept wondering what had taken him so long to return to Valle. "This place is magic," he repeated.

On the way home, we stopped for fresh trout, as mentioned, high up on the pass at around ten thousand feet, at a place that deserves mention… You pull into a Swiss/Mexican chalet type of place, and order up a trout. The fishmonger's comely daughter, you can't help but notice, has her trousers rolled up around her knees, revealing quite shapely legs. She takes your order as your waitress, then casually walks outside to a concrete pool where a fountain constantly adds fresh icy mountain spring water. Without hesitation, she steps out of her sandals and into this frigid tank, which, you realize, is why her pant legs are rolled-up. She fishes around in that tank with an old laundry hamper, coming up with a fresh trout or two, each a perfect pan size. She quickly scoops up the flapping fish and dispatches it with a whack from a tiny baseball bat- a Louisville Slugger. With a flick of her knife, she has it gutted and cleaned.

She carries the order to the grill where the feast is first dipped and then rolled in some secret ingredients and then tossed on a hot grill. Next, our fishmonger's daughter moves on to get your chilly cervesas. The trout girl is highly efficient and quite fetching... even if she does have a powerful fishy smell, and icy cold feet. I find myself fantasizing about her even now. The trout himself was swimming about six minutes ago. Now he is steaming on your plate, mojo de ajo.

Gordy took to the sky at El Peñon like a pro, but he had several landings off the highway a piece, at a place called Club Santana. The LZ there was anything but convenient, being as it was on the wrong side of a small creek and line of trees. As I floated along above, I watched him go in there a couple of times.

Rooster- El Gallo- took right to the flying at El Peñon. He was jubilant about the place. Perhaps that is because he was able to bring his lovely wife Gabriella, who is from Mexico City, and visit in Valle with her parents, too. They all had a great time. And El Gallo had none of the hesitation that Joel had to set off for distant fields. He banged off a couple of long ones up the pass, and followed me to the Divisadero and the lakeside landing in El Zarillo.

But on my flight to Buena Vista, I flew over Los Zaucos high, and found Rooster and Gordy already down in the same field I had used some days prior. I drifted along over Zaucos, making lazy circles on top of an awesome thermal that was drifting my way, and they cheered me on from down below. I couldn't help but crow a little. I keyed the mic, "Hey Rooster, Gordy, is that you guys down there?" Later that night, over dinner, Rooster made me feel really good: "How high WERE you?" he asked. I made it farther that day than any of the Tahoe boys, any other day. I was a happy gringo.

One afternoon Rooster and I landed in Rancho Las Robles, where yet another of God's creatures provided yet more comic relief. I landed first, and when my feet touched I noticed a commotion over by a peasant's shack; a pig was tethered there, and the tether must have been very strong, because that pig was throwing his/her rather impressive girth against his/her chain, in an effort to escape the latest of threats to his/her happiness: myself.

Then, when Rooster lined up for final in the Fusion, he must have really drawn a bead on that porker. Plus, he was coming in much hotter on his Fusion than I had on my Falcon, and he was gliding considerably longer, too. That pig showed his/her dismay by racing around that stake and raising a large cloud of dust. He/she/it squealed in panic. El Gallo flared for a landing, but he had to run it out at nearly eight thousand feet, which brought him even closer to the unhappy pig. It was sometime before he/she/it could relax back to his/her wallow. Settle down Porky.

I am reminded of looking down from the heights, upon the valley just behind El Peñon, a tiny valley of farm fields too small to consider landable, but there are dozens of vague circles down there, each about the same size and each such a perfect circle that I was intrigued as to how they were made, looking back now, and considering the Porky Incident, I realize that these circles are left over from critters that have been tethered there; they eat themselves a circle. These circles are quite vague from the air, and probably invisible from the ground. They are livestock circles, such as I have never seen since.

I was lunching at the Zacazonápan, the wonderful little family restaurant on the highway out of Valle, across the street from the LZ at Tanké de Gas, a favorite place to land because the food and drink are so tasty and so cheap. The daughters aren't hard to gaze upon either. I was marveling once again at how clean the place was. The señora who runs the show there, not only cooks up a mean torta, she also has her kids constantly scrubbing the place. Geraniums and bougainvillea and roses abound.

I had ordered a torta de pierna, a terrific sandwich made on a fresh bun. First, she slices a fresh bolio in two and scoops out a small portion of the bread. This hollow she then fills with frijoles. Next, she throws the bottom of the bun on a hot grill, places slices of onion, avocado and cheese atop, slathers the top with Mayo, and puts a weight on her creation. In about a minute the torta is piping hot. This was served with a grapefruit soda and placed before me, as I waited for Beto. I dove into my lunch and sat chewing contentedly, all well with the World.

It was then I noticed a peculiar thing: outside, the World was raining cornhusks. It started slowly at first, just a few innocent leaves floating gracefully down out of nowhere. Then it became a shower, then a full-on deluge. Cornhusks raining from the sky. I gathered my torta in a paper napkin, and ran out the door to stand in the strange precipitation. I peered up into the sky and tried to focus as high as I could, higher and higher I gazed. I spied cornhusks, I'm guessing two thousand feet high, twisting and tumbling as they fell gracefully, slowly upon me.

Cornhusks have a pretty good sinkrate, I conclude.

The old señora from the Zacazonápan, and her fetching daughters, watched the gringo dash out of her establishment, and were relieved yet puzzled to find him standing in front of their restaurant grinning up into the sky, mayo dripping from his chin. They may have feared I was a diner-and-dasher. She wiped her hands on her apron and came out to see what was up. I suppose she hoped to catch a glimpse of another one of those crazy papaloteros as he turned final for the field across the street, and she was searching the sky when the gringo spoke:

"Milpa," I cried. "Hojas de milpa!"

She saw them too now, yet seemed quite unimpressed, as though showers of cornhusks are a common occurrence at the Zacazonápan. Maybe they are? She beheld the gringo for a moment, then walked back into her kitchen and left me standing alone, contemplating the cornstalks up there in Heaven. The shower rained down for some minutes, and then dissipated as quickly as it had begun. Somewhere, a rippin' dust devil- a 'remolina'- had churned through a cornfield, lifted the leaves a mile high, and deposited them on me and my torta. February in Mexico; WAHOOO! A glidehead's dream come true.

My ol' amigo Clev's Spanish needs work and he was working on it. We were reposing at the Obeja Negra, enjoying a tasty shrimp cocktail and a chilly cervesa. He looked over at me and inquired casually, "How do you say 'I've gotta take a leak?'" This is indeed a key phrase, especially in a land where the beer is so cheap, so tasty and so abundant.

Now, I butcher the Spanish language, I speak a street Spanish, a very Mexican Spanish. But I know there are a number of ways you might say this, just as in English. I suppose that 'Tengo que orinar' is the most proper; *I must urinate.* But it sounds just a little too clinical, what you might say to a doctor or nurse. Then there is 'Tengo que hacer pipi', *I must pee*, but that has always sounded too... well, too girly. It's what your sister might say.

So I thought for a second and then replied: "Tengo que hechar agua". This is what men might say, at least I believe I have heard this before, and it sounds most like 'I've gotta take a leak'; *I must make water.* I'm not even sure it's correct Mexican (Spanish), but it has always worked for me. So I told Clev and he tried it out.

"Tengo que hechar agua," he stumbled. He didn't have it quite right.

I explained again, "Tengo que hechar agua," my accent anyway, was pretty much perfect...

Clev tried again, "Tengo que hechar agua". His accent was improving now, but not quite there yet.

"Tengo que hechar agua."

"Tengo que hechar agua." The exchange went on, Clev was slowly getting it right, practicing, getting it stuck in his head. Soon, I found that I too, had an urge to 'make water'.

"Tengo que hechar agua."

"Tengo que hechar agua." It was our latest mantra.

Suddenly, I detected a presence behind me. I looked over my shoulder to find that our waiter, Miguel Angel, a handsome lad of about twenty-five years, had walked out on the terrace during our exchange. He had apparently overheard the Spanish lesson, and was astonished with us. He grinned at first me, then at my amigo Clev, two grown men, lost in an inane conversation...

Which pathetic old gringo would be first to soil his britches?

But Miguel showed his characteristic charm and restraint of course. He bowed slightly as though granting our wish, and extended an arm toward the doors.

"Hay trono por alli, amigos," he said. *The throne is over there, friends.*

We had a good laugh with Miguel, who just shook his head. Clev went first.

La Obeja Negra

George and Ginny provided us some comic relief, as well. George is a very intense guy. After 25 years or more of hang gliding, George is the kind of gringo you can give any wing to, and forget about him. He will do just fine. But his Spanish is non-existent. He actually turned to me one day and inquired: "Hey Ole, how do you say, 'No' in Spanish?

One afternoon as I was making slow turns atop a thermal, hoping it would drift my way, I was listening to radio broadcasts between the other pilots and Flaco. I hear Flaco ask: "Where are you George?"

George's voice drifts up upon the airwaves: "Well... I'm down here in a field... in a place called... Say Vende."

I have a good laugh at that. 'Se Vende' is Spanish all right, but it means 'For Sale'. You see it all over Mexico, on cars, trucks, houses, lots. On chickens and burros. Se Vende. George had landed at a For Sale sign, thought we could look for him there. I nearly lost it in mid-sky laughing, floating along over San Francisco Oxotitlán. Based on the information George had just imparted, we may never locate the gringo.

Another day, we were all in the Suburban, chasing after George who had reeled off a long one over the pass, into the Toluca valley. In fact, George had apparently just flown the longest flight of the week and he would be stoked. Now we only had to locate him- he had our glider after all.

We keyed the mic as we topped the pass and called for him: "Where are you George? Do you copy? What's your twenty?"

His voice crackled a faint reply over the air. "I'm down in a field next to the highway. You can't miss me."

"Can you be more specific?" The more info you can glean from a lost flyer the better.

"Ahh... well... they're excavating a pyramid here. In fact they're excavating a pyramid across the street, too. Heck, there's pyramids all over this place. I'm in a pyramid zone."

That got more good laughs from Flaco and I There are no pyramids much lees pyramid zones in that part of Mexico, or if there are they are still buried in the Sands of Time. What could George be thinking? Where was he? We traveled along the highway, George's voice getting clearer and stronger. "You can't miss me, just look for the pyramids." Then we saw him, standing along the road, next to some gravel pits. The gravel pits had a sort of triangular retaining wall, so that trucks could back up the rear and dump their load. Maybe they do look like pyramids, if you're a gringo, and if you have a good imagination.

You might almost hear the screams of doomed victims as they are dragged up the bloody stairs and their hearts ripped asunder by an obsidian blade, for Aztec ritual sacrifice!

George's wife Ginny flies too, and she flies well when she sets her mind to it. In fact, her flight might have been the most astonishing of the entire trip. Ginny's first flights were to the Piano field below launch, and that's where I expected her to stay for a while. After all, she had never been over four grand MSL, she had never flown over the back at any site, even back home, and she was flying an itty-bitty Falcon 145. We were just hoping that Ginny would go 'over the back'- to the large fields at Las Peñitas- a much shorter retrieve than the Piano. Imagine our delight then... when one sunny afternoon...

It was George's second or third day ever flying El Peñon. His initial flights had been successful, but nothing truly spectacular. I think he'd landed in the first fields over the back, in Las Peñitas, maybe Tanké de Gas. But the next day George got really stinkin' high, and flew into town, across the lake, and landed at the marina at San Gaspar, arriving there skyed-out. Later in the LZ, with a chilled cerveza in one hand, and a stick in the other, George got down in the dirt and started a diagram, outlining his flight for the benefit of us all. He was very stoked, very animated. "First, I hooked it outta launch, and glided over the back..." his stick slashed and swirled in the dirt. "Then, I got so friggin' high in the second thermal that I just headed for the lake..." The stick raised a miniature cloud of dust. "There were so many thermals along the way," he continued... "it was a gimme." But suddenly, as George was really getting wound-up, the radio on my belt loop sparked to life. A tiny tinny voice came over the air;

"This... this is Ginny... this is Ginny... anybody... copy?"

George was down in the dirt, on his hands and knees diagramming his flight for us all, but not for long. His face registered shock and surprise, and he sprang for his radio buried in his harness. We just weren't expecting to hear from Ginny, who should by now be bagging her cute little Falcon in the Piano, throwing it on the truck for the ride home. But this broadcast was crystal clear, line-of-sight stuff. It could only mean one thing... George pawed frantically through his gearbag and harness, came up his radio, and keyed-up.

"Ginny, Ginny, Ginny...! Is that you? Is that you?" Of course, there were no other Ginnys in the sky that afternoon, no other gringas at all for that matter, especially not broadcasting on 148.50-MHz, in the middle of the Mexico highlands. Of course it was Ginny, who else might it be? "Where are you Ginny? Where are you?"

There was a moment's delay, as though Ginny was temporarily gripped, unable or unwilling to key-up. We waited her word with thrilling happiness and suspense, and then we heard her voice once again;

"I'm at thirteen... grzz... guzz... click..." You could taste the sudden silence. George looked to us for confirmation.

"Did she say... What did she say?" His expression begged enlightenment. "WHAT DID SHE SAY?" he demanded of us.

We all stood there, in an anxious circle, kicking dirt and drinking beer. We were no help at all. But now miraculously, Ginny was back: "Ahh... I'm at fourteen thousand and ahh... and I can't see anything."

George was dumbfounded with emotion, disbelief and dismay. His bride? "Fourteen grand?" he started. His eyes nearly bugged from his head. Then, "What do you mean you 'can't see anything'?" he keyed into the radio. Was she hypoxic? Was she lost in cloud? Was she... blindfolded? Had her eyes frozen shut? Had her helmet fallen down over her eyes? From fourteen grand, over El Peñon, you can see ity all, the lake, the village, it's all laid out below for everyone to see.

Was Ginny Lost in Space?

"I'm so high, I can't figure out where I am," came her reply.

George jumped up and peered back towards launch. He keyed the mic. "Do you see the lake Honey?" he demanded. "DO YOU SEE THE LAKE?"

Another moment's hesitation and then Ginny was back again, "Yea, sure. I see the lake."

"Just point it there!" cried George. "Just point it toward the lake, the LAKE! Point yer toes and head for the lake!"

And so Ginny did. She set out on a glide, pointing the wing at the lake, and George coached her. "Just fly slow when yer vario beeps," he soothed, "and fly a little faster when it doesn't. If yer sink alarm tones, fly faster yet."

Ginny glided and glided and glided some more, making painfully slow progress in that cute little Falcon. Finally, we thought we could just make out a tiny dot under the cummies.

"There she is," yelled George, beside himself with emotion. "Is that her? Yes Jeezuz, and Hallelujah!"

Ginny was SKYED OUT! "How high are you now?" George inquired with pride. The sight of his little lady coming into Valle de Bravo so high had him nearly back on his knees with glee. "How high are you darling?"

"I'm still at twelve thousand feet," she confirmed. From that altitude, on a Valle afternoon, with cummies popping all over the blue Mexican sky, the glide across the lake is a piece of pastel.

"Pull the bar in and glide," ordered George. "I'll help you find the LZ. Just keep gliding!" George jogged across to the lakeshore, seeking a private place to be her private air traffic controller. We followed the drama on the air, listening to the dialogue over our radios. Ginny got closer and closer until she was directly overhead, still with thousands of feet to spare. George did a fine job of getting her into the rather small cornfield at San Gaspár, where a smooth lake breeze comes straight across the field, just off-shore enough to be silky smooth, almost thick.

Ginny dropped in from two feet, a no-stepper, a perfect showing. George was overcome with relief and pride for his bride.

It was finally time for Joel, Clev and I to depart Valle de Bravo, a sad day. Joel went down to the street below Casa Cabrónes, and solicited one of Valle's countless cabbies. We stuffed all of our luggage and gear in his Nissan Sentra- there was a neat trick- and we shoved off for the nearby bus depot. But on the way, the cabbie pointed out a bus going the other way. ¿Is that the camion you want? he asked.

"Si señor!"

The cabbie flagged down the bus, which pulled off the road. There was a quick exchange of luggage and gear, pesos and gringos. The bus was nearly empty, so I took the rear seat, threw open the window, and stuck out my head to catch the last few sensations of this village I love so much, the sights, the sounds, the smells. I was sure gonna miss it.

Almost immediately, a taxi behind the bus commenced to blow its horn. I craned my neck to see what was the fuss: it was Chocho again, my former driver and forever amigo- the same driver/cabbie who had been waiting for me at the station when we arrived two weeks ago. Chocho must have been cabbing along behind the bus, and noticed his gringo hanging out the window. He had a fare he was taking somewhere, but he was all grins and horn, honking and waving with happiness. Joel, Clev, Gordy and I waved a final salute, and Chocho turned off on his mission.

The Swizzle Stick From Hell or, a Turd in Paradise

"**J**ust get the bags out of the truck quickly would you Rodney," said Walter. Rodney looked as though he was about to explode. "Please. Por favor?" A Colima cop was hovering over them in his Policía Fiscal uniform, and even though the Ford-From-Hell was parked in the hotel loading zone Walter didn't like the looks of him. "I'll park and be right back," he promised.

"If you make one more stupid fuck-up!" steamed Rodney. His fists were balled tightly, the tendons in his neck and face were stretched taut in a horrible grimace and his body language spoke loudly of physical violence. Walter had not known Rodney to be the violent type but actually, he didn't really know Rodney that much at all. They were acquaintances more than friends and they were new associates. They had much to learn about each other.

Photo courtesy of Colima Volcano Observatory

Colimotl and Volcan de Fuego

At the moment Rodney's eyes were bulging through his thick glasses. Maybe it was the long day they had just spent lost on the dusty logging roads high on the flanks of the Volcan de Fuego, when they should have been up on the Nevado de Colima instead- Walter's fault again. Maybe it was the problem at the hotel last night when one of the clients had simply opened the nearest door and fallen to sleep in bed-causing them to have to pay for an extra room this morning-Walter's fault again. Of course, Rodney suffered a bit of stress left over from the day before when Walter had projectile-vomited bad oysters all over Rodney's wife's foot- quite evidently Walter's fault. All these issues and more were Walter's fuck-ups for sure, but more likely it was just the cumulative effects of following the gringo and his crazy truck deep into Mexico for the past few days that had poor Rodney in such dire straights. The whole situation was on the verge of boiling over, Rodney was pissed!

"No hay problema Rodney," Walter assured him calmly, trying to settle him down some. They were on a working vacation after all, what could be finer? "We're all here now, safe and sound amigo. Our troubles are over and mañana we fly." Rodney didn't look all that convinced, but Walter popped the clutch and drove off with a wave.

In the last few days they'd been stranded, separated, rained on, took for their pesos, gotten food poisoning, puked it up, paid exorbitant highway tolls and been victimized in numerous other Mexican misadventures. Rodney was convinced Walter was at fault and in fact he was mostly correct. Getting them lost looking for a launch three hours up a marginal dirt road on the flanks of an extinct Mexican volcano was just the latest outrage for Rodney. He would have probably dismembered Walter on the spot except for the fact that... well, that he was even more lost than Walter.

But then, Walter was the guide.

Right now the guide was parking the Ford-From-Hell in the secure hotel lot down the street. He grabbed some clean clothes from his luggage, and returned to the hotel. He was anxious to wash off several layers of Mexican road dust and hit the streets. Walter had settled on the Hotel Ceballo as the group accommodations because it was centrally located in old downtown Colima, and fit their most important criteria: price. The Ceballo is the oldest hotel in Colima, itself an old town on the Spanish Camino Real. The Ceballo certainly met their budgetary needs nicely, two gringos could be housed at about five bucks per night double occupancy. The rooms were cramped, true, and the air-conditioning worked on an occasional basis at best. The plumbing made wild banging noises in the night, and there was a constant cacophony from the street below.

But the gringos were here to fly hang gliders, not hang around some pinche hotel. Besides, the Ceballo was situated on the main square or 'jardine' in Colima. Each room offered a tiny but elaborate balcony overlooking the jardine and all the action. Across the square stood the stately Governor's Mansion, and out on the square itself an orchestra was even now tuning up. The sounds of tubas, trombones and violins floated up through the terrace window accompanied by an occasional clash of cymbals.

Yes, there would be a serenade this evening!

Arriving back at the hotel, the bellman- such as he was- escorted the gringo through the narrow confines of the Ceballo to his room, where he found the shower occupied by Roberto. Roberto was a surprise guest on this first-ever Safari Mexico flying tour. He was a friend of Rodney and Beth's, who had grown up in a tiny village in the very shadow of the nearby volcano, and asked them for a chance to return and fulfill his dream- to fly off the lofty heights. He'd ridden the entire trip with Walter, since the Volkswagen Thing that Rodney and Beth drove was loaded to the gunnels with them and their dog. But Roberto- a street-wise Mexican- had proven to be a resourceful, even necessary asset to the trip thus far. At the moment, Roberto could be heard singing a Latino melody as he scrubbed-down in the shower.

Ese lunar que tienes
Cielito lindo, junto a la boca
No se lo des a nadie
Cielito lindo que a mi me toca!

No hay problema! thought Walter again, excited with this new adventure. *Oh yes I'm even thinking in Español now!* Turning to unpack some things, a loud shout came from the hallway.

"Walter! Waalltttteeerrr!" Turning towards the door Walter saw Rodney again; this time dressed only in a hotel towel and his slippers. His face was still grimaced, his eyes continued to bulge in fury, his anger-level had not subsided at all in the past few minutes. One fist clutched the towel at his hips and the other fist was clenched as though ready to throw a punch. The tendons in his neck were ready to snap.

Walter stepped back, aghast. *Oh God have mercy,* he thought. *This is supposed to be fun, Rodney. What is my partner pissed about NOW?*

"WALTER!" repeated Rodney, only louder this time, like a volcano about to blow.

"Rodney," Walter offered hesitantly, "What's up?"

"This place sucks is what's up," yelled Rodney. Spittle erupted from his lips and knocked Walter two steps backwards. "This place SUCKS!" Rodney yelled it again, as though with all his other faults Walter might be deaf too. "We can't keep our clients here. This place is a pit!"

"Rodney, Rodney, settle down big guy. There's nothing wrong with this hotel," Walter defended himself. "Besides, the price is right, huh?"

"I don't give a rat's ass about the price," hollered Rodney. "I won't spend a single peso here." Something had sure gotten Rodney worked up. Feeling trapped, Walter took a giant stride past his gringo, brushing his bare chest on the way past. The tension in Rodney's life was like a living thing.

"Settle down Rodney will you? And what's the big problem anyway?"

Rodney took one giant stride stage right and pointed an accusatory finger at room 211, the room that he and his wife shared. Beth was another surprise on this trip, having decided at the last moment that she could not let her man just dash off to go hang gliding in Mexico without keeping an eye on him. Was she a guest too? wondered Walter. Or was she in charge? Usually a bossy, tyrannical sort, Beth could be seen now sprawled face-down on a saggy bed, refusing to look at Walter or even acknowledge his presence.

Oh Dios Mio, but I'm an unpopular gringo today! realized Walter with dismay.

Rodney took two more giant steps inside the room and, arriving at the bathroom door, kicked it open. Now he pointed an accusing finger at the porcelain throne and suddenly Walter understood. For there, floating in the toilet bowl, was one of the most prodigious turds Walter had ever laid eyes on. This turd was about the circumference of a bottle of Dos Equis and the same dark color too. It floated on end in the throne, mostly submerged, but with its head above the surface as though gasping for air. Here was a turd to take on all turds, and for a gringo traveling in Mexico, a potential source of pride. While minions of gringos will experience a loose stool on occasion while traveling Mexico—a condition often expressed as Montezúma's Revenge—here was a turd to be PROUD of, a dense, thick and sturdy turd, a turd for all occasions. Montezúma be damned, no loose bowels here. LORD of the TURDS!

Walter didn't really see the problem, his only question, best left unasked was: Who is the lucky progenitor?

But Rodney was still apoplectic and showed no signs of seeing any humor whatsoever in the situation, however scatological, however juvenile. Walter stepped into the baño and yanked the flush handle, which hung on a rusty chain below the elevated holding tank above the ancient throne. A pathetic gurgle and swish of water was released and swirled into the bowl. The turd made a slow, indifferent passage once or twice around the bowl, leaving a brown stain above the waterline like some sick swizzle stick from Hell.

Walter turned once more to face Rodney, whose anger was borderline volcanic. "Ahhh... say look Rodney ahh..." Staying at arm's length as best he could, Walter reached out to the toilet with his toe and dropped the lid, effectively isolating the offensive apparition, if not its shitty aroma. He couldn't stand to see Rodney's twisted face anymore either. The gringo seemed ready to tip Walter up on end and add his head to the vile cocktail in the toilet bowl.

"Ahh... why don't we just umm... leave it... for the maid," he suggested. "Yeah... maybe she's got a plunger or... some... some salad tongs she can lift it out with, or some... rubber gloves... yeah." Walter was backing out of the room. "I'll go find the maid right now!" he offered.

"Aaaaarrrrgggghhhh..." was Rodney's only response, he had been rendered, apparently, inarticulate by a bowel movement. Walter was anxious to make a timely exit. Rodney allowed him a small opening near the door and he made a dash for daylight, for fresh air. He hustled into his own room and slammed the door in disgust where he found Roberto still singing in the shower...

> *Ay, yay, yay, yay*
> *Canta y no llores*
> *Porque cantando se alegran*
> *Cielito lindo, los corazones!*

A Valle Purchase or
Panties From Heaven

The local indigenous women were setting up the market on the street as they did each Tuesday. Walter and Joe sat down for the first liquado of the new season and watched the proceedings. Dressed in their colorful native garb, the Indian women would string up a motley collection of tarps for shade and blankets for flooring and spread their wares and produce at their feet, and sell each other everything from mushrooms to ghetto blasters. It was only the women who seemed to work, while the men folk watched lazily from nearby.

Tianguis

`Marta, the liquado lady, was surprised and pleased to see Walter. Perhaps she was thinking of all the pesos Walter and his loco crowd of flying gringos would spend on her delicious blended fruit and vegetable drinks. "¿Como haz estado?" she asked. *How have you been?* Already she was preparing Walter's nutritious breakfast beverage, from memory.

"¡Muy bien gracias!" said Walter. *Very fine thanks!* "¡Y que gusto de estar aqui y ver de usted!" he flirted. *Great to be*

here and to see you! Marta blushed and giggled at the gringo, her great girth and enormous bosoms jiggled when she laughed. She filled the blender with apples and banana and mamey and granola and nuts and wheat germ and bee pollen and chocolate syrup. She tossed in a raw egg and topped it off with a splash of leche, then hit the 'on' switch. Walter's mouth watered as he waited for the results. This would be his first liquado since he'd departed Valle de Bravo last spring and he'd missed the drink and the daily ritual.

"¿Llegaste hoy?" inquired Marta, now preparing the same tasty concoction for Joe. *You arrived today?*

"Ayer,"returned Walter. *Yesterday.*

"¿Y por cuanto vas a estar?" she questioned. *And how long will you stay?*

"Algunas meses," replied Walter. *Some months.* Sitting there amid the bustle and colorful activity on the streets of Valle de Bravo, looking forward to yet another flying season, Walter felt he might just stay on forever. Just disappear into Mexico and never be seen again.

"¡Que bueno!" said Marta. *Great!* It was good to be welcome, thought Walter, though he suspected again that he was only wanted for the money he and his gringos would spread around town. Marta set two giant liquados in front of them and both gringos sipped their drinks contentedly and watched the local market scene.

"How 'bout all them parapantes?" remarked Joe. He pronounced it 'pair-o-panties'. There had been seven or eight soaring La Torre yesterday when he and Walter had driven wearily into town covered in two days of road dust from the trip.

"We do seem to be in the midst of a proliferation," agreed Walter, savoring his breakfast.

"Why do you suppose anybody would fly one of them things when they can fly a real hang glider instead?" wondered Joe aloud. They each knew there was no good answer to that question.

"Probably too lazy to learn," said Walter. They knew that wasn't true either. Some of the parapante pilots were also hang glider pilots. Alfredo and Miguel most notably, good, experienced glideheads, setting aside their blades to fly a floating baggie, slow and low performance. Like flying a jellyfish. Or bloomers. Bloomers in the sky. It seemed a giant step backward in the evolution of foot-launched flight.

Paragliders?

Walter just didn't understand, and probably never would. "Might be the future of foot-launched flying Jose, who knows? Maybe the joke's on us and we just don't get it..." They sat at the liquado stand and slurped up the last of their drinks. Walter was watching an ancient abuela who had spread her blanket in the hot sun, and was selling women's underwear. No one stopped to admire her goods, the World was just passing her by, and she sat there stoically, indifferent to it all. It looked as though she was in for a long day.

"I just can't believe it..." mused Joe, still on the same subject. "And at La Torre too."

Walter remembered the first time he'd seen a bag in a magazine. 'Parapante' they were called and it would be some time before Walter heard the proper French pronunciation "pah-rah-pahnt". To him and his flyin' buddies, with no Frenchies around to enlighten them, the word had just looked like "pair-a-panty". In the sky they looked like panties too, colorful, slow skivvies floating along and rippling in the slightest turbulence. The pilot hung at the bottom of a V shaped mass of strings that dangled from the canopy, and sat in a most un-aerodynamic harness. Thus had they acquired such derogatory nicknames as 'Dope on a Rope" and "Bag Fags". They had a lousy glide too, and were getting a reputation for not making it out to the landing zone. Thus their new label, Walter's favorite- tree condoms.

Walter shuddered to think of how the bags would collapse in the booming air over El Peñon on a warm February afternoon at, say, 2 O'clock. "I guess if you wanna fly La Torre," he mused, "you gotta do something different just to make it interesting." Launch at the Tower was visible over the rooftops from where they sat, above town, through a chaos of plastic shade tarps and powerlines. The tower sat on a ridge covered in pine forest, in a slot through the trees that had been created years ago for launching hang gliders. It was here that hang gliding had originated in Valle, a lake effect ridge that offered smooth and usually boring lift. Nothing like the kick-butt rippin' thermals that ruled the sky out at El Peñon every afternoon.

Booooooooooring!

"Nope, I reckon we'll go out to the Peñon and fly hang gliders. Good thing we got a stack of 'em". He was still watching the old undies lady, who seemed bored amidst the bustling street, when he had a sudden bright idea... Maybe he could make at least one old lady genuinely happy and have a bit of fun as well.

"Vamanos Jose," he said to Joe. It was a part of Joe's continued indoctrination into Español. *Let's go!* They bid 'hasta luego' to Liquado Marta and hit the street.

Walter strode over to the underwear granny and said, "Desculpe doña." *Excuse me ma'am.*

The old woman seemed startled as she looked up at Walter and Joe, two big gringos who were standing before her offerings. She sat Indian style with bare callused feet, incredibly dirty and colorful blouse and long flowing skirts. More colorful shawls wrapped her shoulders, pink and orange ribbons held her hair in one long and ancient gray braid. It was impossible to guess how old she was, but as she looked up at the gringos with an incredibly weathered face, carved and etched in wrinkles, she resembled an ancient piece of driftwood, painted up in wild colors. Walter noticed that she was blind in at least one eye.

"¿A como salen?" he asked pointing at her goods. *What do they go for?* The old woman thrust a hand toward Walter and made a V of fingers.

"Dos," she answered.

"¿Dos pesos cada uno?" he asked. *Two pesos each?*

"Sí," nodded the vieja, who then scanned Walter from head to toe as though eyeing him up for size. Would he need the extra, extra large?

The panties lay before them, maybe fifty or sixty pair in various colors, some printed with tiny flowers or the days of the week. Various frills and lace. Some were cottony and others silky. He made a quick calculation and then: "Le doy cien pesos por todos," he offered. *I'll give you a hundred pesos for them all.*

There was a moment's indecision there in the crowded streets, as the old lady looked back at the gringos. Maybe she hadn't understood the gringo's Español. Did he say...

ALL?

"¿Mánde?" she asked. It is the Mexican equivalent of *'Huh?'*

Walter reiterated: "Digo le doy cien pesos por todos." *I say I'll give you a hundred pesos for all of them.*

"De veras?" she replied. *Really?*

Walter nodded his own head now and produced the currency from his pocket. "Sí doña, te lo juro." *Yes ma'm, I swear.*

The old lady looked the gringos over again and quickly decided. "¡Sale!" she agreed. *Sold!*

And so the deal was consummated. Grabbing the soiled old plastic bag that she had brought them in, the granny scooped up her stack of skivvies and stuffed them inside. Slowly but surely she stood to her feet, grabbing a corner of her blanket as she did. Walter handed her the hundred pesos, which she snagged with a toothless grin and secreted in her voluminous skirts. She shook the street grime from the blanket and wrapped it around her body like one more shield against Life's uncertainties. Back-pedaling away from the gringos as though to put distance between them before they should come to their senses, nodding her head up and down, supplicating and repeating "Gracias señores, gracias señores..." she spun quickly on a bare foot and disappeared into the crowd, her day suddenly turned for the better.

"What was that all about?" asked Jose with a grin. He looked at the bag of panties and smirked. "Whatcha gonna do with all them? You need panties full of women B'wana, not empties."

"Just doing my part to spread the wealth," said Walter. "Did you see the look on that old woman's face? Best hundred pesos I've ever spent."

"Sure," said Jose. "But why didn't you buy something more useful? Some fruit or tools or something practical?"

"Who says these here panties aren't useful?" asked Walter. "I can think of at least one good use." With a last look, watching as the old lady turn a corner up the street, the gringos themselves hurried off to the truck and a day of flying. "Who says they aren't useful Jose amigo," said Walter again. "I got me an idea about that. We're heading to El Peñon for some fun."

They reached the Ford-From-Hell and jumped in. Walter drove while Jose stuck some tunes in the tape deck. Rumbling slowly through the cobbled and uneven streets of Valle de Bravo, waving to passers-by and shop owners Walter knew, they drove down the steep hill to the lake. Past the marina, the panedería, the florería, and the ferretería. They rattled through his neighborhood Walter had come to realize only last season was known as El Mangito, 'The Little Mango', and soon left the village behind. James Taylor entertained them:

> *Way down here you need a reason to move*
> *Feel a fool running your stateside games*
> *Lose your load, leave your mind behind, baby James*
> *Oooooooh, México!*
> *It sounds so simple I just got to go*
> *The sun's so hot I forgot to go home*
> *I guess I'll have to go now...*

El Peñon del Diablo, The Rock of the Devil, stands out from launch, an enormous eroding lava-dome in a ring of collapsed volcano. Walter steadied his glider, took four hard steps down the launch and was propelled smoothly into the clear blue sky. He turned left and counted to ten. His sleek and shiny wing responded enthusiastically in his hands as if eager too, to join the puffy cottonball clouds overhead. Encountering the house thermal he banked his wing and dug in.

Walter whooped for joy at his inaugural flight for the winter of '92. He resisted the opportunity to ride the very first lift to the clouds, instead pulling down the nose and making a couple of giant, swooping turns at launch. Then he let the glider lead the way and banked into strong lift and circled out. Turn after turn he carved in the wild blue and soon topped-out near cloudbase. Watching as Jose launched below, he waited for him there, and together they turned tail to the wind, gliding for the next thermal at the Zacamecáte. Circling out again, Walter and Jose were joined by a couple of buzzards that flew in close and inspected them. Walter had brief eye contact with the nearest, a drop-dead gorgeous critter who wore an amorous expression on his ugly head. The bird dropped his feet and showed them off to Walter. Maybe the buzzards, too, had missed the gringos?

Walter, Jose and the buzzards topped out again at cloudbase and Walter pointed the glider towards the distant blue lake in Valle de Bravo, heading for home. He glided towards La Torre, which looked tiny beneath him on the ridge above town. His flight path took him out of the rowdy thermal air over El Peñon, and into the smooth marine air from the lake. He looked down and sure enough, as Walter had guessed, there, soaring back and forth over The Towers, was the gaggle of pair-a-panties, colorful tiny dots far below him.

Bagsters!

Walter glided out over the mountain until he was in front of the towers and still thousands of feet above the bloomers drifting sluggishly around the ridge below.

Working his way down with a series of joyous wingovers in the silky lake air, he positioned himself for... the drop.

Carefully calculating the trajectory, and factoring in the wind drift, he reached down to the ballast compartment in his harness where he had stowed the hundred-pesos worth of ladies panties, and opened the compartment part way. Looking back into his own slipstream, he was pleased to see that his plan was working: a flock of colorful panties were falling gracefully through the sky behind him, spinning, swirling, tumbling. He pulled the handle another notch and released some more. Circling back to enjoy the scene, he took in the spectacle again. The panties circled and spun and tumbled through the sky. They appeared to be in perfect position to intercept the bloomers boating below.

Walter released all his lovely ballast to complete the drop, and then pulled the nose down. Gaining all his airspeed, he pushed out and sent the wing soaring in a perfect roll-over. Up and down he swung, making swoop after swoop above the tile rooftops of Valle de Bravo. Reaching pattern altitude, Walter leveled off and held his airspeed. The panties floated down above him, settling gently to the earth.

As Walter overflew the landing field he noticed a tiny figure running across the grass and remembered little Maria Elena, the child who lived in the shack in one corner of the landing area, who was wise to everything about hang gliders, and who would cheer their arrival each day.

Walter turned final and glided into ground effect. He bled off his speed and came upright to flare. He floated towards the center of the field and slowed, slowed, and then PUSHED! The glider stood on its tail and came to a complete stop at three feet. He held the flare and settled gently to the ground.

He carried the glider off the field and noticed the tiny figure running towards him, hair flowing behind and arms stretched gleefully overhead. Hearing her girlish screech, Walter saw Maria Elena, looking slightly taller than last year, but no older. She appeared even more animated than usual and clenched some panties in her grubby fists. Mariela ran towards Walter and threw herself into a big embrace around his legs, harness and all.

She stood back then and looking and jumping towards the sky. She spotted more panties drifting down and dashed off to scoop them up. Her mongrel dog got in the act too, and dashed happily along beside her. They tumbled in the grass and galloped off after even more panties- the dog shook a pair in his mouth. Walter unclipped and stood out from his glider in time to see the last of them filter through the pair-a-panties and settle towards earth. Some of them landed in the lake. Just what I wanted, thought Walter, wet panties!

Walter watched Jose turn final and glide in to land. He admired how the wing cut a graceful and pleasing arc through the air, and then flared to a beautiful stop. Jose kept on running until he set the glider down at Walter's feet. His cheeks were flushed with the chill of altitude and he was out of breath with exhilaration. Before he could even speak Mariela dashed past clutching the panties. She and her dog leapt in delight. Walter realized then what it was she screamed:

"¡Calzones!" she hollered. *Panties!* "¡Calzones del cielo!" *Panties from Heaven!* "¡Calzones, calzones, CALZONES!"

Walter laughed, delighted with her antics. "You made her day too," observed Jose, stepping out from his harness. "Looks like her birthday or Christmas. What's that she's screaming anyway?"

The pair-a-panties still floated aloft on the gentle breezes of La Torre. Walter hoped they too had enjoyed the spectacle as much as Mariela and himself. "*Panties*, Jose. She's hollering *PANTIES! From Heaven!*"

Jose stood and laughed there in the field next to the lake, below the ridge, under the awesome Mexican sky. He laughed easily at first, then harder, then finally with a belly-full he laughed at Walter and Mariela. At panties from Heaven. At kick ass thermals waiting for tomorrow. At the joy of life in general. "I guess you did find a use for them panties after all," realized Jose. "Let's go for a cervesa!"

The Wright Brothers created the single greatest cultural force since the invention of writing. The airplane became the first World Wide Web, bringing people of different languages, ideas and values together.
-Memo Puertas

Soup Kitchen Sally Gets Some Airtime or, Sky Queen for a Day

Miracle Dave ran the soup kitchen in Panajachel, feeding hundreds of hungry peasants, Indians, drunks, junkies and freaks every week. He approached Walter shortly after his arrival, spoke softly and solicited a contribution, calling him "brother". It wasn't until Walter had been in town a week or so that he'd learned that Dave was for real. He could have easily passed for a freaky panhandler.

Dave, everyone agreed, was the real thing- an unselfish, caring person who liked to help others. That he was a trust funder and didn't really have to work at all was a plus for Dave and everyone else involved. Stories abounded about how Dave had sacrificed his own meager income to rescue some unfortunate soul or other. He spent his days collecting donations used to buy food and equipment and pedaling his bike through the alleys of town, scrounging leftover food and the castoffs from the myriad restaurants in Panajachel. This he'd take back to his makeshift kitchen and cook up one big feast a day, for whoever wanted to eat. Dave had few restrictions about who was worthy enough, or unworthy as it were. If you came to his feed and you looked like you could actually afford more precious food, Dave would simply ask for a donation. "For mañana," he might say. His kitchen was staffed by a cadre of gringos and travelers from the far corners of the world. Many strange languages were spoken, many strange costumes worn.

Among Dave's workers, and one of the few who were paid a small wage, was a tiny indigenous woman from a local tribe who most everyone called 'Sally'. Sally's real name was actually quite unpronounceable to the average gringo, coming from some obscure Guatemalan dialect and having several clicking and trilling sounds. Dave said that 'Sally' was about as close as most people ever got- and that she answered to it. Sally was about forty kilos of energy, very friendly and happy-go-lucky.

Sally was just a colorful blur in the hot tropical sun as Walter went to see with his own eyes what Miracle Dave was up to in the backwater crossroads of Panajachel. The gringo sat at Dave's counter to observe, but was soon enlisted to clean and cut a bunch of carrots that was thrust before him. Dave was eager to talk: "I always watch you guys floating around the sky like big birds!"

"You ought to give it a try sometime," offered Walter. "I've got a tandem wing and these sites are great for tandem."

"Tandem?" asked Dave. "What's tandem?"

"Two people," explained Walter. "One pilot and one passenger."

"I thought I saw that the other day," exclaimed Dave. "I saw a glider floating over the viewpoint and I thought there were two people. I couldn't believe it!"

"That would've been me then," said Walter. "So far as I know I've got the only tandem wing in town."

"Dios mio..." said Dave. "I'd be too chicken!" He continued to supervise the kitchen, which was staffed by several dreadheads and hipsters, most of whom looked pleasantly stoned.

"Why don't you come along and watch a time or two?" offered Walter. "It's a pleasant ride up to launch and always an adventure once your feet leave the ground. We've got a fun place to land, too."

"Maybe I'll do that," replied Dave. "Do you fly that thing often?"

"The tandem? All the time. Whenever I get some gringo to break out his wallet that is. I sell rides."

"Really," said Dave. "How much?"

"One hundred bucks, or five hundred Quetzals. Hell, I'll even take pesos. That's three hundred thousand."

"Fantastic!" said Dave. "Do you get many takers?"

"Sometimes... I had three just last week."

"Three hundred dollars!" he exclaimed. "You can afford some of our food," and laughed his easy laugh. "Three hundred dollars!" Walter wanted to change the subject. Nothing like being exposed as a 'rich' gringo in a foreign land, far from home.

"Tell you what Dave: I'll donate one free tandem to the soup kitchen."

Dave's brow furrowed. "What do you mean?"

"You find me someone to donate a hundred bucks to the kitchen and he flies for free."

"¡Bueno!" yelled Dave. "Let's do it, I know several people I can talk into this. They'll LOVE it!" He dropped a crate of onions and stripped off his apron. He yelled to Sally that he'd be back and jumped on his bike. He and Walter pedaled off in different directions- Walter was headed to launch, Dave was gone to find his lucky benefactor.

The next day Walter went to Miracle Dave's kitchen on the way out of town with his gringos, to get Dave and his passenger. A tourist from Minnesota had come up with the hundred-dollar donation and wanted to fly. Walter pulled up in front of the kitchen and was introduced to Big Bruce from Mankato. Bruce was about six-foot-three, 210 pounds; he was out of the question. No way was Walter gonna try to step off launch with this guy. He should have told Dave of his weight restriction, but hadn't stopped to think.

Privately, Walter had been hoping Dave would come up with a woman, anyway. "Aww heck Bruce," said Walter. "No way I'm gonna try to fly with you, sorry."

"Whaddya mean?" asked Bruce and Dave in tandem.

"No offense man, but you're just too damn BIG, or I'm too damn CHICKEN, or maybe BOTH." They looked crestfallen at Walter, so he explained: "Launching and landing are the most dangerous part of any flying. I make it easy by using the right glider, at the right launch, in the right conditions... and with the right passenger. The right passenger weighs a hundred fifty pounds or less. In those circumstances, it's easy. Sorry Bruce."

"But I already gave Dave the donation," observed Bruce.

"And I already spent it!" cried Dave.

The situation was not good, and Walter had to do something to keep this idea from backfiring. It was looking as though he would have to make the cash donation himself after all.

"Isn't there someone else you might enjoy seeing fly?" he asked hopefully. Bruce's eye fell on Sally, the tiny Guatemalan woman. In fact, he'd been watching her work these past few moments. She was dressed, as always, in the costume of her village- Santa Caterína, a small village on the shore of Lake Atitlan only a couple of miles down a burro trail from Panajachel. Santa Caterína was directly below one of the launches that the pilots flew, there was a rickety old hang gliding ramp there that was about to fall several hundred feet off the cliff, and that Walter refused to let any of his gringos even stand on.

Bruce spoke up: "Sally," he said. Sally stopped and grinned at the gringo. "Do you want to fly?" he asked.

Sally wasn't fluent in English, but she was no dummy either. She had, apparently, been following the conversation. Of course she wanted to fly. She was the perfect size too, and as she smiled Walter realized that she was quite attractive in an indigenous female way. Most of them were short and squat and had bad teeth. Sally, though very short indeed, was quite nicely shaped, had a brilliant smile, and was otherwise quite fastidious. She was clad head-to-foot in her colorful native garb, from a rainbow turban that wrapped up her long indigo hair, to the Caterína 'guipil' blouse of every hue, and the straight wrap-around skirt that ran below her knees. The blouse had nursing slots in it to make feeding her small child easier. Occasionally, as Sally went about her chores, one of these slots or the other would fall open enough to reveal one or the other of Sally's nourishing nipples. This type of modesty was not high on the list of priorities for the native women. Shapely ankles and flat shoes completed Sally's countenance. She was identical in most every way to all the other women from her village, a group of females known collectively as Catarinéctas.

Sally was a lovely Catarinécta.

It was also obvious that Bruce was smitten with Sally. Seems that Bruce had made the donation to the soup kitchen largely because Sally might be impressed by his wealth, humility and generosity. Sally, Bruce and Walter piled into the Ford-From-Hell with the other gringos headed for the skies. Introductions were made and the plans laid out. The other flyers were enthusiastic about Sally's upcoming adventure. On the way to launch Walter wheeled the Ford off the road at the rickety ramp above Sally's village. Santa Caterína was spread out along the cliffs below, clinging to them. The crazy quilt of streets and shacks stopped only at the water's edge, where the deep, blue waters began. There was no beach on the shore at Santa Caterína; a few cattails grew along the very edge, where the lake level was subject to minor fluctuations, but otherwise it was all deep water.

They stood on the cliff and looked out at the scene, Walter cautioning all to stay off the wooden ramp. A scorpion was spotted lurking atop a piece of the footing; no one approached except Sally who skipped lightly out onto the perch. Walter cringed as she stood looking out at the spectacular lake view below, and the three volcanoes that stand sentinel across the waters. The gringo tried to coax her back to the relative safety of the dirt road, which also seems about ready to fall off the cliff. Both platforms did not look as though they would survive the next earthquake.

Sally just threw out her arms like a bird and made ready to fly. "Oohh!" she exclaimed. She kicked up one leg like a fledgling little songbird, trying to leave the nest. "¡Vamanos!" she cried. "¡Volar!"

"Aqui, no!" said Walter. *Not here!* The natural cliff launch further down the road, he explained, is much safer, and also farther, making the flight a bit more of a challenge, more fun. "We will travel on to a better spot."

Sally looked disappointed. "Thiz mi pueblito," she said, pointing to the settlement below.

"Oh, we're gonna fly right past here," said Walter. "You just wait."

"We fly there," said Sally. She still stood out on the ramp, her toes hanging off, her finger pointed at the cliffside village below.

Walter laughed nervously. "There's nowhere to land down there Sally. We'd be foolish to even try. There's some cattails down there where we might stuff it in, in case of no other choice, but I plan on making it to town."

Sally looked disappointed, and another gringo spoke: "Where are the cattails?"

Walter pointed out a small band of green along the lake. "Right there... you see a bunch of cattails that grow a good ten or fifteen feet high. I landed there once last year."

"You landed THERE? Why?"

"Just to prove to myself I could do it. I figured if I was planning to come back with a bunch of gringos, then I should make the worst landing available to be sure it could be done."

"How'd it go?"

"Fine. You can simply skim the water and land long. The cattails provide a good cushion. It's like landing in a net. You guys can do the same thing if you must, but I strongly suggest you try to complete the flight into town."

"We not go there?" said Sally. "Mi pueblito?"

Walter laughed. "Not if I can help it," he answered confidently.

Up on launch, getting Sally into the harness was a bit of an experience. She was dressed, as mentioned, in her native garb. These did not include pants, or any kind of leggings at all, so when she stepped into the leg loops they hoisted her dress up around her hips. Sally didn't seem to care, or even notice. So without further delay, Walter showed Sally how to hold her arm around him and they practiced a few runs. Then, they stood at the edge of launch, steadied the wing, and JUMPED!

Mirador tandem flight

The launch was fine, a three-stepper, and soon Walter and Sally were soaring launch. Or trying to... But there was no lift here, and Walter quickly turned towards the distant landing field, far away in Panajachel. He pulled the nose down gently to get the most possible glide, and the wing sunk dramatically. With a sinking feeling, literally and figuratively, the gringo tried to stretch the glide. If they could get into the bowl above Santa Caterína with reasonable altitude, there would be a good chance to work up some altitude there. Into the bowl they flew, sinking, sinking...

Holy SHIT! thought Walter, though he didn't say it. He wanted to scream it, but that would not be professional. How would his passenger feel if her pilot began screaming in panic? *Oh SHIT!* It was a bit of panic now. *This is NOT working OUT!* It seemed that suddenly he was eyeing the waves on the surface of Lake Atitlan, and setting up a tailwind approach for the cattails in Santa Caterína!

"Vamos a mi pueblito?" asked Sally hopefully. *Are we going to my village?* She was gleeful at the possibility, and waved happily to a few spectators below. Walter just grunted and turned the wing hard. One more turn and he was aimed at the shore. The glider skimmed over the water and for a second Walter thought he had miscalculated his approach and would come up horribly short. But the flight path of the final turn was straight downwind, which carried the glider farther than normal. With an incredible rush, it carried its two occupants into a standing wall of cattails ten feet tall, just as Walter flared.

WHUMP!, the glider made a rushing sound at impact, then it stopped suddenly, but gently. The cattails sprung back a bit and when Walter opened his eyes he found himself stuck in several inches of oozing muck at the base of the reeds. His head was more-or-less on dry land, but his feet were in Lake Atitlan.

Sally let out a WHOOP! of pleasure, somewhat louder than anything Walter thought her capable of. Joyously, she scrambled to her feet and let out yet another holler. Walter got to his feet now too, and began to unclip their harnesses. Sally was all grins, and she gave Walter a big hug about his waist. The gringo had to hold the glider firm against the cattails, which were trying to spring back on their intruder and dump them both into the lake. But Sally was overjoyed with gladness. She thanked Walter again, and promptly set off up the bank of the lake, scrambling through the reeds and weeds and over rocks, still wearing the harness. Already, a small crowd had gathered just above the lake, to see who could be in the colorful wing that had descended from their sky; it was a rare day when one of those graceful things swooped in for a visit. Next thing they knew- here comes Sally, raising out of the mud and muck at the shore. By the time she reached the top of the bank one of her shoes had disappeared, sucked off her foot by the muck.

But the crowd loved it. They saw Sally scrambling up the bank and couldn't believe their collective eyes, Sally- local girl- comes flying into Santa Caterína on wings. The last Walter saw of Sally, for a while anyway, was as they hoisted her upon their shoulders, and carried her off for a victory fiesta. Walter was left to break down and drag the wing out himself, but he didn't mind. It had been a big day for the Caterinécta.

If passion drives you, let reason hold the reins.
-- *Benjamin Franklin*

Randy's Whirling Dervish or,
Into The Maelstrom

As Randy stood on launch atop Shaw Butte above Phoenix, Arizona a drop of perspiration dripping off his forehead and dribbling down his Foster Grants, his right wing was picked up by the rowdy launch cycle and he had to fight it back to level. Silently, he cursed the air, and another bead of sweat rolled down his chest. Dressed as he was in full skier's outfit, including facemask and gloves, Randy might have been up at Snow Bowl high on the flanks of Mount Humphries near Flagstaff on a bitter winter day, instead of perched atop Shaw Butte where the temperature had just exceeded the three-digit mark. The city below shimmered with heat waves and it was headed for hundred-plus degrees in the shade as Randy lifted and steadied his wing again.

Below him, out at the vacant lot on the corner of 19th Avenue and Cactus Road, several glideheads had already sunk out. They baked under the afternoon sun and quickly bagged their wagons. Every one of them felt an urgency to get out of those clothes due to extreme heat and to get the wing broke down after landing due to the violent dust devils that patrolled the landing field. Let one of them grab your wing as it sat in the field and you would be in for some repairs- or worse. You might never see that wing again.

Far above Randy a few glideheads- the lucky ones- the ones who had punched-off ahead of him and actually caught the elusive Stairway to the Heavens, were turning into tiny dots thousands of feet overhead. Those guys were happy to be dressed like high-tech Eskimos.

Not comfortable with the balance of the wing just then, Randy set it down. "How about those guys above?" he inquired of just about anyone. The other glideheads and a few wuffos who were gathered atop the Butte turned their gazes skyward and chortled in amazement.

"Skyed-out!" came the chorus.

Randy chomped at the bit, whinnied like a stud. "I'm waiting on a good cycle," he declared. There was one thing certain about Randy- he was a go-for-it kind of dude.

Behind him another flyer, dressed in much the same manner, moved up to stand behind Randy- there was only room for one glidehead at a time to huck himself off the Butte. "Looks like a good one to me," he observed from the on-deck circle. "I'd take this one if I was you." It was a ploy often used to get to the front of the line.

It worked on Randy, or maybe it just felt right all of a sudden, but as the spectators watched he picked up the glider once again, balanced it nicely over his head, and obliged. "CLEAR!" he hollered. With three giant steps and a grunt of effort he threw himself like Pegasus into the sweltering desert air over Phoenix. Randy's race to the sky was ON.

Eight hundred feet below, Walter sat in the shade of his wing- actually sitting on the base tube as a human anchor against the dusties. He had his wing pulled into the lee of his van as added protection against the vagaries of Mother Nature. He had just stripped off his own ski outfit and was removing his flying boots now...

"SHIT!" he exclaimed, while watching the action atop the Butte, "FUDGE!" Walter was one of the unfortunate souls who had sunk out. He had stood atop launch much as Randy just had, he had sweated down his shades, he had picked up the glider a few times, he had judged the conditions, and he had thrown himself out there for better or worse. And... he had judged wrong. Or perhaps his thermaling skills just weren't up to the task. Whatever... "Gol dang it," he exclaimed now. "Phooey!"

Walter had gotten maybe five minutes of flight for his efforts and it had been like flying in a blender- just unidentifiable turbulence tossing him about in all directions. Walter had made one desperate three-sixty and slipped it badly, scaring the BeJezuz out of himself, and then high-tailed it out to the LZ where he had flared too soon and popped into the sky. This maneuver had ended with a loud WACK as he returned abruptly back to Mother Earth in a cloud of dust.

At the moment he was just happy to be alive to try again later. Or maybe tomorrow. He wasn't about to quit though, he was not that wise.

"Good try," said Moe as he walked over and squatted in the shade beneath Walter's Comet 185. "Wet yer whistle?" Walter took a good slug off Moe's water bottle and then cursed his luck again. "SHIT!" he said. Moe laughed at Walter's angst and then, looking back towards launch observed;

"There goes Randy."

Randy burbled around at launch altitude for a while, doing better than Walter had, but not hooking into that wild ride-to-the-clouds. As Walter broke down and bagged his wing he kept an eye on Randy, who now was first above launch, and then below. Randy cranked it, and he banked it. He flew with style and determination. And then... he began to sink.

At about that moment a swirl of sweltering air entered the LZ and formed into a tight little dust devil which danced and snaked its way diagonally across the field, leaped high into the sky, and gave the windsock a twist.

"DUST DEVIL!"

It was a collective cry of alarm as the dustie swirled past Walter who had his wings folded now and was pulling the bag over it. He was forced to grab the whole affair in a bear hug to keep it from blowing over. He closed his eyes for a moment, against the blowing swirling dust. The devil seemed to gain strength and momentum about mid-field where it tightened into a beautiful, if fearsome core, with what looked like miniature explosions at its feet. Atop the dervish, which had grown to perhaps a thousand feet, the dust and debris spouted out like a fountain. If it carried on in this manner for another minute or so, it was bound to cross the busy intersection of 19th and Cactus, where it would likely snarl the heavy vehicular traffic. Here was some turbulence to strike fear in the heart of any flyer...

Well, almost any...

Randy, involved in a desperate dance with the Thermal Gods, cranked his wing this way, and banked it that. He pushed, he pulled, he struggled, he sweated. Yet he was slowly headed down, down into the Hell that was Phoenix, down into shameful disgrace. Redoubling his determination to join his fellow Sky Gods at the glory of cloudbase, Randy determined to never give up. Just then he saw it...

DUST DEVIL!

The whirling dervish had sprung up from the dusty landing field and as he watched, it grabbed the windsock and gave it a wild twist. From Randy's `perspective it looked like some demented and perverse brown fountain, which spouted for no apparent reason into the sky. Except... Randy knew the reason. The reason for the dust devil was intense surface heating, atmospheric instability, and the Coriolis effect. First, the Sun heats the ground unevenly. Then the ground heats the air above it. That air being warmer and less-dense than the air around it, it begins to rise. As the air is set in motion it is affected by the rotation of the Earth and begins to spin- the Coriolis effect. Like a spinning ice skater who pulls in her arms, the rising air begins to spin faster and faster, and gains enough strength to lift dirt, dust, trash and small critters off the planet and carry it all into the sky. Swirling winds in a dustie can hit fifty miles an hour, or more, rising as fast as two-thousand feet per minute. This type of air can rip a fragile wing to pieces!

Randy understood all this of course. This was not his first rodeo. Nor was it the first dustie of his flying career- he was a dedicated desert flyer after all. He also knew that the devil could provide the lift he so desperately wanted if he could just get to it high enough, and so he made a startling decision; he would point his nose at it, he would work that thermal, he would conquer that beast, he would grab that dusty fountain. He would make a pact with that devil...

He would sky-out!

Dust Devil

In Español: remolino- whirlwind

"What the Hell is he DOING?" Walter was unsure who had raised the question, but he turned his gaze skyward and beheld; Randy was making a beeline towards the gnarly dust devil, which had just swept its way through the landing field raising Hell. He was at about five hundred feet- an altitude where most glideheads would be setting up an approach to land, yet he was flying straight at the towering column of energy, and if he held this course he would intersect the devil at about its waist.

"WHAT THE HELL IS HE DOING? TURN AWAY RANDY, TURN AWAY!"

But Randy did not turn away. Instead, he flew straight for the dustie, he hit the dustie, he was flipped over by the dustie, and he disappeared into the dustie!

Now, flying into dust devils is a hang gliding no-no, for sure. In fact, Walter would like to go so far as to tell all who inquire that NO light aircraft should be flying into dust devils if there is any possibility of avoiding such a decision. Walter would like to advise- right here- that if you see a dust devil spring up in your flight path, you should stick yer tail between yer legs, point yer ass at it and RUN!

"WHAT THE HELL?"

The glideheads on the ground began to dash along behind the tower of terror. None of them were entirely sure why they followed, simply that they were compelled to follow. This was High Drama after all, this was Man's Classic Struggle with Nature, and this was Man's Classic Struggle with Hisself. Randy's wingtip appeared through the swirling brown maelstrom a time or two, and it was impossible to determine if he was actually doing the flying anymore, or not.

NOT, was the most likely guess.

The dustie carried him along for a few moments and on the ground the glideheads sprinted along behind. The whole show was approaching the busy junction of 19th Avenue and Cactus, and tall power lines.

Suddenly a streamer appeared out of the side of the snaky apparition. It was a skinny Nylon bridle, bright red. Attached to the bridle was Randy's parachute recovery system. Randy had just ripped the system off the harness container on his chest and gave it a good huck. Apparently our guess that he was no longer doing the driving was an accurate assumption. The 'chute container exited the dustie and stretched to its full length of about twenty feet, and then the deployment bag popped off. The miracle that happened next was just exactly as advertised: the long skinny canopy popped open in a beautiful blue and gold flower, and revealed itself as a parachute. An *emergency recovery system* actually, standard equipment in hang gliding harnesses, an item that may never see the light of day, but an essential piece of safety gear, especially if you plan to fly into Hell. Attached to the other end, the end that was still invisibly lost in the dustie, was Randy and his hang glider.

Walter was breathless and speechless too as he chased the dervish and watched the horrible show. He saw the parachute appear from the side of the dust devil, he watched it blossom, and then he saw Randy and his glider swing out into clear sky. The apparition hung there only a moment however- it might well have been Wile E. Coyote himself- and then the dustie snatched once again at its gritty victim and sucked him back inside. Randy was given another quick spin or two as though tossed in a Wash-o-Matic, and then spit out once again. This time he was looking straight down at the power lines along 19th Avenue.

The nightmare swung to, and the nightmare swung fro. Randy was deposited back to Earth with a thud and his own cloud of dust, narrowly averting the deadly wires as if guided by divine luck. The wing, or perhaps the "wreckage" was a better word, collapsed atop him.

The glideheads arrived moments later as the dust settled and they lifted the wing to peer underneath. Everyone was certain they would find Randy a goner- or perhaps just in the throes of death. Instead, he pushed his helmet up off his nose and exclaimed through a dusty visage:

"Did you see me? DID YOU SEE ME!"

The glideheads unclipped Randy's harness and lifted the glider off him- the control triangle was a broken mess, but there seemed to be little other damage. "Did YOU SEE ME?" It had become Randy's mantra, or maybe his brain was addled and he was stuck on rewind.

"Did you see me?" he asked one and all, as though the other flyers might have been playing marbles all along.

"Oh we saw you all right," replied Dana from amongst the crowd. "In fact, I got it all on video!"

"DID YOU SEE ME!" yelled Randy. "DID YOU SEE ME?"

"Yes Randy. We saw you, and we couldn't believe anybody would be quite as reckless or... just plain go-for-it."

"Did you SEE ME?"

What are dustdevils?

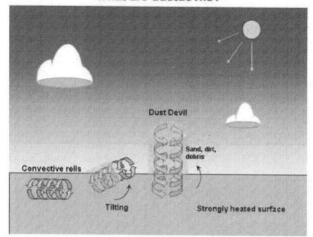

A dustdevil is a whirlwind into which dust and debris gets caught up, making it visible. Dust devils form through a different mechanism than tornadoes, and are much smaller, usually only 10 to 50 feet in diameter, and usually not extending more than 100 feet into the air. They usually are seen in relatively dry conditions, when sunlight is providing strong heating of the surface, and when winds are generally light. The heated land surface can start to produce convective rolls of air (as in the diagram above). Some of these rolls can get tilted upright, producing a dust devil.

Beth Walks the Dog or,
It Was A Match Made In Hell

B eth stepped out of Hotel Del Bosque with her dog on a leash. The train rumbled past behind the hotel, creating an intense racket and enveloping the surroundings in a thick acrid cloud of diesel smoke. Nobody seemed to notice this but Beth. She had one of the most sensitive olfactory systems on the planet, of any human. Smoke, anything but pot smoke that is, was the worst. *Hotel of the Forest Hell,* thought the Beth. *More like Hotel of the Friggin' Belching Rumbling Railroad!* This was yet another example of incompetence from their guide, that worthless Walter. Bring us deep into Mexico and take us to a stinking place like this!

Beth and her dog headed straight for the train tracks, though. It was the one nearby place where the dog could relieve herself and not create a hazard. It was nice to have a moment's peace from the gringos. This particular group, calling themselves 'Team Tahoe', was particularly rowdy. They seemed never to have enough cervesa. Some of them drank it for breakfast, and they call themselves pilots! *Bunch of drunks and maniacs is more like it*, swore Beth. Across a fence the highway ran along the train tracks and was choked with fast-moving traffic. Beth tried to stay far away from the potential danger. She stuck to the far side of the tracks and waited for her beast to sniff out an appropriate spot.

"Come on girl... come on," she implored. The critter sniffed here and there, undecided.

Meanwhile, Walter was at the helm of the Ford-From-Hell, which was indeed packed with a bunch of drunken gringo maniacs. You'd think Team Tahoe was on vacation or something... He swung through traffic, navigating back to the hotel.

Dinner had been delicious and a great success. They had dined at La Cueva, *The Cave,* and drank their fill of Mexican cervesa and tequila. The high point of the evening had come after dinner, when the waiters had sneaked up behind the Farmer and thrown a tequila 'popper' down his throat. The waiters did not realize that the Farmer was a complete tea-totaler of course. Farmer had not had so much as a barley-pop since his release from the Navy many years ago. He was the sober one of the bunch. And the Farmer, in turn, had no idea what was coming.

But the waiters had indeed snuck up on Farmer; while one of them grabbed his head and prized open his lips, the other popped the concoction on the table top to make the contents fizz, and then quickly poured the mess down poor Farmer's throat. Lastly, both waiters had grabbed Farmer by his cheeks and SHOOK his head. Such was the tradition of dining at La Cueva.

The look of shock, surprise, dismay and distress on Farmer's face precipitated a near riot at the table. The gringos began throwing food and drink at him. They sat still only for their own dose of the same swill, the same poison. The waiters obliged, mixing one after another 'popper', slamming them on the table, pouring them down the gringos, shaking, cheap tequila and 7UP. A mariachi band strolled into La Cueva and began playing their own rendition of 'Tequila'.

Chaos reigned.

Walter had finally managed to get the bill paid and all his gringos back in the Ford. Tomorrow they would drive to the mountain village of Tapalpa for some circles, with any luck it would be another long day. He was half drunk and briefly considered letting the Farmer drive. Farmer had remained sober throughout the proceedings despite his ordeal, and was the only truly sober one of the bunch, but Walter didn't trust his navigational skills. Besides, after twenty years of a milk and juice diet, Farmer's system may have been in shock from a double-shot of Moctezuma.

While still about a kilometer from the hotel, the gringos were overtaken by a speeding Volkswagen van. The 'combi' tailgated briefly and then swung recklessly around the Ford and raced on ahead. Beeping its horn as it passed, Walter saw it was being driven by a lovely señorita, who flashed a brilliant smile as she sped past. Indeed- the combi was packed with girls, all of them smiling at the Ford. Some of them waved. One blew a kiss. Walter's gringos went crazy;

"PUSSY!" came the latest rally cry from the back of the Ford. "PUSSY! Wahooo! Go GET 'EM WALTER! Step on it!"

Not willing to argue, and himself intrigued, Walter put his foot into the Ford. Overhead, Royce and Rooster climbed over the glider rack and stood on the hood. They howled and exhorted Walter.

"¡ANDALE!" they shouted. "PUSSY, PUSSY, PUSSY!"

Walter quickly pulled up behind the combi. They swerved in and out of traffic, the girls laughing in delight, the gringos howling with a horny drunken ardor. Finding a break in the traffic, Walter swung around the combi and pulled even, speeding through the streets abreast of the muchachas. His gringos were all standing now, between the gliders. Even the Farmer got into the act, holding his hat with one hand, beckoning with the other. Walter sped past the hotel and raced under a railroad bridge...

Beth's beast finally decided on a place to shit. She settled into a squat just as Beth heard the gringo rally cry. She thought sure it was Royce, or maybe Rooster, but whomever, it attracted her attention just long enough to see the Ford-From-Hell speed past and duck under an overpass.

"PUSSY!" she heard as they disappeared. "PUSSY PUSSY PUSSY!"

That damn Walter, she barked at herself. *That's enough! This guy is a menace to society!* Her dog finished shitting and sniffed at the results. Beth yanked her chain and hurried back to the Hotel of the Friggin' Belching Rumbling Railroad Del Bosque to confide in Rodney what she had just witnessed. Together, they would confront the gringo. Enough of his crap.

Gripped on the tiller of the Ford-From-Hell, grinning foolishly at the racing combi full of splendid señoritas speeding along a short arm's reach away, Walter glimpsed, for a split second, what looked like Beth and her dog, over by the railroad tracks. It had to be them; the dog was squatting and Beth was looking startled, his way. What other dog, amongst the thousands of curs in Guadalajara, would be on a leash? What other gringa would be performing such a chore?

Shit!

The spectacle arrived at a 'glorietta', a Mexican traffic circle. Together, they laid into a hard turn to larboard. The girls had the inside track and Walter nosed the Ford up close to their starboard haunch. The Ford felt top-heavy, what with all the gliders loaded on the rack and all the gringos standing and beckoning. With tires squealing, the procession swung recklessly around the glorietta. Taking the inside lane the women gave Walter quite a chase. For several circles Walter managed to keep the Ford hot on their tail feathers. Then they swerved suddenly outside and disappeared down a main boulevard with much waving of hands, leaving nothing but a scent of pleasing perfume to pursue.

"Chingasa Walter!" hollered his gringos.

"You lost 'em!"

"You blew it gringo!"

"Couldn't you just smell the PUSSY?"

The entire encounter had lasted but a minute, leaving Walter not with the lusty image of carnal Mexican delights, but a dismal realization of the Beth and her beast, registering like a nightmare image on the photo of his psyche. Pablo and Beth were already unhappy with Walter, to say the least. They seemed to resent the fact that Walter was having the time of his life, while they were the most miserable gringos in all of Mexico...

Walter swung the Ford outside too now, and slowed down. He rolled back to the hotel, disgorged his amigos, and went to face the music. There stood Rodney and the Beth, scowling, hands on hips, all business. They were not happy campers.

"You're FIRED!" they declared.

Freemont's Leap or,
A Blast From The Past

With a heave and a huck Stan threw himself off the hill and I was hot on his tail feathers. We were flying a place that Stan called "Freemont's Leap", a spectacular ridge and thermal site named for the intrepid explorer himself, which was about two thousand feet above Freemont Lake in the Wind Rivers range of the Rocky Mountains in western Wyoming. We were flying Freemont's Leap even though this was my rookie year as a glidehead and I was very much the newbie and, most amazing of all, there was nowhere to land.

That's right— Stan and I flew Freemont's Leap in the Rocky Mountains back in my very first year of flight in the summer of 1981 and there was just nowhere to land down below. The objective, as Stan was tickled to point out, would be to soar our way to safety and fulfillment in some distant alfalfa field out near Pinedale, Wyoming, population about five thousand. We would leap off Freemont's Leap and sky out and head south until we could land.

That was the Plan.

Sounds good to me, right?

The problem was the soaring part. As we all know, soaring requires a combination of pilot skill, the right weather conditions in the sky, and reasonable equipment too, which might enable the flyer to reach tremendous altitudes or, at the very least, to extend his glide and get somewhere. Pinedale for example.

What about that? What would happen if we hucked ourselves out there and discovered there were not soarable weather conditions, that we were going down rather than up, and that we would not be soaring anywhere at all, regardless of our skill, equipment and commitment?

What then?

Well then, we were fucked, to put it bluntly. Down below us was nothing but steep precipitous forest, evergreen-type forest, nowhere to land as already mentioned, right down to the deep cobalt blue of the frigid waters of Freemont lake. How well can you swim dressed in a hang gliding harness and attached to a lead, well actually aluminum weight? How well?

Twenty-six years later I was pondering that same question while I pondered the following question too: DID WE REALLY DO THAT, STAN AND I? Were we really that bold and crazy, desperate for air under our feet?

I cannot swim very well; I flunked my Lifesaving Merit Badge when I nearly drowned while attempting to strip off my own blue jeans in the chlorine depths of the pool at the YMCA. The young men at the Christian association had to rescue my sorry ass, pulling me coughing and sputtering from the water, my pants down around my ankles. The Pinedale authorities would have to drag the depths for my corpse, if I was ever foolish enough to put-down in Freemont Lake.

So, did I really do that, or was this my imagination run wild? There was really only one easy way to be sure- find Stan and ask him. Too bad I couldn't find Stan, heck, I couldn't even remember his last name. I had made inquiries within the hang gliding Old Timers' Club. Most nobody had ever known Stan, those few who did had also lost touch. Stan- where the heck are you? Will I have to do this again? Am I that stupid?

Or is it really that stupid? Remembering back twenty-six years to that only flight at Freemont's Leap I remember that it was really, really easy. I took off behind Stan when I saw that he was indeed climbing out exactly as advertised when we had arrived atop the hill and he had dashed madly up to launch where his eyes had bugged with glee and he'd shouted to me:

"IT IS TOTALLY HAPPENING!"

Stan had NOT waited for my questions; he had tossed a handful of weeds and wild flowers into the sky. They'd been snatched up the hill behind where we stood and that was all Stan needed to see. He had spun on his heel with a WHOOP! of joy and dashed off to set up his wing- unzipping bags and spreading wings and stuffing battens.

We were in a frenzy to get set up and hang checked and get off launch, and we skyed-out and turned to little dots in the enormous sky and, well, we'd survived after all. We'd flown out to a beautiful field in Pinedale, Wyoming (population 5,000), where we'd landed and fulfilled our dreams...

Could I really do that again? Sitting at yet another hang gliding site, a very popular and historic site in Draper, Utah called The Point of the Mountain, I was not at all certain. I had been camped atop the Point for some days and my attempts to aviate there had been less than spectacular. I had not hurt myself, but my desire to soar the place had resulted in miserable failure— two sled rides to the fields below, and this at a place renown for its soarability.

Nobody but rank beginners sink out at the Point, yet I did it twice in a row. What crazy notion was in my addled brain that I might perform better at Freemont's Leap, a place were going up was a matter of Life and Death? Was I just plain nuts?

Nevertheless I thought, I can drive up there, get a look at the place. Maybe the trees and bushes had grown up at launch to the point where running a hang glider off was no longer possible? Maybe I'm imagining the whole unlikely episode? Maybe there ain't really such a place as Freemont's Leap after all. Maybe there is only the wild imagination of an aging old fart once-upon-a-time-fearless-flyer. I grabbed my Rand-McNally and I turned it open to Wyoming. I located Pinedale and right next to it Freemont Lake, a long skinny body of icy water oriented north and south just as I remembered and, clearly marked right there on the map and headed up the east shore of the lake along the windward side of the Wind Rivers Range, is a spur road that dead-ends in the Bridger Wilderness Area.

It was much as I remembered.

Or does it dead-end? As I recall, this road was quite the Stairway to Heaven, leading me on towards an aerial nirvana, the type of place I have been in search of ever since. The road was there, does this validate my memories? Just because the road is marked on the map?

It is, therefore I am?

Now, I believe that most glideheads, when confronted by such a precipice, would inquire about the landing areas, and then decline to fly. Maybe they would head back to the Point of the Mountain where many gazillions of successful flights have taken place through the years. Certainly I should do the same.

But the road goes there.

I see the road, therefore I must be?

I decided I'd have to drive on up there to find Freemont's Leap and take me a gander. There was just no other choice. I tried to recruit some other glideheads to meet me in Pinedale with promises of a glidehead Shangri-La, but there were no takers amongst the ridge riders at the Point. Why should they head off on a wild buzzard chase with some old freak, headed off to somewhere they might fly, when they could just stay right there in Salt Lake City and log big hours? Why indeed...?

Good question.

I pulled solo into Pinedale and ran a few errands and asked a few locals about it. "Have you ever seen anyone hang gliding in these parts?" I inquired, soliciting a variety of replies as always.

"Ahh, yeah, they drag 'em up behind boats out on the lake, don't they?"

"Seems like somebody died at that hand glidin' up around Rock Springs a few years back, ain't that right ma?"

"We might be crazy, but none of us is that crazy."

...and so forth. Clearly, none of the locals had a clue about hang gliding around Freemont Lake. Possibly they were all smarter than me. The only character I encountered who had any sage advise at all about what I was contemplating was a lanky cowpoke I met in a local watering hole who observed;

"If you jump off these here mountains in one of them there things, yer askin' fer Big Trouble." He sipped on his Coors. "It's a recipe for disaster," he said.

Really?

Finally, resignedly, I got back in my wagon and headed up the spur road out of Pinedale, searching for the Stairway to Heaven, or Big Trouble, or at least my own self-confirmation. I drove along pastoral ranch land for a few miles until the mountains came out to meet the road, and in the near distance the Wind Rivers themselves dominated my windshield— a wall of awesome snow-capped peaks. One of them must be Gannett Peak, 13,804 feet-above-sea-level, the highest peak in the entire Cowboy State.

Soon the pastures turned into aspen groves and then aspens with mixed conifers and then finally pure pine tree forest. I drove past the entrance to White Pine Ski Area in the Bridger Wilderness Area with little real interest— just barely a glance. Up and up I climbed until finally, around a gentle curve, there was an opening in the forest on the lake side of the road with a paved pullout, just as I'd remembered.

I swung my motor home on in and shut her down and noticed right off a sweet fragrance of alpine air and wild flowers. I jumped out of my hooch and my dog Sarge and I dashed up the last few steps to the ridge top and there... it was... the Stairway to Heaven. Or maybe the Stairway to Hell. But it was Freemont's Leap all right and the steady breeze blew straight up. It was launchable now.

My heart leaped up to my throat and I could scarcely believe my eyes, it was three o'clock of an afternoon and to repeat the words my old amigo Stan had uttered all those years ago;

"It is totally happening!"

While Sarge sniffed happily about I plunked my ass down atop a rock and marveled at the scene before me. The launch is a perfect steep natural slope that faces directly into the prevailing southwesterly and is knee-deep in scarlet gilia, slivery lupine and Indian paintbrush. The slope drops off steeply— about one-to-one, all the way to the lake about two thousand feet below. The lake itself is long and skinny and wind-shadowed at the far shore, white-capped at the near shore. The wind on the water below is clearly straight in, except for those areas where the water swirls from a thermal that has departed the far shore and is working its way across the narrow reach. In short- a glidehead's dream.

Or perhaps nightmare: a perfect launch, but nowhere in sight to land.

Well, I got out my machete and some surveyor's tape and fashioned myself a wind streamer, which I propped up atop the ridge in a cairn of rocks. It was a totally harmless activity that might be construed as a serious effort towards future flying. Then I stood back to admire my work. The wind held the streamers straight out with a bit of the vertical to them. As I stood there marveling at my surroundings a red tail hawk soared past, gave me a look of distain and a holler of "GEEK!" and then sailed off. A shiver of anticipation flew up and down my spine. Am I really going to do this again? If so I would be violating another of the hang gliding common-sense rules of safety, which is:

DON'T FLY ALONE YOU FOOL.

Stan, where are you now, when I need you? You were pretty dang ballzy back then, are you that ballzy now?

I decided to wait on such a decision for a while, I got out my book and my EZ chair and settled in for a bit of relaxation, just to see how things go. I read, I fed Sarge, I made some dinner. Then I slept right there on launch and it was still nicely soarable when I turned-in. I awoke as usual at about 4am to void my weak bladder and I stood on launch as I relieved myself. I couldn't help but notice that it was still blowing straight in a marginal five-to-ten, probably still scratchable out there even at this hour. Standing there in the darkness under the Milky Way with my pecker in hand, that's when I decided.

If it was obviously soarable tomorrow, er, today, at three o'clock I would leap from Freemont's Leap yet again. Stan or no Stan.

Returning to my bunk I slept uneasily as is my wont until sun-up. I laid there restlessly long after my usual rise-and-shine hour, and I told myself that I was a helluva lot smarter now, after twenty six years of flying, than I had been in my rookie year when I followed Stan into the Wyoming sky.

But was I? What if I was REALLY smart? Well, if I were really smart, I would go home, stick my tail between my legs, whatever. That is— I would do something constructive with my remaining years.

Freemont's Leap? What am I, a crazy old fool?

In the morning I spent a few hours perched atop the launch with my lawn chair and my book, and meanwhile the wind picked up gradually until by 10am it was clearly, totally happening. Facing my dilemma, at high noon I dragged my Wills Wing down off the roof and I began to set 'er up. This action caused the very occasional traffic up and down the spur road to stand on the brakes and pay me a visit.

"Are ya gonna jump?"

"Well, that's the idea, yeah."

"When?"

"Uhh... three." A quick look at my wristwatch revealed the time of 1:49pm.

"Why not now?"

"Because I'm too chicken, that's why."

Hesitation, then, "You tryin' to screw up yer courage?"

"Something like that, yes," I replied.

A glance over the cliff. "You ever flown it before?"

"Ahh, well..." I wasn't really sure what "it" referred to; was it the mountain or the wing? The sky maybe? "Yes," I continued. "Once. At least, I think I have. As I recall I have."

"We can't wait for three."

"Mister, I been waitin' for twenty six years," I replied. "I ain't in no hurry now. You just go on..."

"Good luck," he chortled as he drove off.

At high noon it was TOTALLY HAPPENING.

At one o'clock it was TOTALLY HAPPENING.

At two o'clock it was TOTALLY HAPPENING.

At two-thirty it was TOTALLY HAPPENING and I started laying out my flight gear, filling my Camelback and attaching my flight deck. I regretted I had no personal flotation devise in case I put down in the waters below. I regretted I had no emergency locator transmitter in case I put down in the wilderness around. At two forty-five I stepped into my harness and at three pm I stood yet again atop launch at Freemont's leap, with my helmet in hand. It was TOTALLY HAPPENING, clearly soarable, plenty of birds soaring the ridge and skyed-out in the Heavens above. A bit too strong for self-launching however— I would need some help getting to launch. But I was committed. Committed at least to getting my wing up to launch and seeing how she felt. But I would need some wire help.

Suited up in my harness and flight gear, I walked out to the spur road and stood waiting for an assistant or two. I was soon lucky enough that along came three young ranch hands in a pickup. Seeing me standing there waving my helmet in my strange getup, they slammed on the brakes and came to a stop on the pavement. Before I could explain what I needed they started in on stupid newbie questions one-through-ten...

"You gonna jump?"

"That's the idea, how 'bout you guys?"

"Oh man I'd love to... you crazy... don't yer arms get tired... don't it hurt when you crash... I wanna parachute jump... can you swim... blah blah nonsense...?"

"Whatever you guys are up to," I said, "you should just drop everything and get flying. It won't get any easier as you get older." I wanted to encourage the next generation of flyers, but it looked pretty hopeless. What is it about hang gliding that my generation found so compelling, and this generation is so indifferent to?

I took them over to my wing and showed them how to hold on by the wires and how to hold the wings level and to make sure they would NOT let go until I hollered CLEAR and then to get down and out of my way.

Together we moved the wings up into the breeze on launch and brought the wings level and pointed down the slope. Everything felt just about perfect meanwhile and my telltale showed about fifteen to twenty miles-per-hour straight on my beak. It was... need I say it? TOTALLY HAPPENING!

Picking up the glider and steadying it with my assistants it felt so good I immediately asked them to release the glider by hollering CLEAR as instructed. Next thing I knew they jumped down and clear of my wing and I was standing there on Freemont's Leap, ground handling just fine, the wing nicely balanced, light and eager to fly. In fact, I had to hold her back from taking off... This was Freemont's Leap after all, not Freemont's Crash. I stood atop the ridge ground handling like mad, facing the wind, the wing was tugging at my harness and... I came face-to-face with my dilemma.

Should I, or should I not?

"Clear!" I hollered again, mostly for effect this time. It was Indecision calling. I could see my launch crew off to the side, everyone held their breath.

It is often said that every journey begins with a single step. A single step was about all I got out of Freemont's Leap, a single step and my Fusion floated willingly off launch and immediately began climbing. I cast a glance below at my launch crew and yelled them a thanks, they stood with eyes wide and mouths forming 'O's. I gave the bar a shove and squirted for the sky above. For better or for worse, I had just taken Freemont's Leap!

My flight deck sang a happy song and my launch crew quickly became tiny dots on the ridge below me. I focused out front now and grinned from ear-to-ear with happiness or foolishness, hard to say which. I nudged the bar for a gentle right turn and headed north along the ridge— away from Pinedale and the alfalfa fields of Nirvana. What the hay, as long as I was climbing, I might as well enjoy the view.

I boated along the ridge as far as I dared, climbing all the while, and when the lift trailed off I turned back towards launch. Now I was at least a grand above, plenty of room for my first three-sixty, which gave me an awesome view of the Wind Rivers towering snow-capped before me. It was then I saw, and it was then I remembered— The White Pine Ski Area!

In the middle of my first circle over Freemont's Leap I looked down with sudden relief on a beatific meadow and the enormous parking lot of the ski area below. Suddenly I remembered more of Stan's advise from so many years ago...

"If," he said, "we can just get five hundred feet, we can easily glide over the back and land at the ski area."

I was SAVED!

Stan and I had indeed gotten those five hundred feet, in fact we had dialed it right up in bitchin' lift to fifteen thousand feet or so, we had turned into tiny dots, and then we'd vanished into the sky. We had left White Pine Ski Area forgotten in the dust. But now, looking down upon my salvation I couldn't believe my eyes... White Pine Ski Area was apparently hosting some sort of search-and-rescue-EMT-firefighters jamboree and the area below me was dotted with men in orange and yellow emergency-type gear, ambulances and fire trucks were scattered about on simulated life saving missions. I was more-than-saved, I was RESCUED!

There was only one place that I was going to land, no doubt about it now, I had found my own Nirvana! It was as though the Sky Gods had made prior arrangements for the arrival of the winged old fart on a dangerous mission. I hollered at the top of my voice, so that all might hear;

"WahOOOOO!"

I continued to climb into five figures on my altimeter, until I had climbed above the topmost lifts at White Pine Ski Area and then I pointed my nose at the lifts. I glided over the meadow and the parking lot, now thousands of feet below me. My spine tingled with excitement, my central nervous system had the Willies. Freemont Lake was forgotten now, the scene around me and the opportunity below me held me in thrall. As I flew out over the parking lot I dragged my shadow, a rather vague and indistinct shadow but visible nonetheless, over a few of those fire trucks, a sort of announcement of my imminent arrival. Soon I was soaring the tops of those peaks and climbing out towards the Wind Rivers. I was the only glidehead for hundreds of miles, and yet I felt quite at home, happy even. My salvation lay spread out below me, the Paramedics' Jamboree.

Then suddenly I noticed a number of these vehicles form a line, load a bunch of personnel like tiny ants, and roll out of the parking lot. "Hey wait!" I hollered, even though it seemed unlikely I was audible from such an elevated perch "Hey WAAAIIIT!" I yelled once again. "You can't leave now! Here I come!"

I quickly decided that my re-visit to the sky above Freemont's Leap had been realized, and I bailed. I banked the wing up steep and dumped the lift. I was heading DOWN! Down I spiraled, first this way and then that. I set up my approach to bring me down in the middle of the parking lot where my wheels would work best. I turned final and skidded in, touching down on my wheels and chest armor. It was inelegant perhaps, but painless.

I had SURVIVED!

I stood up and shed my harness and helmet. I raised my arms in a victory salute, fearless flyer once again. Smarter this time, and with the Gods on my side. A pickup headed in my direction and I could see it advertised the White Pine Ski Area itself across the door panel. The driver rolled up with a concerned look on his face.

"You all right?" he asked.

"Mister, I am better than all right," I replied.

He gazed over his shoulder towards the top of the ski lifts. "Where did you jump off?" he wondered aloud.

I pointed over yonder ridge and said, "Over yonder ridge." This had him very confused now, since it was a direction quite the opposite of the ski lifts.

"Where?" he inquired skeptically, turning his head.

"Over the ridge there, from the clearing alongside the road above the lake. Freemont's Leap." I hoped the sincerity of my voice was evident. The fellow got out of his pickup and looked me over.

"You didn't jump off the ski area now, did you?" Doubt was scrawled across his face.

"No sir!" sez I. "I jumped from Freemont's Leap, just like I just said." The fellow looked me over once again and then asked the obvious...

"Why did you do that?" he said. It was the Ten Thousand Dollar Question.

"Well, because there's just nowhere to land," I explained.

"Because uhh... because WHY?"

"Because there is no where to land. You see, I did this twenty-five years ago when I was young and stupid, and now that I'm old and wise I wanted to do it again. Because there's nowhere to land. Sort of a life confirmation I guess. One of those 'because it's there' things, you know?"

This information was met with a blank stare for a moment, and then a chuckle. "Well," he asked. "How was it?"

"Man," I said, "it was faaaaaantastic!"

Wyoming's Wind Rivers Range

Encounter At Los Zaucos or,
A Bargain at Any Price

Like a giant, noisy and happy centipede, the eight small Mexican boys carry my glider from the field where I landed, and deposit it at the small tienda. I, the gringo who fell from the sky, have only to haul my gearbag and tag along behind, supervising and encouraging. We arrive in our own small cloud of dust and take refuge in a spot of shade, thirsty one and all. A faded wooden sign on the door announces our location: Tiendita Los Zaucos Oxotítlan. This is my first visit. Here, should my generosity compel me and my pesos continue to flow, I could buy us all a frosty soda pop.

I ordered up the drinks and we enjoyed them in the shade of an enormous blue agave. Israel, the oldest, largest and boldest of the bunch speaks up: "¿Usted es casado señor?" *Are you married sir?*

I look forlornly at Israel and reply sadly, wistfully, "No amigo. ¡Que lastima!"

"¿Porque no?" asks the child, his brow knit with dismay. *Why not?* Genuine concern is etched across his grubby face. Israel is wearing a New York Yankees ball cap. He glances at his amigos, who mirror his concern.

"Pues, nadie me quiere," I lament sadly. *'Cause no one will have me.*

"Hay que buscar," he encourages me with conviction. He throws up his hands to punctuate his thoughts. He slurps the Coke while his amigos nod in agreement- *You must search.*

"He busce por todos lados." I assure them. *I've looked everywhere.*

Israel spreads out his arms like scrawny wings and gestures to the cluster of shacks around him. "Buscate por aqui!" he exclaims. *Look around here!*

Los Zaucos is one of the first towns a glidehead comes to as he sails up the pass toward Toluca, just a collection of cinderblock and cardboard dwellings spreading humbly over fields of sustaining milpa. A high place already, the earth rises from here to the snow-capped summit of the Nevado de Toluca Xinantécatl at 15,600 feet above sea level. A glance through the window of the tiendita frames a view of the snow-capped volcanic heights towering above a local campesino, who is struggling with a plowshare and a brace of oxen.

"De acuerdo," I agree. *All right*, and I nod my head. I just may after all, who knows what mystery life holds for us? Israel and his amigos seem in accord with that. They continue to enjoy the cokes, their pleasure evidenced by a round of loud slurping. A mangy spotted dog wanders across the highway, flops down next to Israel, and licks his foot. It's time to pay my little posse of helpers a few pesos each for their labors with my wing. Figuring Israel as spokesman is also the boss, I ask,

"¿Quanto seria amigo?" *How much will it be friend?*

Israel's countenance brightens at this suggestion.

"¿Quanto page usted señor?" he inquires. *How much do you pay sir?*

This question I ponder deeply, and I let my face brighten as I arrive at the perfect solution. Then I suggest: "Le pagan con el puro amistad." *I will pay you with pure friendship...*

Israel, underwhelmed at my generosity, scrunches up his face at me and consults his minions. They also are not exactly thrilled with the offer and they squirm uncomfortably in their seats.

"¿Esta bien?" I ask. "¿La amistad?"

This brings more squirming from my new amigos, and some obvious disappointment. A moment ago, Israel was going to help me find my bride. Now, he's not so sure that I'm worth the trouble.

"Bueno," I decide, "Un cancion, entonces?" *A song, then?*

This offer brightens the whole bunch and they nod their collective heads. This, at least, may be some more tangible reward. I burst out in a few bars of When You Wish Upon A Star. I sing loud and strong, trying to be worthy.

When you wish upon a star,
makes no difference who you are
When you wish upon a star,
your dreeeeams come truuuuuue!

I sing the first verse twice while my amigos look on, astonished, but delighted. They giggle as I juggle a few stones for them, and then finish my song-and-dance with a flourish. "Esta bien?" I ask. Is that all right? I jingle some monedas in my pocket.

Israel is indeed happier now, but clearly disappointed, too. "Es muy codo, señor," he replies. *It's very cheap sir*. To drive home his point, he slaps his elbow a time or two. This is the Mexican hand signal for 'cheapskate'.

It is said that you can count your wealth by the number of your friends. Israel has friends aplenty, but he is no philosopher. He wants Coin of the Realm. I relent, pull out the monedas, and give them all five pesos each for their efforts. In return I receive a heartfelt gracias from all before they retire to fantasize over their newfound wealth. I expect them to bite the coins, for authenticity, but they do not. Israel gives me a limp lifeless handshake; it is the Mexican way.

I calculate what this encounter has cost me: five pesos per kid times eight kids cost me forty pesos. Eight refrescos at 1.5 pesos each brought another twelve, totaling fifty-two pesos, or just under six bucks. It had been a pricey retrieve, but there were lots of amigos, and it was a long dusty trail.

Jake The Human Cannonball or, High Adventure Over Shaw Butte

"**H**ey guys, check it out!" hollered Andy. "Jake's loopin' again! WaHOO!" Walter was bent over zipping up his glider bag when he looked up above Shaw Butte in Phoenix, Arizona, and sure enough, Jake was letting 'er rip. As the rest of the 'Beauties' watched, Jake stuffed the bar, bringing the nose straight down. When the glider reached maximum airspeed, he let off the bar and ripped into a loop, pushing over the top. They were long, graceful loops, and you could hear the wing shred the sky, even from this great distance- a delayed flutter, traveling for several seconds before it reached the observers in the landing area.

"Shit!" declared Leslie. Maybe he didn't approve but Jake didn't care. From his lofty place in the sky, he couldn't hear anyway. As the glider ripped over the top of the loop and dove straight down, he stuffed the bar again and started another loop.

Walter had seen this display before. Jake was known as one of the more radical pilots who flew the Butte. He was the type who was not happy just to thermal or soar the ridge lift like most glideheads. He needed more thrills, wilder thrills, bigger thrills. But having seen it all before, Walter bent to his task again, zipping the bag.

Suddenly Andy cried out again, "LOOK!" he hollered. Walter looked. The glider was right-side-up now as it should be, but something was weird. As Walter took a double take, his eyes nearly bugged right out of his head. The glider was upright, all right, but it was also... empty! Jake was nowhere in sight! Walter blinked, thinking his eyes were playing tricks on him. But, no! The glider floated along nicely and was buffeted by some mild turbulence, BUT IT WAS EMPTY!

"Did you see that?" asked Andy. Walter could only shake his head in the negative. He was still speechless. "Holy shit!" said Andy; he was the only one who still had his tongue. "He disappeared behind the mountain!" he exclaimed.

"Shit!" said Walter, finally coming to his senses.

"Shit!" said Stony.

"Shit!" said Leslie.

"Shit!" said Andy. "Let's GO!" Without another word, the Beauties jumped into Andy's truck and sped off around the Butte. "Shit!" Andy cursed a red traffic light.

"You think there's any hurry?" asked Walter. "No one could survive a fall like that. It must have been a thousand feet. Let's not crash in our hurry."

Andy popped the clutch, squealing rubber. He only glanced at Walter. "SHIT!" he said again.

Sweetwater Lane winds around Shaw Butte and through a residential area before arriving at the dirt-road gate up Shaw Butte. Andy lead-footed the throttle recklessly and Walter wished he'd grabbed his helmet.

"SLOW DOWN ANDY!" he begged. But it was no good. Andy raced for the back of Shaw Butte like it was his own life that depended on it. Glancing up, Walter caught a glimpse of Jake's glider. It still floated around the sky and yup... It was still empty. The glider was now pointed downwind and traveling at a good clip with a tailwind.

"Slow down, Andy fer chrissake," said Leslie. "You'll kill us, too!"

But again it was no use. Fortunately, they soon reached the end of the paved road where Andy was forced to slam on the brakes. He flung open the door and jumped out with his key to unlock the gate, all in one motion. "Jake might be DEAD!" he observed. It was a foregone conclusion...

"Might be?" said Walter. "I don't think I want to go any further."

Andy threw open the gate. He jumped back in the truck and spun gravel in his hurry up the road behind the Butte. Recklessly, they rounded a couple of steep turns and were shocked to see Jake walking down the dusty trail towards them. He still wore his harness, he had a foolish grin on his face and what looked like a great bundle of laundry in his arms. At least, that was Walter's first impression. Then he realized that it wasn't laundry at all, Jake was carrying his emergency recovery parachute in his arms. He didn't even have a limp. The glideheads roared to a stop next to him.

"What the heck?" they asked, in unison. "What the...?"

Jake grinned some more and dropped the laundry in the bed of the truck.

"Thanks for the ride fellas," he said, and jumped in back. For a man who had just looked Eternity in the eye, he seemed very calm, more like he maybe really had been stuck at the laundromat all afternoon. "Let's get outta here," he suggested with a glance around.

Andy looked at Walter as if he'd just seen a ghost. Then he maneuvered the truck around on the narrow road. "What the heck?" he asked.

They drove back down the road as Leslie asked, from the back of the truck, "What the Hell happened?"

"I broke the connection," Jake explained fatter-of-factly.

"You broke it?" asked the others in unison. This was a difficult thing to do- that was the idea of a connection. In fact, none of the Beauties had ever heard of a broken connection. It was a First. But Jake was flying with a fancy piece of hardware called a 'pitchey' for a connection and so it was somewhat suspect. Still, it was not supposed to fail, and if it did fail the back-up piece of hang webbing was supposed to catch the falling flyer before he fell more than an inch or two; that was the job of the backup.

"Yep," said Jake. "I've been meaning to back it up." He smiled sheepishly... "Never got around to it."

"You mean you didn't have a backup?" Hang gliders are generally supplied with a backup loop of webbing, so that in case the impossible happens, as it just had over Shaw Butte, the flyer would not find himself in free fall.

"Then what happened?"

"Obviously," Jake stated the obvious, "I threw my 'chute."

"But you were so low!"

"Tell me about it. That was as low as I've ever deployed. Those years of skydiving came in handy yuk yuk!" This was met with incredulous nervous laughter from his fellow flyers, all of whom made a mental note to return straight to their wings and check their connections.

"I guess!" said Andy. "Well... what was it like?"

"I suppose it was scary," confessed Jake. "But I was too busy to be scared."

"What did you do, exactly?" asked Walter. He was new at this stuff, and he wanted to know how to behave if the unthinkable ever happened to him.

"Well..." said Jake, "when I came off the bar I felt right at home."

"God!" said Leslie.

"I skydive too, remember? So I stabilized and looked down. The ground was coming up FAST!"

"Then?"

"Then I realized this harness is not built for a terminal deployment. I knew it would likely fail..."

"Shit!" sang the Beauties in unison. "SHIT!"

"So I threw the 'chute and gripped the bridle, so to take up some of the deployment shock..."

"And...?"

"And, well... The canopy opened and then my feet touched."

"Just like THAT?"

"Here I am, ain't I?" said Jake, the Human Cannonball, and then added; "Burned the shit outta my hands." He held them up for all to see where the recovery system bridle had singed his flesh- his only visible injury. "See?"

"Wow!" sang the Beauties.

"Kinda busted my ass to when I hit, slipped on a rock." Jake rubbed his sore spot, as they cruised back down the Butte.

Five miles downwind of Shaw Butte, Harvey and Maude Clashan settled into the chaise lounges poolside at their lovely new home in Paradise Valley. They tipped a toast with a couple of extra dry martinis- Boodles gin shaken, not stirred. Harvey was reading the newspaper. "Honey," he mentioned casually, "there's going to be a meteor shower tonight. Maybe we should take a trip out in the desert where we can see better."

"Oh good idea, Harvey. We'll bring along a thermos with these martinis."

"Should be a great night for star gazing. Not a cloud in the sky." Harvey glanced up from the paper and something in his peripheral vision caught his eye. Suddenly, he couldn't believe what he was seeing. "Honey..." he said again, but no more words came. Harvey was looking at an empty hang glider, tailwinding along, streaking for his backyard. Then "Holy shit!" he exclaimed.

"What's the matter Dear?" said Maude, but just then the wing sliced into the Clashan's palm tree and spun sideways. It hung there for a moment and then crashed backwards into the pool.

"Holy shit, ma!" said Harvey. Maude just stood there with a martini at her lips, a olive in her mouth. They looked back and forth at each other, and at the empty glider, astonished.

"What do you suppose...?" said Maude.

"I suppose we'd ought to call the Sheriff," answered her man, "or maybe the preacher."

"Don't look like there's any particular hurry," observed Maude. "I guess this fella finally got tired of holdin' on."

"Oh Harvey!" said Maude. She couldn't look at the wreckage anymore. "This is just AWFUL!"

"You call the Sheriff, Honey. I'll get the camera. Wait'll they get wind of this back in Kokomo."

How NOT to hang glide 101
Listen up boys and girls… DON'T TRY THIS AT HOME!

Prop Stopped Over Four Corners or, Hang 'em High!

Walter had been enjoying the flight as best he could under the circumstances; the Four Corners area of America is a spectacular place to fly. But he was sure getting tired of concentrating on Willy, who always seemed to be a tiny speck on the distant horizon. Every now and then Willy would crank a one-eighty and head back to Walter. He would quickly close with Walter, fly a few circles around him and wave the "high" sign a time or two. Then he would level out and pull on ahead again. It was a pain in the ass, not just because it forced Walter to focus completely on Willy so as not to lose him in the big sky ahead, but also because it forced him to fly so fast, pulling on the bar until he ached all over.

The two flyers had left the hangar at Pleasant Valley outside of Phoenix two days ago. They had spent one day buzzing about the volcanic craters outside of Flagstaff where they had learned to hang glide some years ago, and then departed for the Airmens' Rendezvous in Telluride, Colorado. Since just after dawn, Walter had been pulling on the bar for hours.

"SLOW DOWN!" yelled Walter. But of course Willy couldn't hear him, it was an exercise in futility without radios, he could yell his dang-fool head off and Willy couldn't hear him, not only because they were in separate aircraft doing around sixty miles-an-hour, but also because Willy was dang near deaf. And Willy couldn't really slow down much either; he was flying a Cosmos Ghost 12 after all- a little rocket ship of a wing, while Walter was flying an Air Creation XP-15, larger and considerably slower. All Walter could do was clutch the bar under his arms and lean back into the seat and hold the wing steady- there was no hope of catching Willy, or even keeping up.

Or was there?

Slowly, a crazy notion was creeping up on Walter's brain... "No!" replied his conscience "Can't do that! Carry on, ignore the ache, keep Willy in sight."

But... wouldn't it be nice... for just a moment... ease off all the pressure... yet keep up the speed... indeed, even go a bit FASTER? With less effort? Doesn't that make sense?

And that sharp ache in my lower back...?

Gone.

No no no no no NO!

Crazy idea, nuts.

The machine just wasn't built for that.

His conscience was speaking now...

Something about maximum thirty degrees of pitch, so says that factory dude, the guy who designed the whole mess...

Wouldn't that make more than thirty?

Much more?

Maybe so, maybe no...

I guess there's just no way to find out short of giving it a try, decided the flyer. Tentatively, he pushed the bar out to the front strut to make a little room to move, flying as slow as possible now, wings level.

But the objective was quite the opposite- to fly ever faster.

So, with a quick look out front at the far horizon, and with one last quick glance at Willy The Dot out there in the distance, Walter swung his body down and out to the left side in the seat, and ducked under the bar. Then, he sat up again- now on the FRONT side of the bar, the wrong side of the bar as it were, the FAST side of the bar- a place he'd NEVER been before, the idea being that he could just lean back now, and fly faster than ever with less effort...

Great, right?

There was one small glitch that Walter had not considered however, one little detail particular to only this trike, well, only this make of trike... One minor detail that was designed into the trike as optional safety equipment, and this became horribly obvious in the blink of an eye, in the *flash of an eye*. The "optional safety equipment" was the shoulder-restraint seat belt that was part of his harness. This shoulder restraint was clipped onto the lap belt by means of a small E-Z clip rivet. It also had a recoil spring to spool the belt back up after use, the same idea as the seatbelt recoil in a car. Apparently, Walter's act of bending forward so was just enough to un-clip that buckle off the rivet. And apparently, the recoil spring was not capable of doing its job in a sixty-mile-an-hour blast wind. Walter didn't even have time to register surprise as the end clip of the shoulder restraint went whizzing past his nose, *in the flash of an eye*. Next thing he knew, there was a nasty, horrible WHACK, and his Rotax 503 snapped to a ghastly and unexpected stop with a fearsome shudder, it had all happened *in the flash of an eye!*

Suddenly there he was, a hapless flyer in the wrong place at the wrong time, and everything was frightfully quiet. Only the wail of the wind through the wires accompanied his flight...

"WWWWSSSSSSHHHHHH"

Then the nose of that XP pitched down, and Walter was offered a startling new view of the desert below him, obstructed only by the thin front strut. His conscience was yelling at him in protest too; "WHOA!" it cried, "I TOLD YOU SO!" and,"DUMB ASS, WHAJADOTHATFOR?"

Quickly, Walter tried repeating the move in reverse, ducking back under the bar with a twisting-wrenching move that dragged the corner of the control triangle painfully across the middle of his back. But this time, as he raised his head up now back on the "correct" side of the bar, the side of the bar that God and the designer had intended all along, the rear edge of his helmet caught on the basetube causing it to rotate down over his face, tearing painfully at his ears, eyebrows, nose and lips.

"NNGGAAAHHHOOOWWWW!"

Blindly now, and with both hands gripped for control, gripped for Dear Life, Walter tilted his head far back where he could just barely see under the visor of his lid, and discern that the wing had banked up to a horrible angle during his stupid struggle. It had also pitched up at an unusual attitude since being released from its nose-down angle, something the pilot knew without looking- he was familiar with the feel of high "G" forces. Walter gripped the bar with both hands now, glimpsed the cockeyed horizon out from under his lid, and remembered the Manufacturers Operating Limitations which prescribed just how this machine was recommended to be flown. Desperately, he fought the wing level. With his hands finally free, he swung the helmet off his face to have a look around and re-orient himself. He gave a quick glance over his shoulder at the prop, which now resembled something from a tired old Coyote vs. Roadrunner rerun.

There would be no problem deciding where to land however- the wide two-lane dirt road that the trikers had been flying along was like an enormous empty runway stretching into the distance. All was terribly quiet in Walter's sky as he pulled the nose down, this time following the manufacturer's recommended technique, and dove carefully on in for a gentle approach to a landing.

"ZZZZZZZZZZZZZZZNNNNNRRRRRIIIIINNNNNGGGGG"

Ten minutes later and Walter could hear Willy's little plane returning now. He had removed the screwdriver from his tool kit, and was distractedly trying to extract the shoulder belt from the engine drive hub. His three-blade IVO prop was nothing but sad looking flecks and strands of fiberglass, and mangled steel torsion bars. It would never spin again. When the belt had hit the propeller the prop had simply exploded and then sucked the belt in buckle-first, spun it up and cinched it incredibly tight around the drive hub, stopping fifty-two horsepower in a very abrupt instant, and trying to rip the recoil belt mechanism completely off the trike mast. The housing dangled pathetically by one bent bolt, the other had disappeared completely. Now, the situation looked hopeless, the only worse possibility, a likelihood it seemed, is that the Navajos hereabouts should appear on the horizon, capture the sorry beligani, and stake him out on an anthill slathered in honey.

It just wasn't looking good... *Wait 'till Willy gets a look at this.* If Walter'd had a jar of honey along, he'd a just got started on the slathering. *I wonder how ants like shit...?* he asked himself. He was knee-deep in that.

Walter continued to dig despondently at the shoulder strap as Willy gave him a buzz job, did a graceful one-eighty, then set his wagon down on the road and taxied over.

"What's up?" he inquired.

"Broke my prop," replied Walter without a glance.

But Willy had already grasped the obvious. "I guess so!" he laughed. "What the heck did you do?"

"Ahh, the shoulder belt got away from me. I guess that recoil spring didn't work as advertised."

"You got the... what? How did the shoulder belt get away from you?"

"Well, you're not gonna believe it but, ahh... I was trying to keep up... with you."

"Trying to keep up with me? What do you mean?"

"Ahh... I decided... I mean... if I was on the other side... you know. So I ducked under the bar and... the danged clip popped off the lapbelt. Whizzed right past my beak, straight into the prop."

"Holy shit!" laughed Willy in wonder. "I'm glad you're all right. What did you do then?"

"Well I got back where I belonged pretty quick. Then I dove down and landed here. Looks like I'm a hitch-hiker now."

"You mean because of the prop? Good thing I've got another one."

"You've got another PROPELLER?" Walter should not have to ask. Willy was loaded down with all manner of stuff, including a crate of fresh avocados and a crate of fresh peaches. In fact, Willy's wagon looked like some weird cartoon caricature of a flying machine; Jethro Bodine Goes Triking. He walked around back of his wagon, started tugging on a long, skinny cardboard box, and soon beheld a fresh sixty-eight inch, two-blade IVO prop.

"Incredible!" declared Walter digging again at the stuck belt, but with renewed interest now. "Let's get this old mess off here before we get scalped."

SOS Mexican Style or,
MAYDAY! MAYDAY! MAYDAY!

It was late when Walter punched off El Peñon del Diablo- the Rock of the Devil. Most of the other flyers had already circled out and were somewhere over the back, or headed in to Valle de Bravo. He turned for the house thermal and was kicked around for a few minutes, sinking out, until he finally cored the lift. He was rewarded with the familiar tone of his variometer, singing happily and showing thousand-plus rate of climb. The wing climbed at one of those bizarre nose-high attitudes that Walter craved, an unlikely angle against the skyline that set his heart pumping fast with adrenaline. The ride to the top of the house thermal went quickly, and the gringo bailed over the back.

The flying actually got better as Walter glided to the near edge of the Zacamecáte. Dark cumulous clouds had gathered a mile above the ridge, and he glided for where a redtail hawk was banked over and circling in strong lift below him. He dove in above the bird and felt the tug of rising air. He pushed out and the vario began to sing yet again. As he circled out Walter carefully observed the bird and his every move, while far below the peasants labored in the milpa.

Walter kept the bird below him as long as he could, finally diving on the feathered beast as the animal's superior sinkrate and slow-speed handling out-flew the gringo. Abruptly, the bird flared in a tiny core-within-the-core, and disappeared above Walter's wing. As he flashed past the leading edge at an improbable attitude, Walter heard the bird's gleeful scream;

"KREEEE!" he called. It was a screech of pleasure, thought Walter, or maybe of disdain. Whatever, it was probably the last he would see of that halcon, at least until mañana.

The gringo flyer craned his neck in the thermal, searching above the wing. For a second, he thought he saw the bird, already a speck above him. He saw too that cloudbase was rapidly approaching. Of course, it was just the other way around- he was approaching the clouds. He leveled his wings and glided away from the center of the thermal. It had lost little of its ferocious energy, but become quite smooth. And fat. There was plenty of lift all over beneath the cloud, and now it was simply a matter of slowing down, and holding just a few degrees of bank.

Walter pushed out.

He moved over to the edge of the cloud where things were considerably mellower. He realized that his hands were very cold; he had his gloves handy, but there just hadn't been time to pull them on. He zipped closed the neck of his jacket and flight suit first, then pulled up his facemask and pulled on the gloves. Cozy now, he scanned the last few circles under the cloud, scanning the skies for other glideheads. He could hear the chatter on the radio. *Just like another bitchin' day in the sky above Valle,* he thought. With that he pulled down on the nose, leveled the wing, and dove for town.

Arriving over La Torre, the launch above the village, Walter was surprised to see another glider, poised to launch. It was a weekday, so there were few other pilots in town. He figured everyone had gone to the Rock of the Devil. Then he noticed a strange vehicle and a couple other gliders, hidden in the trees in the setup area. Must be some newcomers had arrived in town. As he watched, the glider on launch wobbled for a moment, and then took flight.

The glider cleared the trees and kept flying straight. To soar La Torre often requires a quick left turn, to stay in the marginal ridge lift next to the hill. From high above, it was impossible for Walter to tell for sure if the glider was climbing or sinking, but he knew that if the pilot continued straight on, he would sink out. That was okay, there was a large field on the lakeshore below; the official landing zone.

Walter took a little ride over to the jardin in Valle, made a few circles far above the iglesia, and then checked the other glider's progress: now it was out, a little over the lake, it looked as though it had still not made a turn. He'll have to turn soon, thought Walter, just to get back for an approach. From his windy perch he willed it to turn...

TURN!

But the glider did not turn. It just kept flying straight. It flew straight, and flew straight some more. In front of the glider was about five miles of lake. No way could he even come close to gliding THAT far.

Turn fer Chrissake, TURN!

What a GEEK!

But in spite of Walter's admonitions, the glider just kept flying straight. There was nothing out there, nothing except cold water, a few whitecaps and a fisherman bobbing lazily in his dugout pirogue, his line cast into the lake. Walter floated thousands of feet above, disbelieving that anyone could be that stupid. To fly out in the middle of a lake was... Well, was to DIE. Most likely anyway... To drown. To make them get out the search fleet and drag the lake bottom for your carcass while the carp nibbled on you. Here in Mexico, it was more likely that the rescue services would simply sit around drinking caguamas and wait for your bloated and disfigured carcass to float to the surface, then stick you in a box.

WHAT THE CHINGADA WAS HE THINKING?

Walter was about to stuff the bar on his Airwave Magic Kiss and point the nose towards the LZ, uncertain what aid he might offer, when he noticed the glider finally make its first turn of the whole sorry show. It wasn't much of a turn really, maybe sixty degrees to larboard, but it was a turn. The pilot had actually made some decision regarding his own destiny, it might have been too little and far too late, except that it set the glider on a heading that would take it right over, or maybe right on top of, the pescador. It was a quick turn, slightly over controlled, and the glider oscillated back and forth a bit. It also turned the glider slightly off the wind so that it picked up speed dramatically. The pilot got the wings level again and suddenly Walter could see from the shadow below it that the wing was LOW. So low, it was about to crash into the tiny canoe.

The small tail of blue smoke that trailed the tiny boat as the pescador trolled his line became a swirling puff for a few seconds, and the boat surged sluggishly out of harm's way. The glider flashed over the canoe and splashed into the lake at a high rate of speed. Even from far above, Walter could see the impact. The glider stopped instantly, then floated gently on the surface, but Walter knew it wouldn't float for long. Shortly the pilot's orange helmet popped into view, behind the sail. The flyer, depending on how much buoyant foam he was wearing in his harness, would have only a few minutes to get disconnected, before the wing started a slow glide for the bottom, dragging him with it. Walter could see the pilot thrashing around now. To call him a pilot was a bit of a stretch, thought Walter.

A Newbie maybe... a Goner, was more like it.

But there was hope! The fisherman had turned his tiller a bit, and was now coasting along next to the floating wing. As

Walter watched, he gunned the throttle again, and slid up next to the trailing edge of the wing. Then he tucked his nose up to the pilot, who threw one soggy arm aboard.

Suddenly, it looked like the day was saved by a pescador.

Walter hung over Valle de Bravo and over La Torre watching the drama unfold, enjoying the show now that it was unlikely that the gringo would have to be shipped home surface freight. The fisherman and the glidehead hung together for a while. Apparently, it was a delicate maneuver to get such a load into the tiny craft, he would certainly have to get out of a soaked harness first. A wet harness alone, without a wet gringo, might weigh fifty kilos. Finally, the gringo was shipped aboard and flopped into the tiny craft like an oversized and exhausted fish. Straight above now, Walter saw the gringo laying on his back, catching his breath. The gringo must have seen Walter too, but he made no visible motion of recognition.

Meanwhile, the fisherman ran a line from the stern of the canoe over to the nose of the glider, which was now a foot or so beneath the white caps. All was ready to head for shore, so the pescador gave his throttle a good twist to get the show moving. A cloud of blue smoke appeared to trail the boat, but it seemed to go nowhere. The fisherman backed off the throttle for a few moments, but then he must have gathered his resolve and twisted the throttle once again, really laying on the horsepower this time, because the cloud of blue smoke became very dense. They started moving towards shore ever so slowly, but that glider had never been designed to operate in such a dense atmosphere as H2O. It couldn't, wouldn't and didn't withstand the drag. Instead, it simply folded up as the crossbar or some other tube failed, and turned into what looked from above, like a giant colorful lawndart.

The gringo sat up in the canoe then; maybe he had noticed the sound of crunching aluminum or tearing sailcloth. Even from far above he could be seen waving his arms at the pescador. The canoe stopped and sat idling in the water. It idled for quite some time while, perhaps, the gringo assessed the damage, agonized over his cruel fate.

Finally the aviator lay back again, the pescador's exhaust became a trail again, and the tiny canoe started tugging, only gently this time, the wreckage to shore again.

Well... there's one knothead we won't have to worry about mañana, thought Walter, and he headed back to terra firma.

Oh, that I had wings like a dove,
For then I would fly away,
And be at rest.
-Psalms 55:6

The Yellow Peril of Glide Mountain or, My Field of Dreams

"**S**hould I just bail?" asked Jeffro. Desperation was etched across his face. Looking back on that day with perfect hindsight, we should have encouraged him, "Yes Jeffro. Get over the guardrail quick and punch. Give 'er heck," but we didn't.

If we had just shoved Jeffro off the cliff I'm sure he would have done fine, instead of waiting for us and getting sandbagged behind us, the aging "experienced" glideheads of the bunch, the "wise guys" so to speak. He wouldn't have had to watch as we rocketed out of Glide Mountain on a powerful gust front. He wouldn't have been standing on launch when the proverbial shit hit the proverbial fan. He wouldn't have had to break down his wing in the sixty-mile-an-hour winds, blowing dust and driving rain at launch. And he wouldn't-some days later- have had to listen to us old farts gloat with happiness and glee.

But there was a big fat cumulonimbus cloud out front of launch that day, with a curtain of rain hanging half way to the ground. Could we really send him out in that? True, the cloud was not going anywhere, was not showing any wind or movement at all in fact, not flashing lightning, not growling with thunder... For a storm, this one looked downright docile. Directly below Washoe Lake was yet a glassy mirror. But I wasn't willing to help Jeffro. I guess Kelly wasn't either.

"Don't look like any wind in that cell at all" declared Jeffro. He was a picture of desperation: the hungry glidehead newbie, just gotta get some air under his feet or... or perish! "What the Hell should I do?"

Jeffro looked to us for guidance and inspiration because we are the "experienced" glideheads. Did I say that already? 'Old farts' would also describe us. "Good Judgment says 'wait my child'," declared Kelly. Or was it I said that? "Wait a while and let this cell develop or... or let it move on. Maybe ahh... maybe someone else will bail first, a wind dummy."

So wait we did... just sat up there on launch while slowly the cell dropped its rain and just petered-out right there in the sky, for all to see. Meanwhile, the thermal cycles continued to be very friendly, drifting straight up launch at five-to-ten. I took a short siesta under my wing. Kelly fiddled with his new gizmo called a GPS. Jeffro paced back and forth on launch like a hungry cat. My respite was interrupted only when a tourist appeared in a rental car and inquired in an excited voice "You guys gonna jump? You guys gonna jump?" I looked at my watch; it had been a forty-five minute siesta. If we were really going to commit aviation today, it would have to be soon...

I glanced over my shoulder once as I was clipping into the wing. I was looking at the windsock in the tall pine tree above launch but I couldn't help but notice the black sky up that way- over Mount Rose Meadows and beyond towards Lake Tahoe. The over-development was NOT finished for the day and, since the time was only one o'clock it seemed likely that we were in for an exciting day, one way or another. Kelly was suiting-up behind me, and Jeffro too. There was doubt in their eyes and I must admit, there was doubt in my heart and mind. But this is what we've come to love about hang gliding- the uncertainty. Just huck yourself out there and see what happens. Hope for the best, then just go for it,

So I punched. I lifted the wing and felt it balance. I leaned forward down the Glide Mountain cliffside. I pointed the nose at emptiness, and gave the wing three hard steps...

"KAWABUNGA!"

As a reward for my audacity, I was lifted smoothly off launch and straight into a big fat thermal. I banked the wing over and pushed the nose up and reveled in that indescribable sensation of climbing out in a strong tower of rising air, higher and higher, and still higher yet, My vario sang a thrilling song. As I circled up I watched Kelly step over the guardrail with his wife Nancy's help and bail too; it seemed like he hardly even hesitated on launch. Together now, we circled out, drifting in a strange direction- taking the thermal north and slightly east out towards Washoe Valley and in the general direction of Reno, Nevada. Jealous of our free ride, a buzzard sliced into our thermal and put us both to shame.

Drifting over Sky Tavern the lift really turned on and we soon had a view over Glide towards Tahoe, an unpleasant purgatory where lightening etched a stormy blackness of tortured clouds. Suddenly the radio sparked to life as Nancy called in. "It's blowing sixty here!" she cried. Her voice was stressed and filled with concern. "A gust front has just hit launch, Jeffro's wing is getting totally thrashed!"

I glanced down at launch where we had stood not ten minutes ago and now the cars were like tiny toys and I could see Jeffro's wing being thrashed about by the wind. A few pathetic humanoids scurried about like ants, taking cover. Somehow Jeffro got sandbagged.

I just didn't have much time to worry about the earthlings however, I was climbing out in a fat and strong thermal, eyeballing my buddy Kelley and drifting north over Sky Tavern. Despite the trauma below we were having a fine time of it when suddenly... Holy Shit! I saw it— a Yellow Peril!

Just up from Sky Tavern the gust front had hit the pine forest and was raising a cloud of yellow pine pollen from the forest. From my perspective in the sky, it looked like an explosion had just happened, as though someone had detonated a bomb on a windy hillside. The yellow cloud was being billowed up by the gust front, and then blasted down by the wind at sixty miles an hour. In moments that bomb blast would be directly under us. It was TIME TO RUN!

"Kelly!" cried Nancy from launch on the radio, "What do you want me to do?" It was a reasonable question: Nancy had volunteered to drive retrieve for us, now she just wanted to know where to go, but there was no reply from Kelly. Either there was something amiss with his radio, or he was just too danged gripped on the control bar, too white-knuckled-out to key the microphone in answer.

I glanced at the Yellow Peril again and the cloud held my gaze all the way around the turn. In more than twenty years of flying the High Sierra I had never seen the likes of that! Happily, my amigo and I were circling out like homesick angels, each circle putting another few hundred feet between us and danger, each turn like a blessing from a higher authority. Super-cold and heavy air from the downburst was falling down Glide Mountain and Galena Canyon, blasting through the trees and colliding with the super hot and light air that we were soaring. The cold air sinks while the hot air rises, and takes a couple ballzy glideheads er, ahh... Old Farts... with it.

Suddenly, overwhelmed with pure fright and adrenaline, I knew what I wanted to do, what I HAD TO DO: at fourteen thousand feet above sea-level I keyed my mic and uttered one word several times:

"Peavine, Peavine, Peavine!" I cried, and then, "You copy that Nancy? We're headed for Peavine!"

I could see it on the near horizon- about ten or fifteen miles north of Glide and just the other side of Reno was Peavine Mountain, another flying site from my newbie days. I had made my first ever big-mountain flight there and was quite familiar with the terrain. A cloud street paved the way, and Peavine too was showing signs of over development, but there was blue sky also. In fact the flanks of mountain were baking in Sierra sun. The place would be booming. I glanced once at my buddy Kelly (what's wrong with the radio friend?) and I bailed. I might have yelled too- WAAAAAA! - but I don't remember. Certainly, there was a shout in my spirit, but whether it left my throat or not I don't recall. Probably more of a terrified whimper than a rebel yell... there was no one there but me to hear anyway. I pointed the nose north over the Sierra Nevada and bailed for Peavine.

I was at 14,000' and I was gliding faster than best glide and I was still going up. Up, up, the air was rising everywhere.

I held the bar at chest level with my elbows while I zipped up my flight suit, adjusted the balaclava down over my face and pulled my gloves on one at a time. Finally, dressed properly for the setting, I held in the bar and raced north for safety, still climbing. Comfortable now, I ran for my dear life from the Yellow Peril of Sky Tavern.

WahOOO!

Kelly and I fled the thunderstorms, staying in the High Sierra to avoid the controlled airspace at Reno-Tahoe Airport. We sped along the mountains getting an awesome glide, stopping for circles only a time or two when the lift was too sweet to pass up. As we dove past the gun barrel of Reno's runway two-seven, Peavine was a shining goal before us, bathed in bright sunlight and capped with beautiful cumulus clouds. From the looks of our glide we would get there plenty high for safety. Behind us, only blackness laced with gray and angry-looking clouds, punctuated by flaming bursts of lightning. A few times, I dangled my head to peer under my toes at the Yellow Peril but I don't know what had become of it. A momentary, unlikely phenomenon I suppose, it dissipated as the rain closed in.

We arrived high over the flanks of Peavine and quickly centered solid lift back to altitude. Now we were looking north at yet another of our favorite flying sites- Zulu Ridge, and once again the clouds behind us threatened to ruin our day. I heard Nancy call on the radio, "Kelly, I'm driving Highway 395 north of Reno. Where are you?" But there was again no answer from her man. I knew where he was though- circling with me in the same thermal, in the same threatening sky.

"I got him Nancy!" I hollered at the radio. "We're headed for the landing area at Zulu!" Earlier in the spring Kelly and Nancy and I had been out for an evening glass-off at Zulu. We had soared the ridge lift up to a thousand feet or so that evening and landed on the dry lake below. Now, here we were coming at Zulu from the south, only this time we were stinkin' high, skied-out a mile or more above the ridge. We were so high that the ridge below looked like flat land and I needed to study the scene to find the Zulu launch and landing area.

"Roger that," replied our ace driver. "Here I come!"

But we were still busy. Now, thunderstorms were sweeping down from the mountains and pushing us east into the Nevada desert and the Great Basin. The terrain below Zulu Ridge is an enormous dry lake. Today there were swirls of dust devils and wisps of alkali dust from what must be strong lift and gusty winds. I began to spiral down there, hoping Kelly would follow me to safety, but my circles yielded a net climb, not the descent I had hoped for; we were still in strong lift. There was no point in trying to get down here.

In the distance something caught my eye: a runway, or a wide and straight section of road, at that distance and altitude I couldn't be sure. Whatever it was, it seemed to be a fairly easy glide. Plus, it looked like I could simply stuff the bar and race along generating lots of drag: I would get somewhere safe and GET DOWN TOO! I followed along the ground with my gaze and traced the road back to Highway 395 where I knew that Nancy was racing along for retrieve. Then I called her with directions, "Take the road to Zulu launch Nancy, and just keep going on pavement. We'll be about ten miles along. You copy?"

There was only a slight hesitation, "The road for Zulu launch, stick with the pavement," repeated our driver. "Copy you. I'll follow it about ten miles looking for you guys."

"Roger that," I confirmed. "As soon as I land I'll call you." With that, I pulled down the nose on my wing and dove as fast as I dared given the rowdy air, and bailed for the haven in the distance. From the base of the clouds at my altitude, it looked like Manna from Heaven. The closer I came the more certain I became that what I was looking at was an airfield and not a road— a private airfield in the middle of nowhere. I didn't really care what it was however, as long as it was wide and smooth enough for my landing.

Well... perhaps "landing" would be a dignified way to describe what I do when I return to earth. "Beaching" would be about as accurate, even though there was no beach around for hundreds of miles... As a gnarly ol' fart, I don't land my hang glider on my feet like the birds anymore, those days are over, that would be far too painful. Instead, I skid in on my chest skidplate and roll in on my hurkin' training wheels. This procedure is more like how a whale might land if he could fly, than a bird. I just skim the ground at a few inches and fly slower and slower until... PLOP!, I sort of plunk down. Not really a landing at all, but for this, I need a smooth flat spot, the longer and smoother the better. Golf course fairways are the best choice- like skidding on velvet, but an airfield works well too.

Racing now for a beaching, the dirt strip out in front was looking better and better. Down to a thousand feet and straight above the strip my suspicions were confirmed by the presence of a windsock and a hangar. Looking at the windsock I could have whooped for joy: the wind, about ten miles an hour by the looks of it, was blowing right straight down the pike. Perfect for a gnarly ol' fart beaching... I knew I could land smoothly and safely here.

I called Nancy on the radio, "Nancy, I am directly over an airfield about ten or twelve miles down the Zulu road, on the west side. Do you copy?"

"Roger that," came the reassuring reply from the ether. "I'll be looking for you."

With that, I banked the glider steeply and raced for the ground. As I circled I studied the sky for Kelly's glider, finally spotting its profile about a mile off and several thousand feet above me. Kelly did not look to be in such a hurry.

But I was. I wanted DOWN, and I wanted DOWN ON THAT STRIP!

I banked the wing and spiraled down over the windsock, which all the while looked very reassuring. At pattern altitude I began a blazing aircraft-style approach, flying downwind with the bar stuffed, groundspeed just a blur, passing along above a hangar-house meanwhile. Then I banked hard-a-starboard for a combination base leg and a quick turn onto final. I felt tremendous relief as a beautiful dirt strip lay before me and I was directly over the centerline, I might have whooped for joy. I flew over the fence at maybe a hundred feet. I settled into a roundout and flare in very nice smooth air and touched gently back on Mother Earth.

"Wahoo!" I hollered.

I had dodged another bullet!

I wasn't just alive...

I was ALIVE!

Joyously, I hoisted my carcass up in the control frame and un-hooked from my wing. I stepped out from under the Dacron and looked up; there was my amigo Kelly all right, still a few thousand feet off the desert floor. But just beyond him was a nasty black cloud and what appeared to be a giant gust front churning through the desert, raising a hellacious cloud of dust. Could Kelly get down in time? We must have both been thinking the same thing I guess, because as I watched my flying friend he circled away from the squall, pointed his tail feathers at the advancing cloud, leveled his wings and sped off across the sky like the scared glidehead he probably was.

Run Kelly, RUN!

Suddenly in a hurry to bag my wagon, I was stripping off my harness when I noticed a small sedan pulling out of the ranch house driveway and coming out to the airfield; the Welcoming Committee? I pulled off my helmet and tried to assume my calmest demeanor and a pleasant smile. I wiped the snot off my nose, the drool off my chin. The car pulled up, an attractive housewife at the helm, her hair done up in curlers. She rolled down a window and was just about to speak when the gust front abruptly hit us:

WHAM!

Instantly, I was holding the nose wires of my wing as it bucked and thrashed about like a demented beast. "Hello," I said, trying to smile and act casually. "How are you?" As though hang gliders fell from the sky onto this dusty airstrip in the middle-of-nowhere every day- a common occurrence.

"What are you doing here?" asked my hostess, in what I thought was an incredibly lame question. Was I lost? Was I shopping? Was I playing 'buzzard'? Was I Sky King looking for Penny? Wasn't it just as obvious to her as it was to me what I was doing here? I WAS GETTING DOWN, is what I was doing here. I WAS SURVIVING! I WAS BAGGIN' MY WAGON!

I WAS ALIVE!

"Ahhmmm well, I just landed here," I stated. It was simple fact, and there was no denying it. But my hostess was not so enthused.

"Oh no no no," she exclaimed. "We can't have that!" I thought this was nearly laughable, and I might indeed have laughed if I hadn't been busy holding my thrashing hang glider. How deny the past? How change history? 'Oh no no no, we can't have that...?'

I was holding the glider with both hands against the advancing gust front. Rain was only a few short yards away, the air was delightfully cool and smelled heavy with ozone. Now lightening was my big worry. "I beg your pardon?" I asked.

"I said we can't have anyone land here," explained the lady, a look of genuine concern etched across her face. "Our insurance just won't allow it."

I stood holding the bucking glider and watched as the rain advanced upon us a little closer. The hot desert wind had suddenly turned cold. "All I want is to get out of here ma'am," I stated. "I'll just bag this wagon and leave, be gone..." But she wasn't through yet.

"My husband asked them if his partner could land here under our policy and they said 'no'. They said if anyone at all landed here but us they would cancel our coverage." It was news to me. Didn't sound too unlikely though, coming from an insurance company... Take the money any way you can, just be sure to limit the liability as much as possible, and whatever happens, avoid the payout.

"Sure am sorry 'bout that ma'am," I yelled over the increasing maelstrom. "Now, if you could just hold this here glider for a minute... I could pull some battens."

"There's no one else coming is there?" she asked, glancing worriedly around the sky. Kelly was a tiny dot on the horizon now, she didn't even see him, and for that we were both grateful. From my perspective he looked to be getting an awesome tailwind glide as he disappeared to the east.

"Well ma'am, I don't know for sure if anyone's coming. Can't never be sure," I said, glancing about the sky. "But I suppose... if you build it... they will come. A field of dreams."

"What was that?" she asked. "Who will come?"

"I said, if you build an airfield someone's likely to land on it someday. I for one, am very grateful!"

"My husband would be very angry," she chimed.

"Well then let's do us all a favor, and not tell him," I suggested, and grabbed the radio. "Nancy, I'm down at uhh... what's the name of this strip?" I inquired of my hostess.

"H Bar H," she replied.

"I'm down at an airfield named the H Bar H, Nancy. Do you read?"

I bagged my wagon as Nancy roared up in the truck. She was concerned for her man Kelly and in a hurry to chase him, and we were getting drenched with fresh rain as we tossed the last of my belongings into the pickup. I finished tying down the glider and was jumping in the truck when I yelled my thanks and farewell to my hostess. "Don't worry ma'am, I won't be back!" I yelled. I slammed the door and turned back to Nancy. "¡Vamanos!" I suggested.

"What was that all about?" asked Nancy.

"If you don't want airmen to fall onto your airfield, then don't build one." I declared. "Let's go find Kelly," I said, and pointed over the horizon.

"I suppose he kept going downwind?" surmised Nancy. "There's lots of nothing out that way... except Palomino. Off we go."

Kelly did indeed fly out to Palomino Ridge that day, tail-between-his-legs and running for his life. He outran that squall at the H Bar H and made a beeline for yet another hang glider launch on Palomino Peak. Kelly flew four western-Nevada hang gliding sites that day: starting with Glide, he flew Peavine Mountain and Zulu Ridge before brushing me off at the H-Bar-H and continuing on to an alfalfa field below Palomino. He'd climbed out at the first one, flew over the next two stinkin' high, and landed at the forth. It was not an extremely long flight as hang gliding goes, but it was exciting, thrill-a-minute flying, starting with that cloud of Yellow Peril back at Sky Tavern. When we finally rendezvoused with him in the landing field below Palomino I asked him for his impressions:

"How 'bout that cloud from the forest at Glide?" I asked.

"Holy heck" exclaimed my friend, very animated. "I was tryin' to get some life from my radio when I looked over and saw that I didn't know if I should shit or quit"

"It was time to get out of there for sure" I agreed.

"Did you hear me on the radio?" asked Nancy. "Poor Jeffro waited just a few minutes too long and got shot down there on launch. It blew down so hard and so suddenly he had to chase his wing across launch It almost went off the mountain without him!"

Why we laughed at that I'm not sure- the image of poor Jeffro chasing his glider in the teeth of a gust front that chased us for the next hour or so brought us to nervous laughter I guess- it certainly wasn't hilarious. We were sorry for Jeffro, but we were just glad to have survived. We had dodged a bullet, it was more like a blast of birdshot. We had dodged a blast of birdshot.

"My radio wouldn't broadcast," said Kelly. "But I could hear you yelling 'PEAVINE, PEAVINE, PEAVINE!' so I just pulled in the bar and followed. I wanted out of there, too. Wahoo!"

We loaded Kelly's wing on the truck and hit the wind. Turning back on the highway, looking towards the southwest from where we had come, Glide Mountain was nothing more than a tiny bump on the distant horizon.

Holy Mary, Jesus and Joseph! or, The Mystery at Magdalena

"**M**agdalena traffic, this is Cessna seven-two-three-seven-Gulf inbound for a landing. We'll be turning left base for one-eight."

As Ivo Zdarsky banked his Cessna 172 on the downwind leg to a landing approach, he spoke into the headset. We were on the last leg of our southbound journey, the purpose of which was to pre-fly the route for the UL Rally Southwest, where we will return in September to fly the same route in trikes. Below us lay the inviting tarmac of Magdalena/Tacicuri airfield, tucked into the Santa Cruz valley some fifty miles south of the US- Mexico border. An idyllic, sleepy setting, Magdalena was to be our first of three stops in Old Mexico.

Ivo had done a terrific job at the helm thus far, piloting his heavily laden aircraft throughout the desert southwest. My French associate Thierry Caroni rode shotgun, busily capturing GPS waypoints for our planned return six months later. I was crammed in the back seat along with the way-too-much junk the Frenchman and I had dragged along. It was a beautiful spring day and I wanted out to stretch.

"Magdalena traffic Cessna seven-two-three-seven-Gulf turning final."

There were already some aircraft parked near the small terminal, about which I was intrigued. This would be my fourth visit to Tacicuri, the first in an N-numbered aircraft. I had never seen any traffic here in past visits, so I was mildly surprised. But it was, after all, Semana Santa- the Holy Week- and all of Mexico was on the go. This must be just normal holiday traffic, right?

Imagine our surprise then, as we braked past the tiny terminal and glanced over that way: there were at least a dozen soldiers behind sandbag bunkers... and they were pointing fifty-caliber, tripod-mounted machine guns at... at US!

Worse- there seemed to be an entire squadron of Federáles in their trademark blue uniforms- Mexico's most arrogant and feared warriors, automatic weapons slung from their shoulders.

Ivo glanced over his shoulder at me in the back seat but didn't need to say anything. "What have you got me into now?" he might have inquired. He wheeled the 172 around and taxied slowly back towards trouble. He swung the plane around so we were pointing at the adversary and stopped the prop. A silence fell over us as a pair of Federáles approached in a business-like manner. Ivo broke the spell.

"You get out first," he demanded.

I couldn't argue with that. It had been my decision, just a suggestion really, a stupid suggestion I suddenly wished I had forgotten, that the UL Rally Southwest fly through Mexico. My prior flying experiences here had been among the most satisfying of my career. Now I had my doubts.

Ivo slid his seat forward to make room for my exit, and I stuck out my leg. My right leg was asleep as my foot touched Mexican tierra. I crawled stiffly from the rear seat wondering what I would say? As the Spanish linguist of the bunch, it would be up to me to make a good first impression.

The Feds were quickly beside the plane, stern-faced. Their guns were at the ready, though pointed still at the ground. I opened my mouth and stuttered for a moment, then out came this:

"Caballeros!" I cried, "Venimos en paz!" *Gentlemen! We come in peace!*

The Feds were not deterred. They did not put down the automatic weapons. They did not burst into song and dance. They did not smile or offer a welcome; they motioned with gun barrels that all should exit the aircraft.

"¡Sale!" came the command. *Get out!*

"Somos touristas," I began repeating. "Somos touristas!" *We are tourists!* I glanced sideways towards the terminal and was surprised to notice that besides the soldiers in battle-green khakis and the Federáles in dress blues, there were also a number of gentlemen in suits, and their stylish women, gathered in the shade of a run-down terminal. Looking unsurprised and uninterested by our arrival and subsequent treatment, they seemed completely indifferent to our plight. Damas and caballeros, I could smell the perfume from here. All were dressed in black, as though mourning. Something heavy, no doubt, was going down at Magdalena/Tacicuri.

But what? What had we stumbled into...?

The Feds quickly checked out our cargo, looking for weapons. When you are a traveler headed south in Mexico they are looking for guns. When you turn around and head north they look for drugs. We had neither, we were tourists.

At the first opportunity I lurched across the few remaining feet of tarmac separating me from the dignitaries. I approached the nearest and most regal looking of the bunch and offered my grubby paw. I felt a little foolish dressed as I was in a grimy Cosmos T-shirt, soiled Bermuda shorts and smelly Tevas. Ivo Zdarsky, expatriated Czech flyer, looked even wilder in a tie-died T-shirt that read "JUST FLY" in large block letters across his chest. He could easily have posed as a gunrunning commie-pinko mercenary. Thierry Caroni, the Frenchman, had dressed in casual Euro-elegant style and, with attaché in hand, was clearly the brains of the bunch.

"Caballeros," I repeated. "¡Venimos en paz!" I was stuck on the phrase now, and waving my passport. "¡Somos touristas, somos touristas!" The mood was somber though, no matter how much I grinned. I shook hands with a number of the suits and at least one shapely, fragrant female. They all demurred yet remained stoic. Dsperately, "¿Por que tanto gente?" I asked. *Why so many people?*

The suits looked at each other and then at me. Finally, one of them stepped forward. "Ustedes llegaron antes que el

Gobierno de nuestro Estado," he stated. *You have arrived ahead of the Governor of our State.* Imagine my surprise again, as I absorbed this bit of information. The Governor? This explains the heavy security; we had arrived in front of a political dignitary.

"¿El Gobierno?" I asked, dumbly. I could see the Feds had lightened-up the search of Ivo's plane and were now demanding his papers. Why the Hell hadn't they briefed us back in Nogales, Sonora when we filed our flight plan for Magdalena de Kino that we would be arriving at an awkward time? They must have known. What was going on?

"Uh..." I repeated, "El Gobierno?" It was my latest mantra. "El Gobierno?"

"Si Señor," said the suit. "Hoy es un ocasión muy triste para nosotros." *Today is a very sad occasion for us.*

"Hoy?" was all I could say as I grinned foolishly. "Porque hoy?" *Why today?*

"Este dia de hoy marka exactamente tres años hace asasináron nuestro hijo Luis Colosio," I heard, and it all became clear. *Today it's exactly three years since they assassinated our 'son' Luis Colosio.* It all rushed back to me then, I had been working on an animal census with my trike at the time in this same state, counting deer and javalena on enormous ranches around Hermosillo. It had been Big News of course: Luis Colosio... hand-picked successor to outgoing President Carlos Salinas de Gortari... Colosio, native Son of Sonora rises to the Top... Luis Colosio... the NEXT president of the Republica de Mexico... gunned down in the streets of Tijuana while campaigning... murdered by a drug cartel... the whole country in mourning... especially Sonora. Especially in... MAGADALEDNA de KINO, his hometown!

"Nació aqui", concluded the suit in sorrow. *He was born here.* "En Magdalena." I looked back towards my associates now. Thierry Caroni was busy explaining to a heavily armed Federále why he carried a half a case of French wine stashed under the rear seat. Ivo looked back and shrugged, grinning weakly. I cursed our poor timing. What would be our fate...?

Now, I suppose most of you gringos don't relish the thought of being in our shoes; you and your plane surrounded by gun-toting Federáles, etc., but, and this is why I love Mexico so; there was a happy ending after all. Reasonably happy for the gringos anyway. The Feds accepted our alibi, the Governor's plane did arrive on schedule. He stepped from his sleek machine and was quickly escorted from his plane to an armored limo. The whole assembly boarded their vehicles and left Magdalena/Tacicuri and the hapless but relieved visitors, in a cloud of exhaust, dust and burned rubber. They were off to honor their fallen leader, and we were quickly forgotten.

We stood around briefly wondering how the chingada we would get into town some three miles distant when, to our mixed relief, a Federáles de Caminos (Highway Patrol) slowly entered the field. We explained our predicament to these caballeros, and were offered a lift to the nearest taxi. That is how we ended up in the back of the Mexican cruiser- yet another new and dubious Mexican experience- and were delivered to the central square in Magdalena de Kino; the jardin. There, we were deposited in front of a startled cabby who was alarmed to see the Fuzz headed his way, but who was relieved when three gringos jumped from the cruiser and thanked the officers.

Of course I was the only true gringo.

I explained to the cabby that they had just released us from the carcel (jail) and we needed a lift and a refreshing beverage. With an astonished look on his face he said "¡Porsupuesto!" *Of course!* Next thing we knew we were settling in to a sumptuous Mexican comida, cervesa in hand. Mariachis strolled through the plaza, and a gentle breeze cooled our jets.

We spent the afternoon chuckling about our latest experience, and viewing the ancient bones of poor Padre Kino in his last resting place, as well as the new tomb of the assassinated next-president of Mexico, Luis Donaldo Colosio. We witnessed the proceedings in his honor briefly and then cabbed it back to Ivo's Cessna. We departed wiser, and none the worse, for San Carlos.

What I have learned from my years of travel and flying in Mexico, is to expect the unexpected. I look forward to my next visit.

Breakfast Kauai Style or,
Such a Lovely View!

"**I**s it always this... bumpy?" came the query through the intercom.

"Ah, well, it has smoothed out considerably the past few minutes. Can you tell?" There came no reply. "You comfortable back there Al?"

They had left the worst of the turbulence behind on the lee side of the island Kauai, a big rock that sits isolated and alone in the Pacific Ocean, being constantly washed by strong Tradewinds. The windward side Tradewinds were considerably smoother than the lee-side rotor Tradewinds, since they had traveled thousands of mile over open water. They were strong 'Trades' today, but very smooth. Walter had tried to even-out the ride through the rotor with gentle pitch inputs and by simply holding the bar level, but the Trades were really kicking today, ferocious in fact. While the wing felt all of the turbulence in the wind, and so did Walter's arms, the ride in the back seat could be somewhat better for his efforts; just hold everything level and absorb the worst of the bumps. Even so, there had been some nasty knocks a while back-lifting him and Big Al right out of their seats and into their lap belts, rolling the wing first this way, then that. For a split-second, the wind had even snatched the bar right out of Walter's hands, sent it knocking up against the front strut, which was when Walter had snatched it back! And...

They were only halfway around the Garden Isle. There was bound to be more of the same treatment on the home stretch. Walter tightened his grip on the bar, tried to sound relaxed, and commenced a climb where he hoped to find smoother air.

Big Al spoke finally, "Yeah... I'm fine." Walter thought he heard a burp in there too, but he couldn't be sure. Big Al claimed he was two hundred eighty pounds, and it was all Walter could do to wedge himself in the trike with him. As it was, Walter's pitch-range was considerably reduced— when he pulled the bar in to fly fast his elbows poked Big Al in the gut. Walter imagined one trike, two trikers, and a watermelon.

Hold that melon Al.

Even worse, back at the field Walter had been unable to fit the smaller of his two helmets, the one the students usually wore, on Big Al's head. So they had been forced to swap. It was not what Walter liked to do, he preferred to always wear the same lid, but for his forty-bucks-an-hour wages he was forced to make concessions. Now, they turned the corner past Kapaa and headed for the Kong Rock, flying in very smooth windward air.

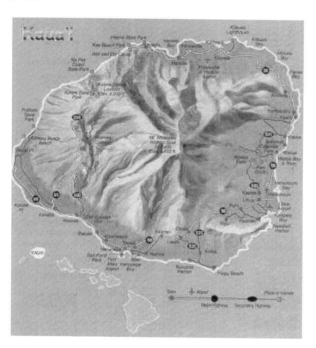

"Weaaalll," said Walter. At times like this a little flyer's twang on the intercom could go a long way, like those jet jockeys in The Right Stuff, or Top Gun. It could inspire confidence. "Weaalll Al, we might be getting more turbulence when we get around by the Na Pali and turn the corner in this wind. But from here, we've got little choice. We're just about mid-flight, equidistant either way we go, smack dab in the middle of this here rock. I suggest we keep going. Beautiful views up ahead." Walter and Big Al were out on a two-hour flight. They were circumnavigating the Hawaiian island of Kauai, and they were one hour out. Ahead lay Kilauea Lighthouse, Hanalei Bay, and the spectacular Na Pali Coast; the most awesome part of the trip. Walter was looking forward to it. They circled the lighthouse once, and moved on.

"Up ahead you see Hanalei Bay," he intoned. Big Al just grunted. He had done some of the driving earlier in the flight, but now he simply sat behind Walter, holding the watermelon, and grunting occasionally. "Hanalei Bay," said Walter again. "Do you realize Al... that Hanalei Bay... is that place... where that rascal Puff, the Magic Dragon... once allegedly frolicked in the autumn mist?" Walter liked to tell his rides that. He was a baby-boomer after all. He remembered clearly the first time he'd heard the news about Puff- he took it for gospel. He and his delinquent friend Greg Walker had split a tab of Window Pane in celebration. It had been great news, *Puff the Magic Dragon!*

Big Al just grunted again.

"In a Land called Hanalei," intoned the pilot.

Suddenly Walter, who was pressed pretty close to Big Al after all, felt a terrible convulsion in Big Al's watermelon and he knew instantly what was coming up, but a little bit too late to do anything about it. Big Al's voice was cramped and distressed when he said: "What happens if I feel hic burb nauseous, MMbwAAHHH!"

And with that, he puked a gusher.

"Oh shit," exclaimed his pilot. "You okay back there?"

But Big Al was not okay, of course. He puked again, only harder this time- a real blow. Walter did not like this sort of thing, didn't like it at all. Besides the unpleasantness of someone else's vomit, there was always the possibility that Big Al might swallow his tongue and die right there in the back seat. How would THAT feel? And how would it look in the 'incident report'? *Cause of death- puking.* Like Janis Joplin or... or Mama Cass. Maybe Al would swallow his tongue and die in spasms?

Plus- it was Walter's helmet that Big Al was barfing into, and there were still three more hours of flying booked for the day. The tourists arriving at the field right about now would soon have to deal with Al's mess. There had just been no warning... Walter always inquired about his clients' comfort without fail, and he didn't just mean comfortable in the seat, dressed warm and what have you. Airsickness, like all motion sickness, is a result of an inner-ear thing with which Walter was not plagued, thank the Gods. Airsickness was not something that Walter or any pilot for that matter, liked to bring up before flying- "Ah... by the way... does flying make you puke yer guts out?" Just not good for business. Then again, airsickness is also a bit psychosomatic too, any suggestion of the likelihood might make matters worse, make puking even more likely.

So he didn't say,'Hey sorry fuck you gonna puke?' like he wished he had now. That would just not be professional. Instead, he had soothed: "You comfortable back there big guy?" He had asked Big Al that a half dozen times. Big must have had SOME notion that he was about to puke. But had he responded?

Nope, nothing!

Well, there wasn't much that could be done now. There wasn't much that might have been done, anyway, but given some warning Walter might have at least explained the Proper Puking Procedure: 1) lift your face shield away from your face, 2) move the microphone boom away from your lips, 3) turn your head over your right shoulder away from the boom and 4) let fly, 5) try to get it all in the slipstream of the trike. If done properly, that puke would hit nothing but Wild Blue Yonder and the propeller. At least the ride home might still be pleasant.

But Big Al had blown it, literally and figuratively- he hadn't even lifted his face shield. Now, he sat behind Walter and heaved again.

"RRRAAALLLPPPHHH!"

Walter reluctantly glanced over his shoulder at poor Big Al and nearly regurgitated himself. Big Al's breakfast was plastered all over the inside of his face shield. A true gusher- a projectile, apparently Al had started the day with a big breakfast. There was vomit hanging from his eyebrows, his eyelids, his glasses, his nose and his beard. It oozed off the microphone and the wind blew it down his neck. As Walter peered over his shoulder Big Al pursed his lips and drooled puke down his chin.

"Bahh!" he remarked.

The substance might have once been biscuits and gravy, or perhaps it was that ol' timey Hawaiian favorite, Spam and eggs. Walter turned away, back to the chore at hand. It would be no good for HIM to start gagging too; who then, would fly the plane? He spoke calmly, reassuringly, twangily: "You might be a bit more comfortable Al, if you lift your face screen. It should improve the view, anyway. We're about an hour from home." Big Al just groaned again. "You all right back there?" The Princeville Airport was sliding along underneath them now, a private airstrip where Walter knew he could land in case of emergency. In fact, maybe he should. Drop in on Princeville and let Al get a hold of himself. The NaPali coast and Kalalau Valley lay ahead- some of the most beautiful turf in the sky.

"How ya feelin' Al?" He tried it with his best piloty twang.

"I ahh... I feel b... better now," said Al without conviction. He was trying to be cheerful though, make the most of his flight-of-a-lifetime, but his declaration had been punctuated with a dry heave convulsion.

"ERP!"

"Great, Al. We'll be back on solid ground before you know it. Hang on now." With that thought in mind Walter poured on the coal, pulled down the nose, and sped for home.

The Wisdom of Panchito or, No es mi Culpa!

The sun was setting as Walter put his TrikeZilla to bed for the night. The giant red orb dipped dramatically into the Sea of Cortez at Bahia de San Carlos and splashed wild colors back into the sky. Just south of where the glowing ball would soon be extinguished, the stark mountain peak called La Tetakawi jutted up in ancient splendor and cast long shadows over the sleepy fishing village. It was shaping up to be another night in Paradise for the gringo.

Quickly, Walter chocked the wheels, tied the wings down and stripped off the seat cushion to bring along. There wasn't much more to do and of that he was pleased. Already he could see a sunset-pink roostertail of dust approaching up the dirt road- Consuelo, in her sporty little Jetta, roaring up to meet him as planned.

Walter dreamed of her smooth honey-brown thighs and lovely white smile. He recalled how eager and willing she had been to make love to him just last night- 'mi piloto' she had called him with an impassioned moan as she wriggled beneath him. He hurriedly rechecked the tie downs. He didn't want to keep her waiting, but he didn't want his trike blown away in the night by a sudden lust, er, ahh... gust either. Consuelo roared through the gates to the airfield and skidded to a halt in a swirling cloud of dust, as was her wont. If there were one complaint Walter had about this hot, pint-sized little señorita, it was how she drove. Two speeds, it seemed, was all Consuelo knew: full throttle and full brake. Actually a skillful driver, she nonetheless made Walter nervous. He really wasn't in that big a hurry, but it is the Mexican way.

Consuelo waved a greeting to old Panchito, the tiny and ancient Yaqui Indian who, ostensibly, 'guarded' the airstrip, and who now stuck his wrinkled old face out from his bodega. Here in San Carlos, everyone knows everyone. They are probably related too for that matter... Panchito waved back and grinned a toothless grin. He hobbled a few steps in their direction.

Walter climbed aboard the Jetta and squeezed Consuelo's knee. Suddenly and acutely aware of the growing tumescence in his shorts, the gringo glimpsed the last rays of sunset shine through the señorita's frilly blouse, revealing a fine up-turned breast and a chocolate dipped strawberry nipple. There was hurry now all right: back to the hotel, pronto.

But Panchito wanted to talk, it appeared. He stood with the gate open but signaled them to a halt. Consuelo, in characteristic style, popped the clutch and roared the last few meters between them, where she stood on the brakes. The Yaqui reached through the window to Walter, shook the obligatory hand.

"Nos vemos mañana," said the gringo. *We'll see you tomorrow.*

"Desculpe señor, pero creo que usted olvidó algo," returned the old man. *Excuse me sir, but I think you've forgotten something.* Respectfully, he pointed a bony finger at the gringo's trike.

"Sí?" asked Walter. He looked over towards his 'Zilla. The trike was tied down nicely on four spots; both wings, the nose and the tail were anchored to the ground. Nothing has been left behind, nothing forgotten or overlooked... A gentle breeze blowing in from the sea caused the prop to spin slowly on the clutch, but this was entirely normal to the machine. Not until the engine was started and the operator stepped on the gas would the clutch engage and start to shove. Meanwhile, it was free-wheeling in the breeze. It wouldn't stop unless it was tied down. "Que?" asked the gringo. *What?*

"El helice esta voltiando," exclaimed Señor Panchito profoundly. Perhaps... the gringo's eyes were not so good. Maybe... he was simply blinded by the sexy señorita in her shameful little... minifalda, or his brain was otherwise addled. *The propeller is spinning* you foolish gringo.

"OH!" exclaimed Walter "Er umm ahh esta bien señor, asi esta bien," he explained and nodded emphatically. *That's fine sir, as it should be.* He squeezed Consuelo's knee as if to suggest that she pop the clutch again, there were other, more... urgent considerations than this old-timer.

But Panchito stood his ground. He shook his head and wagged the crooked finger at the gringo while Consuelo revved the throttle.

RRRNNNRRRNNNRRRNNN!

"No Señor," said the old man "Hay que parar lo." *You must stop it.*

Impatiently, Walter tried to explain more carefully. He spoke very slowly to be certain the old Yaqui would get it this time, "El helice tiene garra, amigo. Esta bien." *It has a clutch on the prop my friend. It is OKAY.*

Panchito wiped his face with a paw made of old parchment. Apparently, he would have to make his directive more succinct. He shook his head with conviction, leaned his weathered old head in the ventana, and explained his position more clearly: "No señor... Si despegue este avion, seriá mi culpa." Now Walter understood ol' Panchito's position: *No sir. If that plane takes off they will blame me.* He settled an elbow on the roof of Consuelo's Jetta and looked sage. He waited for Walter to find the wisdom in his words.

Walter looked at Consuelo, glimpsed a lacy brassiere cradling a caramel delight. She bent forward slightly, enhancing Walter's perspective, and grinned invitingly at him. She wiggled her eyebrows in fun. The last time Walter had peeled off that undergarment, the first and only time, he had discovered tiny fresh lilac blossoms tucked inside. He could smell lilacs now- his pecker throbbed painfully. He desperately considered explaining the situation to Panchito one last time, but it didn't seem like the most expeditious solution. Obviously, old Pancho had never considered that an airplane must make a whole bunch of noise before it would actually jump from the ground and take flight. That a prop freewheeling on a clutch was no threat to anyone's responsibility. But Pancho had obviously never seen a prop that spun when it wasn't about to take off. The old peasant had put two and two together... first you spin the prop, then you take off.

The gringo slipped his hand between Consuelo's hot satiny thighs and gave her a kiss on a fragrant bare shoulder that begged to be bitten. He jumped from the Jetta and sprinted to his 'Zilla, surreptitiously shoving his bulging pecker off to one corner of his shorts as he ran, an exercise in modesty. He stopped the spinning prop with one hand and fumbled into the tool bag with the other. Extracting a bungee chord and, hooking one end over a blade, he hooked the other end over the engine mount.

That should do it- this plane won't be making any unplanned departures now. He dashed back to the waiting Jetta, to Consuelo and her warm little pot of honey.

Panchito looked happy now. He winked at Walter. "Muy buenas noches Señor," he said with an exaggerated wink and a conspiratorial glance down to Consuelo's aromatic charms. Dignified by the exchange, finally certain that all was right with his world, he turned and walked back to his humble shack while Consuelo popped the clutch.

Hammer Bound For Hell or,
NICE PRE-FLIGHT, DUDE!

The High Sierra peaks were still aglow to the west when Walter shut down the spark for the night and rolled easily up to the hangar door. Old Pedro, the ancient Mexican from the trailer park next door to the Lone Pine airfield was the only visitor, the only member of humanity to have any interest at all, really, in Walter's activity. But Pedro, at least, seemed genuinely pleased with his luck. He grinned at Walter as the gringo climbed out of the funny-looking aircraft and removed his helmet. Pedro grinned his toothless grin and zoomed and swooped with his hands and dove and swung like a bird- spread his arms, and made a circle or two for emphasis. To a distant observer it may well have appeared that the old paisano had lost his mind or was staggering drunk. But no... Pedro was just giving his best imitation of Walter's flying- not flying to get somewhere, just hanging around the patch and flying touch-and-go patterns- swooping down to kiss the runway, then pouring on the throttle and going 'round for another. Flying for the heck of it.

Walter loved it too, landings were the fun part of flight if you really wanted to know- the difficult and precise part which required practice to perfect and which, when perfected, was also the easiest and most fun. But at the moment the hurry was to get the trike crouched-down to fit through the hangar door and then bed her down for the night. Walter swung into action even as Old Pedro continued to gesture and exclaim about the show.

First he pulled the pins to remove the front strut and set it aside in favor of a much shorter "hangar strut" which would allow the seat to hinge down and lower the wing until it was just a few inches above the floor. With the trike thusly crouched down for clearance, it was then a simple matter to shove it inside, under the low hangar door. Well... a matter made even easier when a claw hammer was dropped into the tiedown loop about half way out the wing opposite the camera mount. The hammer balanced the camera mount over on the other wing and, with the hammer dangling there the wing was perfectly balanced for shoving through the hangar door. It was just a simple claw hammer- light framing, but it did the job well. As Walter gave the trike a gentle shove, Old Pedro pointed an aged brown finger at the hammer and exclaimed, "Por que esto amigo?" *Why this friend?*

"Balancear lo, meter lo dentro el hangar." Walter explained. *To balance it for shoving under the door.* The tool must have looked pretty silly to Old Pedro. In any event he grinned some more and pointed and laughed. Then he waved farewell and turned his back on the gringo and his funny-looking flying machine. Shaking his head he retreated for home.

Walter conceded the hammer did look a bit foolish- it just happened to work perfectly for the job of counterweight and was easily inserted into the tiedown loop and dangled there quite nicely. It must have weighed almost exactly as did the camera mount because its weight automatically leveled-out the wing. Walter reminded himself yet again about the tag he planned for the hammer- a common flyers' reminder warning, a warning that Walter figured more as a gag than a necessity. He would purchase one of those red aircraft warning flags that read REMOVE BEFORE FLIGHT, and hang it on the hammer— light framing— just for laughs.

Walter stepped out from the hangar and reflected, in the twilight of the evening, on his short flight. The air had glassed off and was silky smooth between the snow-capped high peaks of the southern Sierra and the burnished ridge of the Inyo Range- a rare event indeed in the Owens Valley. By the time Walter had shot more touch 'n goes than he could count he was drooling with happiness, the slight breeze had stopped altogether and all was very still outside the hangar- a perfect flyer's evening. Traffic whizzed by over on Highway 395 and Walter softly cursed the travelers- they were entirely indifferent to flying, to Walter, and to his amazing flying machine. That would be a good way to describe the vast majority of humanity when it comes to sport flight- indifferent.

Sheesh!

Walter shook his head in sad disbelief as he carried his helmet to the truck and headed home for the evening. Still reflecting about the sorry state of sport flight, he drove off realizing that he was going broke as a flight instructor, that the writing was on the wall and there wasn't much he could do except go get a real job pretty soon... Or go down with the ship. The simple dang truth was that the vast majority of humanity, and certainly the entirety of those motorists driving by on Highway 395 this evening as Walter made landing after landing were indifferent. 'Completely oblivious' would be an even better way to describe the situation, they were completely oblivious to Walter, and his bitchin' funny-looking plane. Only Old Pedro paid the slightest attention.

Since the dawning of Civilization and down through untold millennium Humanity's Oldest Dream had been to fly like the birds. As humanity toiled and traveled painfully at the pace of a burro or camel or horse, the birds took wing and effortlessly covered great distances and were graceful and awesome. For the untold centuries and millennia mankind's struggle had been completely earthbound, while his gaze turned skyward in wonder. And now... Now for the last 100 years... Flight is here! It was all around us! Incredible flying machines in all shapes and sizes, available to nearly everyone! Here! NOW! And yet...?

Indifference.

Oblivion.

WalMart greeter.

It was the only other job Walter qualified for. *How's that for Irony*, thought the flyer— from flight instructor to ignominy. Walking back to CampZilla Walter heard a blues song on the radio. The singer was repeating a soulful refrain.

If I could only fly...

If I could only FLYYYY!

"What, I say WHAT is WRONG with these people?" thought the gringo aloud. "Have they not looked to the sky? Do they walk around with their gaze constantly tuned to the shit about their feet? Are they totally oblivious? Can they not crane their necks? Do they not realize that it is SO EASY that nearly EVERYONE can fly? You get out there and do whatever it takes but... YOU FLY!

Then the silly fool could change his refrain.

Now I'm flying,
Now I FLYYYY!

Shit!

How many times had some gawking Groundogon walked up to Walter and his pretty little wagon and said something like "Wow, I've always wanted to try that!"

And just exactly as many times the gringo had replied emphatically "Load 'em up partner, your time has come. It is YOUR LUCKY DAY!" At which point the pedestrian had often decided, whimpered, "Oh no. NOT TODAY! I just couldn't."

Simpering fools...!

Shit and two is eight! A guy spends his whole life wanting to do something until he is actually confronted with the reality sitting right before him on the runway and then... NOT TODAY! Where would we be now if Orville and Wilbur had been so friggin' pathetic? Shit!

Well, tomorrow is another day indeed. Walter decided then and there to give Whitney another go. He turned and looked west at Mount Whitney looming just a few miles away. The peak is the loftiest place in the forty-eight States at 14,491 feet above sea level, and was just a brooding dark silhouette under the glowing sunset. Walter had flown close to its haughty summit but never actually over it. Would the little plane really fly that high? Walter wasn't entirely sure, but decided to give it a try- tomorrow at the crack of dawn. He would go light- flying solo and with just half a tank of fuel. He would go in the brisk morning air when engine cooling was not an issue. Tomorrow, he would go. Screw 'em!

"Lone Pine traffic this is ultralight Delta niner-nine rolling for takeoff on zero-seven. I will be turning westbound for Mt. Whitney, Lone Pine traffic..." At this hour there was no one around to listen anyway, so Walter pushed the throttle to the floor under his foot and shoved the nose up for takeoff. Delta surged ahead and quickly popped off the runway. The Inyo range was still dark with leftover night but Walter stood his wagon on a wingtip and cranked a turn through 180 degrees. This changed his course by 180 degrees too, and now his little craft was climbing out straight at Mt. Whitney, perhaps ten miles distant.

Walter backed off a little throttle and settled into a rapid climb. From field altitude at thirty-seven hundred feet Walter had more than eleven thousand feet to climb if he hoped to see over the back of the Sierra. It would be a long climb. The air was perfectly calm though, a deep stillness that was left over from the night before. At least at this altitude, the air was perfect for a summit attempt. Walter pushed the nose up gently and straight-armed the bar. This would help the rate-of-climb too. Glancing out his left wing, Walter squeezed the shutter release for his camera and watched as the tiny eye in the lens winked, confirming that the shot was taken. Every few minutes along the climb Walter took another shot...

The curtain of light cast by the sun rising over the Inyo range behind the flyer and falling down the high Sierra was a dramatic sight that Walter enjoyed as he climbed out over the Alabama Hills. Shadows played upon the strange rocks below, and dawn, heralding yet another day in Paradise, was splashed across the profile of a hundred miles of snowcapped peaks.

Walter, caught in the middle of the show and purring along under his friendly little wing, was just amazed. How could anyone miss this? he wondered. How remain oblivious to such wonders? A chill floated up and down Walter's spine as he soaked up the wonderful new day in the mountains when...

Suddenly, something caught Walter's attention through his peripheral vision, a sight that really ruined his whole morning. Turning his head sharply to the right the flyer was stunned to see his claw hammer- light framing- dangling from the tiedown loop at mid wingspan! The hammer! Walter had forgotten to remove the hammer before taking flight! Oh shit! The gringo's left hand went automatically to the throttle and chopped it back to idle. As he did so the nose dropped through the horizon and Delta began to glide.

What the chingada!

Shit!

I forgot the hammer!

Slowly, he came back on the throttle, realizing that there was really no danger. In fact, the hammer hung nearly static, almost motionless in the perfect morning air. It was far enough out on the wing not to be a danger to the propeller even should it fall free. In fact, falling free was probably the BEST thing that might occur...

Walter eased into more throttle and settled back in his seat, consciously trying to ease the tension too, to calm his hammering heart. *There is nothing really wrong here... there is nothing really wrong here... there is nothing really wrong here...* It was the gringo's newest tune. *There is nothing really WRONG!*

What's wrong with this picture?

Walter glanced at his altimeter and watched it spin up past ten thousand feet. Still the air was very still and the hammer hung quietly under the wing. But at eleven thousand feet the air took on a decided chop. At twelve thousand feet the bumps were much more dramatic and Walter concluded he had a headwind- an upper-level west wind which was falling, cascading down the High Sierra peaks, hammering him, so to speak, on the nose. Holding the wing level Walter stared hard at the hammer, which was now jumping and flailing about the leading edge spar as if suddenly alive. *Can a silly claw hammer- light framing- be a serious danger to a triker while*

dangling from a tiedown loop at thirteen grand above the Owens Valley? It was a consideration that sullied all of Walter's thoughts, as Delta remained pointed for Whitney's lofty summit, her motor purring smoothly along.

Suddenly, the little plane pitched and lurched wildly to larboard and the bar was ripped from Walter's grasp. Grabbing and pushing and shoving, the triker leveled off as best he could, only to be shoved wildly in the opposite direction. *Shit!* thought Walter. *I'd better shut down this prop and turn around!* Fumbling with a gloved hand for the switches, Walter shut off the motor and gasped with relief. Yanking the bar through 180 degrees to point his tailfeathers at the Sierra ridge and his nose out to the valley, Walter noticed another blur in his peripheral vision to the right, but this time when he looked, the claw hammer— light framing— was gone, disappeared... adios! Walter craned his neck behind and below him but all he saw was vast square miles of wilderness where the tool was heading now like a hammer bound for Hell.

"Wheeoosh!" Walter hollered with relief. Chickening out, he headed home for the hangar, the craft gliding silently now, his new destination thousands of feet below. Enough excitement for one morning. Mt. Whitney wasn't going anywhere- it would be there tomorrow.

Travels With Trikezilla or, Most Folks Got Better Sense

Walter stood out on the tarmac and kicked at some imaginary dirt with a toe. "But surely señora," he implored. "There must be... some... posibilidad?" The señora shook her head slowly back and forth while her eyes stared up in wonder at the most unlikely flying machine she had ever seen.

The airport at Nogales, Sonora, just south of the US border, is a quiet place; only a few planes were parked on the tie downs and light breezes rustled the bougainvillea. A few buzzards—*zopilotes*—whirled and soared overhead. Walter was rapidly warming up under the clear blue winter sky and could feel his fingers and toes coming back to life. He unzipped his flight suit. He'd landed on his way south to Hermosillo for the necessary documentation for entering the country; primarily a tourist card and entry permit for his TrikeZilla. He just wanted to continue his journey south into Mexico.

"Lo siento mucho Señor." *I'm very sorry, sir.* "Pero no se puede usted." *But I can't allow you.* The Comandante was a middle-aged woman in an official blue government uniform who stood about half Walter's size; an unlikely specimen for such an commanding office. Walter had met few Mexican comandantes before, none of them had ever been women.

"But Señora," continued Walter. "Manaña is Día de Aviacion in Mexico. I have no choice. I must go!" This was true, and a little-known fact; Mexico has an official day for flight, the second Saturday in January. If you are a flyer in Mexico, this holiday is like a cross between Thanksgiving and your birthday.

The señora peeled her gaze from Walter's strange looking apparatus for a moment of eye contact. This gringo had the look of a desperado and maybe he meant it—that he had no choice—she thought. She would explain the problem once more: The entry permit required an "N" number from all gringos and also a pilot's license and further documents to be properly completed. Since the Señor has none of these, then he must not really be a pilot at all, and could not enter the country in an aeroplane. Any aeroplane. But most of all not in this... this... funny-looking... thing.

Whatever it is!

Walter had heard it all before of course, so he was not surprised. Though trikes are quite popular in Europe, they haven't made inroads in the States yet, and are even scarcer in Mexico. Still... TrikeZilla squatted there on the runway looking battle-ready. She sat on three off-road type balloon tires that Walter had scraped the knobs off by hand. Her wing, an Air Creation XP-15, was all white with a red leading edge and a silver slash underneath. Her tubing was finished with a brushed gold that sparkled in the sun. Walter had built her chariot by hand, cutting all the tubes and drilling all the holes, torquing each and every bolt by hand just so. He was unimpressed by mere skeptics.

One way or another Walter vowed, he would continue south. Perhaps an explanation would help...

"In my country you do not need a license to operate an ultralight, Señora, and Mexico has adopted those same rules." Walter had said this several times. It sounded good, he thought, but was a complete lie; there were no ultralight regulations at all in Mexico and indeed, what the Señora said was true. Any flying Walter did in Mexico would be illegal flying. To the gringo, it all seemed so ridiculous.

"That may be so Señor," replied the Comandante, "But this is MY airport and I am responsible for all who enter here. I'm sorry Señor, but there is nothing I can do..." She looked back at Walter's Ultralight with a bit of a shake of her head.

TrikeZilla was loaded down for travel. There were five transparent fuel jugs holding a total of twenty-five gallons of Chevron eighty-seven octane. Two daypacks of luggage hung on either side of the jugs and a gear bag with bedroll, ground cloth and sleeping pad was stashed under the seat. A case of two-stroke oil peeked out from under the load and the tool bag bulged. A torque wrench was lashed to one landing strut and a large machete to the other. The wing bag was Velcroed below the propeller and two streamers of surveyor tape trailed off each wing tip. Walter thought they added a festive look. From the kingpost flew a tiny Mexican flag. *If the gringo was heading north I could have him searched on pure suspicion*, she concluded. *Well, he going back north now.*

Walter was untying the trike and stashing the tie-downs in the wing. Again he stood before the woman who was Comandante at Nogales, Sonora. Conspicuously he jingled the coins inside his pants pocket. "Surely Señora, there must be some…. way," he reiterated.

"Noooo, Señor," she intoned. "I'm sorry sir, but you'll have to return to your own country." How could Walter explain? Sure, it was his country by birth. But Walter didn't want it, and somehow always felt more useful, alive and… vibrant, in Mexico. Besides, he'd been sent there on a mission to open the country to the joys of triking and couldn't just turn around and go home. Give up? Furthermore, when Walter had left the hangar and headed south for the border the other flyers back in the hangar had been placing bets on whether they'd ever see him alive again. Or his plane, for that matter…

There were places to go and things to do.

Walter wished he'd never stopped here at this airport in the first place. His tiny engine burned car gas anyhow, it was available at any PEMEX, and he planned to avoid airports from here to his destination. Where ever that turned out to be. *To Hell with this dumpy little bureaucrat,* he thought. What possible harm could come from such a journey? She was just a typical pathetic bureaucrat. *Out of my way!*

"Desculpe la molestia," said Walter politely with a slight bow. *Excuse the trouble.* "Ya me voy." *Just let me outta here quickly*, he thought. Walter sat in the trike and reached up to spin the prop'. "Gracias por la hospitalidad," he said facetiously. With a glance around he hollered, "¡LIBRE!" *Clear prop!*

The engine popped with a whirr. A small crowd of spectators had gathered around the strange contraption and now they stood back to watch. Walter added some throttle and rolled down the taxiway, awash in indecision. He cleared traffic in both directions and turned onto the active runway. A breeze had set in, blowing down from the States that morning, so Walter took off headed north, like a good gringo should. But as soon as his wheels lifted, he cranked a hard one-eighty and pointed his 'Zilla south as a good gringo definitely should not. His flight took him back over that same little piece of tarmac and the terminal there in Nogales. The small crowd that Walter had left on the apron was standing on tiptoe now and waving all arms as he flew by overhead. All except the Comandante that is. Walter could see her standing off to one side, hands on hips, watching his progress across the clear blue sky. Maybe she'll think the gringo's lost, he thought. *A lost gringo!*

But then, maybe she'll call in the Fuerza Aerea Mexicana. Was there even a Mexican Air Force?

¿Quien sabe...?

Walter added some throttle and pulled the nose down. Suddenly he knew how Hernán Cortéz must have felt when he landed at Vera Cruz in his tiny boat with his stinking band of thieves: unwelcome and headed for strange lands. That's it, thought Walter. He felt like a damn conquistador!

Did Cortez Cry?

Back home, Walter was the Mexico guy. His flying buddies considered him as very 'sabe' about Mexico. Walter knew all the hang-gliding sites in tropical Mexico and had flown many of them on a regular basis. Walter was the first pilot to have flown from Cerro Jocotítlan and land back home in Valle de Bravo. Walter was proud of that flight. He'd had to fly around the Nevado de Toluca, which stands in the way at about fifteen thousand six hundred feet and had in fact soared to eighteen grand on that flight- enough altitude to fly over it. Walter was the first and only pilot to land on launch at El Peñon del Díablo- a narrow, rough slot in the trees. In fact, no one else had ever considered that trick and it had earned him a reputation as a bit of a loco gringo.

"Hey goater, did you hear what Walter the gringo did today?"

"¡Como!"

The loco gringo flew El Peñon ninety days in a row one winter, a feat that the locals were still talking about. Those were the Good 'ol Days... Yet there remained so many mysteries in this country that Walter would often despair of ever figuring things out. Now, as he sped south in TrikeZilla, he considered a few...

Like, for example, the night the nuns exploded bottle rockets over the sleeping village at 3AM, like they had done that night in Valle de Bravo; Nuns, fer Chrissake? They let nuns have bottle rockets? And fire them off from the front steps of the church, no less? And why was Walter, clad only in Bermuda shorts and sandals, the only one to rush out into the street and complain loudly?

Also... why would much of the village get so drunk on Sundays that very little could get done on Mondays? Is this Mexican tradition? Walter hated Mondays.

And the banks, the banks were horrible. Every week or so the gringo would need to go into the bank and get pesos with his dollars. They knew who he was and that he just wanted a quick money swap when he entered the bank, yet they always insisted he sit down with a manager to show identification with his cash dollars, cash! And then to have his dollars scrutinized carefully like they might be home made. Forms would be validated in triplicate and the whole process was painfully slow.

And the telephones... Oh dios mio, the phones! thought Walter. There were credit card phones in Valle now; spankin' new phones, and when Walter dialed home to wish a Merry Christmas to his mom, he could hear her just fine, but poor mom kept saying over and over, "Hello... is anyone there? Hello? Merry Christmas... Hello?" Walter was pissed. He'd reported the foul up with the local phone service but of course they hadn't fixed the problem. They were losing money but the attitude was that the gringo was the problem. If the gringo would just go away, the problem would go away too...

Just another mystery.

Walter had recently solved one riddle however. Ever since he had returned this winter to Valle the children had been greeting him with a strange name: Kalimán, and Walter had no clue. Then one day while driving through Mexico City, Walter had turned on the radio and discovered, "Las Aventuras de Kalimán, el Hombre Increíble." Intrigued, Walter had listened as best he could as the signal faded in and out, even pulling off the highway looking for a strong signal and a clue to the mystery.

Kalimán? Hombre Increíble? Walter remained puzzled. Why would the Mexican niños call him such nonsense? Kaliman the Incredible Man? Walter thought himself no closer to unraveling the truth.

Yet another mystery...

But soon thereafter, Walter was walking an errand back in Valle and as he strode through the cobblestone streets a small boy of eight or ten years ran past and tagged him and called shrilly "¡Kalimán!" Sprinting, Walter caught up to the niño and offered him a Popsicle at the store next door. The child was eager to agree, and as he sat there with helado dripping off his chin, Walter was enlightened: Kalimán, it seems, is a Mexico radio soap-opera hero who airs nationwide at four o'clock each day and has so for some thirty years. He and his sidekick, an adolescent by the name of Solin, have been fighting the forces of evil throughout the world so long that everyone in Mexico knows them.

"¿Pero porque yo?" Walter inquired. But why me? Walter didn't feel like a superhero. Matter of fact, at the moment, Walter felt kind of mystified; like a stupid gringo.

The child's eyes wandered up Walter's face and came to rest on his turban. Walter had worn the turban frequently since having bought it for $4.95 at a Bailey's Food and Drug Store for Halloween. The turban was a good alternative to helmet-hair after flying, and it fit easily in his harness. There was a blue stone on the forehead that highlighted the gold lamé cloth. When asked, Walter liked to say that he'd received it as a gift from a little snake-charmer gal down in Marrakech, but of course that wasn't true.

Now the child revealed a secret that would forever change Walter's existence in Mexico: Kalimán, it seems, wears a gold turban with a stone, a 'zafiro' on the forehead- just like Walter's. The stone had mysterious powers which only Kaliman could harness. Well, Walter's turban was just like Kalimán's, realized Walter. The child explained to his new amigo that Solin was Kalimán's close personal friend and he hoped to form a similar bond with some like emissary someday, perhaps with the great Kalimán himself.

"Well," offered Walter. "If I can play Kalimán, Hombre Increíble, you can certainly be my Solin. I may not have the same powers as Kalimán, the Incredible Man himself... but I can fly." And so it was agreed. Cementing the deal with a high-five and another helado, Kalimán and Solin strode through the streets of Valle de Bravo.

Feeling much wiser now and even somewhat empowered, Walter had headed for launch. It was only fitting that a man of my stature should go flying, he had decided.

The Lost Gringo Meets FedZilla

But now Walter was an hour south of the border and about sixty miles removed from his futile encounter with the Comandante in Nogales. Here, he was just an illegal alien in an illegal aircraft, cruising along at two thousand feet. He didn't feel like a superhero or conquistador any more. Indeed, he felt about ready to burst into tears.

As the Mexicans say: 'iQue pendejo!'

He wondered how the Hell he ever got here anyhow. What had possessed him to disobey the Comandante back at the border? Only a madman or a fool would have continued, he knew. Now Walter wished he'd shown better judgment and simply admitted defeat. Matter of fact, Walter fervently hoped he could someday find happiness just to stand around on the ground like the rest of humanity. What was it that compelled him to do such stupid things, take such crazy risks?

A Mexican airshow?

The flyer felt the insignificance of a speck of sand on the immense desert below his wings, and knew the meaning of humility.

Walter saw an enormous storm cloud flash with lightening on the distant horizon and felt the significance of respect.

He was severely hammered in some sudden heavy turbulence and felt outright fear.

The gringo nearly collided with a red-tail hawk, which flashed by in the blink of an eye, and felt like pissing his pants.

Instead, he flew along the Santa Ana riverbed that heads south from Nogales and then followed the divided toll road straight south. It stretched away into the distance like a long emergency runway, and provided some solace, some small peace-of-mind. Walter's TrikeZilla purred along nicely, but he realized that sometimes flying just wasn't so much fun; he worried about every little thing...

Would the weather hold?

Improve?

Worsen?

Deteriorate altogether?

Was the carburetor jetted right, not too rich, not too lean?

Was the prop pitched right and were the bolts torqued properly to specs?

Were the tires holding air?

Would any gear blow off and into the prop?

Would the wings break and/or collapse?

Disintegrate?

Diverge?

Was there enough fuel?

Was there more fuel to be bought somewhere up ahead?

Would the Federáles be waiting in ambush at the next gasolinéra when Walter flew in for fuel?

Was there enough daylight to get to Hermosillo International before dark?

Where was Hermosillo International, anyway?

There seemed to be an infinite amount of variables in keeping this machine in the air and heading south, an endless list of worries, and they all seemed to Walter to be aimed towards his total failure and ultimate destruction. Now, here was something more to worry about: Walter was an illegal alien in an illegal airplane and he was advancing deeper into Mexico with each spin of the prop.

The gringo leaned out of his seat to glance at his fuel jugs and found that he was running low- something else to worry about. He would have to land soon, but just long enough to transfer fuel from his auxiliary tanks into his burn jugs. Also, his bladder was about to burst.

He saw that he was approaching a small village along the highway, so he swooped low to read the highway road sign: SANTA ANA, just a dusty little village in the middle of nowhere, but a name which did nothing to set his mind at ease. Antonio de Padua María Severino López de Santa Anna y Pérez de Lebrón, after all, was a scoundrel from the Mexican Revolution. He had held the office of Presidénte eleven times in Mexican history, he had left a legacy of disappointment and disaster, and he enforcing a "take-no-prisoners" policy at the Alamo which, of course, is about the only thing about him that gringos remember.

Take no prisoners...

Lining up on a narrow two-track winding through the desert, he hit the switches to stop the prop and slipped his 'Zilla on in, touching down on a two-track in a small field next to the pueblo. Walter would have preferred to land next to a mini-mart or a hospital, somewhere with service availability, maybe there was a town somewhere named 'Jose Jimenez'? But this field would have to do for a quick fuel transfer.

He swung the trike around and looked back towards the village. A crowd of small children were running his way and squealing with glee. TrikeZilla always attracted lots of attention. How frequently would someone aviate into Santa Ana? Probably not very often he imagined. Taking off his helmet, he quickly relieved his bladder and then set to work, spinning off the lids to his fuel jugs and getting the siphon going. The villagers were arriving in droves now—first the strongest and fastest children, then the adults, and finally the grandpas and grandmas all turned out. Walter worked furiously, transferring fuel and simultaneously performing a flight check. The crowd that gathered was vocal but respectful. It dawned on Walter that they must figure him for some kind of narco traficánte, loaded down with evil drugs for sale to senators' kids.

Suddenly, there was a distant roar of four-barrel carburetor over near the highway that caught everyone's attention. Walter looked up in time to see a sinister black Dodge Ram pickup aimed at him from about three hundred yards out, and closing fast. As Walter watched in dismay, the truck ran through a barbed-wire fence without regard, smashed over an irrigation ditch with abandon, and kept on coming. The driver really had his foot in the throttle, and was making a beeline for the gringo. Whoever they were, they meant business.

"Oh shit," cried the gringo. "¡Me llevo la chingasa!"

Not knowing what else to do, Walter reached into the side pocket of his luggage and came out with... the turban. As a safeguard it wasn't much, but he smashed it over his head and turned to face this latest peril.

Kalimán Escapes Their Clutches

The pickup truck was a nearly new model, though covered with dust, and topped by a bank of floodlights and red and yellow emergency beacons. Twin spotlights were available to the occupants in front of the doors. An official sticker on the side identified it as a government wagon of some sort... FEDERÁLES DE CAMINOS. The crowd parted like the Red Sea as the sinister looking vehicle skidded to a halt in a cloud of dust. The doors swung open and out jumped four heavily armed men in civilian clothes who quickly closed on the gringo. They held Uzi-type weapons and pointed them at Walter's head. It was the first time anyone had ever pointed a weapon at Walter. He felt a sudden weakness in his knees.

"¿Que estas haciendo aqui?" barked the hefe. He wore an officious looking hat with some type of badge on the crown but was otherwise dressed in civilian clothes. He sure acted like the leader though, a mean hombre. Now he invaded

Walter's personal space with a grimace, nearly bumping chests with the gringo. His eyes and the tendons in his neck bulged in anger and stress. Spittle flew from his mouth and pelted Walter's flight suit. Now, in Spanglish, he repeated his query, "Whad arr jou do heer!?" Walter just couldn't afford to just tell him the truth;

Well sir, umm, see señor, I'm an ahh illegal alien with an illegal airplane and I just had to take a pee and fuel up so I'm only here for a minuto or dos. How do you like me so far?

Surely, he'd be locked up for an indefinite amount of time- probably until someone paid his ransom- and worse, he would never likely see his faithful TrikeZilla again. Walter would just have to lie. He only hoped his Español was up to the task.

Stepping out from under his wing and slightly away from this most recent threat, Walter cast his glance skyward and squinted against the hot Mexican sun, as calmly as his nerves permitted under the circumstances. He squinted sharply and scanned the horizon, Clint Eastwood style. Craning his neck he looked briefly straight up, as though seeking Divine intervention.

The hefe exploded once more and took a stride forward, now stepping on the gringo's toes, "¿Que estas haciendo aqui?" he demanded again. "Whad arr jou do heer?"

Walter brought his gaze down and looked the hefe in the eye. In the most convincing voice he could summon, the flyer lied with the first words that came to mind: "Ando buscando a Solin, Señor," he said looking up again. "No haz visto de el?"

I'm looking for Solin, Señor. You haven't seen him? It was very simple Español but it stretched Walter's vocabulary to the limit.

A murmur went through the crowd of locals and Walter heard the magic words he'd been hoping for. The children picked up on it first: Kalimán they cried, KalimánKalimánKalimán! The gringo decided he'd better run with the idea, and make it good. He looked the commandante in the eye and said, "Siempre anda perdido Solin."

He's always getting lost, that Solin.

The hefe stole a quick glance towards the sky as if he too were anxious about Solin, and then sternly back at the gringo. One or two of his compañeros actually scanned the sky, gazing hopefully for their little amigo. More of the children took up the chant now: Kalimán! they cried with joy. They too, searched the Heavens for Solin.

But the hefe was not so easily distracted, "Donde vas?" he roared. "Wherr arr juu goink?"

Walter liked this line of questioning better; he would not have to lie. Mañana was Día de Aviación Nacionál after all, and Walter was going south to participate in the festivities. "Voy a la Festival Aereo en Hermosillo, Señores. Van estar ustedes?"

I'm going to the airshow in Hermosillo, sirs. Will you guys be there too?

The traveler grinned as best he could, knees still shaking, pointing south with a finger. These guys were probably after drugs, he figured, and heading in a southerly direction would belay some suspicion from Walter. After all, who takes buns to the bakery? Walter hoped they didn't get to snooping around and search the inside compartment of his wing however. What might they find there? He felt a bead of sweat drip down the back of his neck and dribble down his spine.

But the guns were coming down now as Walter kept grinning, and they were starting to point at the ground. But the hefe hadn't given up yet: "¡Deja me ver su permiso!" he spouted. "Led me see juu permeet!" This is what Walter feared most. He had no permiso and as such had no right to be standing here on Mexican soil, or flying Mexican skies for that matter. But at least now, Walter would not have to lie about it. He held up his hands in a supplicating manner, Mexican sign language for 'I take no responsibility for events past, present, or future', he grinned weakly at the hefe and gave it to him straight.

"Yo no tengo permiso, Señor," he stated, matter-of-factly. *I have no permission sir.* Hey! If you're Kalimán, El Hombre Incréible, and the Mexican Federáles close in on you, you don't need no steenkin permits! The guns were pointing at the dusty Mexican tierra now, and the hefe had deflated. With shaking hands, Walter turned and busied himself spinning the caps on his jugs. The fuel transfer was done. He stepped out from under his wing again and took a walk around his plane, giving it a quick pre-flight. The crowd yielded as he walked. More sweat rolled down his brow, he was feeling weak in the stomach too now.

Returning back to the hefe he asked his own question; "Y ustedes, quien son?" *And you guys, who are you?*

"Somos los ántitraficántes señor," came the answer. *We are the dope chasers sir,* and all the guns came back up as a point of pride, aiming not at Walter now, but at the clear blue sky. Time's right to make an exit, decided the gringo.

"Mucho gusto," he said and walked to each in turn to shake hands. "Tell you what I'm gonna do now," he continued in his broken Spanish. "I'm going to taxi my plane over there," he pointed, "and I'm going to take off VROOM right through here," waving now, gesticulating with both arms. "Please keep these people out of my way."

The guns came around towards the villagers now, who all started a respectful retreat. Some of them threw up their hands with joy: Kalimán! KalimánKalimánKaliman! It was the day Kalimán had descended upon Santa Ana, wearing his turbante and flying a very strange avioncito.

Walter pushed his plane around and sat down in the cockpit. He reached up to spin the propeller. "Hasta la vista amigos," he intoned by way of salute and then, "¡LIBRE!" he hollered, and gave a good pull. TrikeZilla popped once, and then settled into a pleasing whir. Walter taxied to the fence at the far end of the field and turned his wagon around. Once more he faced the villagers and the Federáles too. He added full throttle and TrikeZilla leaped into the sky. Walter pulled the nose down to gather speed and made a low pass at around eighty kilometers an hour. He saw the villagers flash by with a blur. He cranked a big turn and came back for another pass over the crowd, now just head-high. TrikeZilla blazed overhead at full cry and made a tremendous racket above sleepy little Santa Ana. As his tiny plane climbed out, Walter gave a glance back over his shoulder.

There in the field lay the prostrate bodies of the children, the men and women, the grandpas and grandmas of Santa Ana- and four of Mexico's finest, waving Uzis at the azure Mexican sky.

Sanctuário

Walter headed south along Highway 15 best he could towards Hermosillo, no happier for his narrow escape. But tomorrow was indeed Día de Aviación Nacionál, and from Walter's experience, this was too good to pass up. All aviators and aviation enthusiasts were treated as heroes at least one day a year in Mexico, and tomorrow was going to be that day. If it flies, it once flew or someday might fly, the Mexicans would drag it out of some hangar or bodega and dust it off, spin it up, make some noise with it, and maybe even aviate with it. The craft in question may or may not be capable- no matter. They would shove it out, blow it off and attempt to start it, make some racket anyway. Walter knew that if he could just avoid any more trouble between here and Hermosillo International, he'd probably be safe on arrival. His confidence grew with each revolution of his Rotax 503 and with renewed spirit Walter began to think of the advice Guillermo had given him over the telephone before he'd departed Arizona.

"Yo te invito," Guillermo had said. *I'm inviting you.* He'd continued by directing: "Juss go to de ol tower on de leff an axe for mi."

As Walter approached Hermosillo now, just a cloud of smog on the southern horizon, ol' Mister Doubt began to creep back into his brain. He could almost hear his amigo's broken Inglés but the words did not make good clear sense. The old tower on the left? This implies that Guillermo knew from which direction Walter would arrive. Of course he did; all gringos come from the north. Everyone understood that... But, what if Walter got lost, overflew the airport, and had to backtrack to his destination. Would the directions still apply? What if Walter went instead to the new tower on the right, and asked for his amigo Guillermo Camu? What would happen then? A misunderstanding might ensue, and Walter might have to explain to some other Federále why he had just landed on Mexican soil, no- at an International Airport- with no permits, no license, no radio and no 'N' number. Walter just couldn't predict how the Mexican authorities might react and he didn't want to speculate too much now. He suspected that back in the Land of the Free, such behavior would result in his possible incarceration, confiscation of his 'Zilla, and hefty fines. Walter hoped the Mexicans would show more... amistad. Be more accommodating. Especially on this, the eve of Día de Aviación.

A range of mountains grew off Walter's starboard wing, over which drifted a brown cloud of pollution, a sure sign of a major metropolis Walter guessed, and so he added throttle to climb on up for a better look. Cresting the ridge Walter flew between two tall communications towers and, spread out before him like a dirty desert oasis lay his destination; Hermosillo, a farming and industrial town of a million or more souls. He knew from the chart he carried strapped to his leg that the airport lay on the perimeter of the city, so he cranked a right turn to fly around town. As he did so he spotted the smoky contrail from the exhaust of a jumbo commercial jetliner climbing away from the runway. Walter could not see where the plane had come from but there could be little doubt where he needed to go. He realized then that his stomach was tied and knotted with stress due to the uncertainty of his immediate future. Like Hernán Cortéz himself when he stole that boat out of Hispaniola, there could be no turning back now.

"Que será, será," say the Mexicans: whatever will be, will be.

Approaching the airport over an expanse of humble Mexican shanties, Walter put his head on a swivel. Constantly searching the sky around him for other air traffic gave Walter a strange ease, as though well, if this were all he could do to protect his ass from danger, then he would do it all right. It gave him something to do with these last few minutes of flight. Something else he could do to avoid heavy air traffic was to fly extremely low. No point in a collision or even a close encounter with other traffic. That just wouldn't do at all to improve his welcome. Blazing over powerlines and rooftops the flyer waved to the *gente* below, and made a beeline for the old tower on the left.

Walter pulled up over Hermosillo International at five hundred feet and throttle back on his motor. Flying circles to clear traffic, he checked out the layout of the enormous facility. There were two commercial airliners- the big boys- nosed up to a large terminal where there was a flurry of human activity across the runways. Walter hoped they'd stay parked right there and let him in on the taxiway next to the runway. He descended to two hundred feet over a taxiway and commenced to circling. He circled and circled awaiting a signal from the tower. With no radio communications with the gringo, they were going to have to drag out their lights. Walter circled a few more times, concentrating on the tower each time he came around. Finally, after what seemed an eternity, Walter spotted the green light, he was cleared for landing. Here goes nothing!

He reached down and closed the throttle. In the sudden quiet, with only the wind through his sails, Walter banked his 'Zilla into a tight spiral and descended towards pavement.

He turned a quick base and final and nosed down on final glide. There were a collection of old buildings at the east end of the runways and Walter hoped this was the old tower on the left. Whatever, he decided to cast his fate in that direction and, a second before his wheels touched, he adjusted his trajectory in that heading. 'Zilla's big balloon tires touched down with a squawk. They were not made for, and unaccustomed to, pavement. Walter let 'em roll in the direction of the old tower. The building had an all-glass facade, covered with reflective film that made the whole building into one massive distorted mirror. Walter watched himself roll to a stop in TrikeZilla, a strange apparition indeed: sunburned, windblown and loaded down with gear in a plane with no nose, no tail and no cockpit. He hoped he didn't look too much like some bizarre freak from the sky.

But the flyer had little time to reflect, so to speak, as the mirrored door burst open and out strode a splendid Federále indeed. Shocked by this latest apparition, he stood before Walter with a look of pure wonder. Dressed in the crispest uniform Walter had ever seen, he stuttered for a moment as if speechless, and expectorated as he groped for words. His outfit was pressed from shoulder to pant-cuffs; twin creases traveled from the epaulets on his shirt down his chest and waist to join perfectly with those on his trousers. He wore ribbons on the shirt too, flowing down from one to another; they formed a colorful array in the afternoon sun. His shoes were spit-shined and showed not a scuff. Topping this whole apparition was a magnificent hat with an impressive brass badge on the brim: FEDERÁLES DE TRANSPORTES. Walter glanced at another small placard over the man's chest: 'O.M.RUELAS' it read, COMANDANTE.

Walter opened his mouth to deliver a respectful greeting. Something like: *Muy buenos tardes Señor, a sus ordenes*, would have done just fine. He fervently hoped to make a better impression with Señor Ruelas than he had with his last comandante back at the border. Instead there exited only a hoarse and mildly painful croak. Walter realized suddenly how truly parched he was, and at that same instant Señor Comandante Ruelas regained his wits.

"¡Señor!" he fairly shouted, "¿Como esta usted?" Walter was glad to hear the formal you: 'Usted'. This implied respect. It was unlikely after all, that any Federále would call you 'Usted' as he was throwing your ass in the hoosegow. Señor

Ruelas stood there with his arms wide as if ready to offer the gringo a bear hug. Walter unclipped his chinstrap and took off his helmet. Extending his hand he opened his parched mouth and tried again:

"Tengo mucho sed Señor," he croaked. *I am very thirsty sir.* This seemed like a safe opening to Walter, and was certainly the truth. Much better than the truth, the Whole Truth and Nothing But the Truth; *Well you see sir, I'm an illegal alien sir, flying this here illegal airplane sir and I must have just violated a bunch of your Federal Air Regulations by landing here beg your pardon sir, and my ass is sore and I'm burned out, and I'm almost out of gas, and my ears are ringing and, oh yeah, I could sure use a refreshing beverage. Would you help me out this once sir, before you toss my ass in the carcel?*

"Tengo mucho sed..." It was a croak, more than a statement, but the words seemed to work magic as Señor Ruelas, galvanized into action, quickly turned back to the mirrored door from whence he'd come,. Putting fingers to lips he blew a shrill whistle and barked a sharp command, as a comandante is wont.

"¡Cervesa!" was all he said, the magic word.

With the Comandante's back was turned, Walter reached into his saddlebag and pulled out his turbante. Might as well go for broke he realized. He pulled the turban over his head. Ruelas turned back to face Walter and as his eyes focused on Walter's headgear his face grew wide with wonder yet again. The door burst open just then, and out came a small boy, maybe ten years old, who struggled under the weight of a case of cervesa Tecate, which was crowned by a heaping mound of crushed ice. There was a parade of people behind him, all wearing grins or looks of astonishment as they first beheld Walter and his strange TrikeZilla. Or maybe it was...

Kalimán?

Señor Ruelas unburdened the boy of his refreshing cargo and presented Walter with the first beer. Grabbing one himself he gave it a good shake before popping the top and unleashing a spew of brew, a salute to a thirsty flyer. "¡Bienvenido, Señor!" he exclaimed. *Welcome!*

Walter heaved a sigh of relief as he popped the tab himself, and slaked his thirst on the first cervesa he'd ever been offered by a Federále. From the looks of the frosty case at his feet, it would not be the last...

Hotel Bombero

A crowd quickly gathered around the flyer as he quaffed his fill of frothy swill. A fiesta atmosphere prevailed as Señor Ruelas dispatched his first cold one, and then with a happy belch he helped himself to another. Everyone was very curious about Walter and TrikeZilla and the questions came in a flood:

"De donde viene Usted, Señor?" they asked. *From where have you come?*

"Phoenix," replied Walter. He felt proud of that now- an accomplishment. All self-doubt had been quenched with that first Tecate.

"¡Phoenix!" The word spread like wild fuego. *"Phoenix! The gringo came from Phoenix!"*

"¿En este aparato?" *In this contraption?*

"Claro que sí, Señores, vuela muy bien," said Walter: *Yes, of course. It flies very well.*

At this news came more looks of incredulity and delight. Señor Ruelas was matching Walter beer for beer and Manuelito, his tiny helper, returned with another case, which was quickly dispensed among the growing crowd. Ruelas was obviously the Hefe here and everyone stood respectfully aside as he passed. He strolled around TrikeZilla and shook his head in wonder. He seemed fascinated by the machete lashed to the landing strut. Manuelito meanwhile, was similarly mesmerized with the gold turban on Walter's head. Walter explained the obvious- that he had come to participate in the 'Festival Aereo' to be held mañana and he hoped he was welcome.

"Porsupuesto," declared Señor Ruelas with a smile. *Of course.* There was a quick discussion in rapid-fire Español with his men, and then Ruelas turned to Walter. "Donde va quedar usted por la noche?" he inquired. *Where will you spend the night?* Walter was loaded down with camping gear, and thought that the grassy lawn next to the terminal would provide adequate comfort. Explaining this, Sr. Ruelas laughed: "¡Como que no Señor!" *Of course NOT sir!* Walter was buzzed by now and gave silent thanks that they'd all commenced to regard him as 'Señor'. "Aqui somos muy agradable," explained the Señor. *We are friendly here.* "Dejame preguntar de los bomberos." *Let me ask the firemen.*

Bomberos? Bomberos? Ask bomberos what, wondered the gringo?

Someone handed Sr. Ruelas a two-way radio. He called down the airfield to the firehall and explained that a gringo dignitary had arrived for the Festival in a wild flying machine, and was there any posibilidad that he might find somewhere to bunk in the fire hall? Arrangements were soon made to accommodate Walter. Señor Ruelas consulted his watch and explained that the bomberos were about to serve dinner... If they hurried he would arrive just in time. Then, as Ruelas and his growing legions pushed TrikeZilla from behind, the whole entourage followed and laughed and carried on about this trike-traveling gringo and his long journey, shoving him down the tarmac.

Walter began to smell the firehall from a half-kilometer away, a wonderful aroma of garlic, chiles, limón and lard. Hunger stirred his belly-full-of-beer and Walter was elated to notice that the bomberos too had more refreshments for him. They pushed Walter and his TrikeZilla under the overhanging roof at the firehall and Walter produced tie-downs from within his wing. Securing the aircraft, Walter was escorted into a comfortable dining room where the aroma of Mexican cooking was nearly overwhelming. As Ruelas pulled a chair out for Walter, he noticed a mother-daughter team, slaving away over a hot stove and an enormous pot of posole stew. Since it was Friday Walter was served a steaming bowl with a generous serving of fresh Sea of Cortez shrimp with cebolla and repollo, cilantro and oregano, wedges of limón to top his stew, three flavors of salsa roja and two of salsa verde.

There was also fruit and vegetables, rice and beans and, of course, hot tortillas. As Walter savored the aromas, the old Señora scooped a bit of dough from a bowl and quickly rolled it into a ball. Placing it in a press, she leaned on the handle to squeeze it flat, and then tossed it on a hot plate with a practiced motion. There it bubbled and sizzled invitingly-pockets of air forming inside. The señora's delightful assistant smiled shyly at the gringo and tossed the tortilla into a basket where it joined a dozen or so more in a stack.

This will be worth writing home about decided the gringo. As all present watched, he gave thanks to the Sky Gods and dove into his meal.

The Promised Land at Last!

As Walter devoured all they set in front of him, he met one by one, all the bomberos who worked at Hermosillo International. In twos and threes they strolled into the fire hall and stood by the gringo and shook his hand and grinned widely. They would cluster around TrikeZilla and gawk at the trike. They gathered around the plane when someone produced a Polaroid camera and grinned for posterity. They insisted Walter wear his 'turbante' for the photos.

The Capitano of the bomberos arrived and hustled in to greet Walter, and to assure him that he was welcome in their midst, they were anxious to make him comfortable, and that an armed guard would be posted on his strange flying apparatus. Was there anything else he needed? The Capitano was a very handsome man in a very handsome blue uniform. He beamed with pride as he spoke to his visitor. He introduced himself: "Fran Carlo Aramburo a su servicio señor. Sus deseos son ordenes," he said: *At your service sir, your wish is my command.*

Walter assured the Capitano that he was indeed comfortable and felt welcome too. The food was delicious and plentiful and the drink was generous. If there was anything he needed, well... his fuel tanks were nearly empty. Was there any possibility...?

But Walter didn't even finish the question. Fran Carlo turned to one of his men and barked an order in rapid Spanish. The man departed at full sprint towards the fuel depot across the parking area. He soon returned driving a Chevy tanker truck full of one hundred low-lead, and began filling TrikeZilla's tanks. Meanwhile Walter, in an effort to return the hospitality, offered his services to the Capitano.

"Me gustaría volar con ustedes," he offered. *I'd like very much to fly with you all.*

The Capitano seemed pleased with this notion. Walter was relieved as well, because he didn't know what the official response to his continued aviation might be here in Mexico, especially at an international airport. But if he could get the Comandante himself enthused well, the Sky was the limit. So when Señor Fran Carlo himself sidled up next to him and asked, in a conspiratorial manner:

"¿Es possible... que usted vuela... con mis hijas?" *Is it possible you will fly with my daughters?* This request brought an unsolicited response from the other bomberos as they yelled their approval with catcalls and whistles. Of course Walter would fly the Captain's daughters- anything he wanted for that matter. Before he could respond, another of the bomberos, sidling up beside Walter, put his mouth next to Walter's ear as though to offer a big secret.

"Muy buenas suerte señor, son muy guapas señor," he confided. *Good luck sir, they are very cute sir.*

That settled it, and it was quickly agreed. Next morning at 8AM Capitano Aramburo would bring his daughters to the field where Walter would be given a special clearance for departure.

Meanwhile, the bomberos were hospitable indeed, offering Walter anything to make his stay pleasant. A soldado was posted over TrikeZilla, although Walter figured such drastic steps were ridiculous. Hermosillo International Airport appeared quite peaceful to him for one, but it also seemed a rather wild notion that someone might creep up and steal her; they couldn't even fly her. Her guard, well equipped with the latest in light weaponry, kicked back under 'Zilla's wing and promptly fell asleep.

Next, Walter was offered a foot-tour of the terminal by Ruelas who- in spite of the considerable buzz he wore from copious amounts of Tecate, still looked starch fresh in his gleaming uniform. They strolled through the modern terminal and made a casual beeline for bar. Ordering up two tequilas, Ruelas made a big fuss when Walter attempted to pay for them.

"Son gratis," he said. *They're on me.* "Mi casa su casa."

They tossed-back the fiery distillate in the traditional Mexican manner- a sprinkle of salt, a slice of fresh lime, a gulp and a grimace. The liquid burned down Walter's esophagus and started a warm glow in his stomach. Together they made quite a spectacle as they continued their stroll through the terminal: the Comandante and the Hómbre Increíble. Walter decided they had only to link arms to complete the masquerade.

They were sauntering past the rental car area when Walter heard his name called. Turning toward the sound Walter found a familiar face standing there looking astounded. It was Christine, a schoolteacher from up on the Navajo Reservation, where he had paid a visit some months previous, flying up there in TrikeZilla.

"Walter?" she asked again, as though incredulous.

"Hi Chris," He approached and they shook hands. "What are you doing here?" Ruelas had followed along and remained beside Walter. He too wore a look of surprise as if to ask, '*You know these people?*'

"What am I doing here?" she said. She looked Walter over, his scruffy boots, his tattered flight suit and the turban on his head. She looked Ruelas over, his shiny boots, his crisp suit and his crested hat. "What are YOU doing here?"

"Well... I heard it was Día de Aviación," said Walter. "So I flew on down in TrikeZilla."

"You WHAT!" she asked. She turned towards another gringo who was vaguely familiar as well. He too looked stunned, but before Walter could react, Sr. Ruelas stepped into the scene.

"¿Amigos?" he asked.

"Sí," said Walter. "Amigos de Arizona." *Friends from Arizona.* Christine stood with jaw agape as Señor Ruelas politely offered his hand.

"Mucho gusto," he said. "¡Bienvenidos a Hermosillo!"

Christine was still speechless and so Walter explained, "We're having a little stroll. Would you care to join us?"

Her gringo spoke up. "We're trying to get to Bahia Kino," he said.

"Too bad," observed Walter. "Mañana we will have an airshow. Looks like it could be a nice time..."

Chris was still amazed. "You FLEW down here?"

"Sure did."

"How did you get across the border?"

"Umm... Let's not go into that right here," muttered the gringo. "But I'm quite relieved, believe me, to find such hospitality. I was hoping they would not throw me in jail, and these folks have been great!"

Next morning brought a tremendous crowd to Hermosillo International. They thronged the airport and brought chairs and coolers and shade tents. A public address system screeched and growled and moaned, a nearly unrecognizable litany. A large circus tent was set up for the local dignitaries. Slinky Señoritas in Budweiser dresses were paraded before the crowd. They were met with catcalls, whistles and ululations. The airshow commenced and wowed the crowd. Katty Waggerstaff was the star, she shredded the skies in a fantastic display of skill and daring. The crowd was astonished when she appeared for autographs, all hundred pounds or so of her.

Other performers worked the crowd, Walter and his host Guillermo were given a few minutes to fly their TrikeZillas. He felt a little foolish circling the field with his amigo. But the crowd adored them, like all the other acts. Walter made a few high-banked turns, a couple of low passes, a touch-n-go. It was his first festivál aereo, for one afternoon he was a star.

Carla Consuelo Spreads Her Legs... er, WINGS!

Next morning while Walter was giving his 'Zilla a pre-flight, a car pulled up and out jumped Señor Fran Carlo Aramburo. He beamed a smile at Walter and offered a greeting. He walked around the car and opened the door for his Señora, a very lovely woman. The Capitano's daughters stepped out next and Walter was floored. To say they were "muy guapas" was to understate. Two Mexican beauties stepped from the car. Fran Carlo made the introductions. Ciena, the youngest, looked to be about sixteen or seventeen years old. She was tall and slender, green eyes in a gorgeous face. Carla, her big sister, was absolutely stunning. Raven hair, ruby lips, tall and slender, wrapped in a tight cotton dress, she wore a green ribbon in her hair that matched her eyes. Her smile flashed and almost knocked the gringo over. She held a hand toward Walter and a spark passed between them.

Carla looked to be about twenty years old. She had a tiny little waist and ample breasts, joyous mounds that jutted towards the gringo. Walter couldn't help but notice luscious dark circles of her nipples through the tight cotton Sundress. He put on his reflector sunglasses, the better to admire her surreptitiously. "Mucho gusto," she said. *Much pleasure.*

"¡El gusto es mio!" stuttered Walter. *The pleasure is mine!* Carla held a hand to her lips to hide a flashing smile. She tugged at her tight dress as the gringo admired her long legs, two delicate stems that descended from Heaven, and disappeared into high-heel shoes. The whole family was dressed as though for a dinner party, rather than a day in the sun. This was not airshow attire. At the gringo's inspection, Carla blushed through skin the color of fancy-grade bee honey. Señor Fran Carlo spoke to his daughters.

"Quien va primero?" he asked. *Who's going first?*

Walter wanted to laugh. These girls were NOT dressed for flying. Carla's outfit reminded Walter of the latest smash hit song on Mexican radio: "Renalda, Renalda, quitate tu mini falda!" *Renalda, Renalda, take off your mini skirt!* There would certainly be no way to accommodate them in the 'Zilla with any regards for her virtue. But Carla did not hesitate. She held up a finger and wagged it at Walter. With a giggle, she stepped towards the trike.

"Eres volador?" asked Walter. *Are you a flyer?*

"Quien? Yo?" she answered. *Who? Me?* She looked around as though confused.

"¡Sí tu!" said Walter. "¿Haz volaste?" *Yes you! Have you ever flown?* Carla shook her pretty head and said no, she hadn't. "¿Nunca?" asked Walter. *Never?* Carla looked to her father for support.

"Nunca," she admitted. "Pero es mi sueño." *I never have, but it's my dream.*

"¿Entonces esto va a ser tu primero vuelo?" asked Walter. *So this will be your first flight?*

Fran Carlo explained: "Quiere aprender volar. Tiene mucho fe en usted," he said. *She wants to learn to fly. She has much faith in you.* The gringo nearly went down on a knee to confess his ever-lasting love and devotion, right there on the tarmac, where Carla, Fran Carlo, and all the rest of the World would have no doubt. For a lone gringo triker, far from home, Carla looked like the Promised Land. But how would she get in the trike wearing that sexy little minifalda? And what did she have under there, besides the obvious? Underwear? Panties? Walter waited no more to find out. He gestured towards the machine.

"¡Vamanos!" he commanded. *Let's go!*

Carla raised a shapely foot and hooked a high heel on the foot peg. Walter grabbed her around the waist and hoisted her into the back seat. She settled in there like a princess on a throne, smiled excitedly at her family, and tugged at her skirt which was creeping up her thighs. She giggled some more.

Walter pulled a helmet over her head, using the opportunity to steal a glance down her blouse. He just couldn't help it, such a wonderful bounty.

Peace and Plenty!

He fastened her lap belt and spun the prop. Now came the tricky part. Walter didn't see how he would get between those slender shapely legs without causing considerable embarrassment for his cargo. Carla's long legs just wouldn't permit it. As it was, the cotton skirt had crept impossibly high up her thighs. *We might just as well leave it behind*, thought the gringo. He grabbed the nose of the 'Zilla and turned the trike away from Carla's family, pointing it towards the runway of Hermosillo International. Then he sat down in the front seat.

Carla kept a tight grip on her modesty considering the circumstances, clasping tightly with her knees. She seemed to be unaware that there was a need for her pilot to get between her legs, for her to spread her knees, and to let him in. Walter leaned forward as best he could while fastening his seat belt. Meanwhile, Carla's knees poked him in the spine. But if they were indeed to visit the heavens above, then he would have to lean back at some point. She would have to yield.

With a twisting motion of his shoulders, Walter opened, just barely, Carla's lovely legs. She allowed him only a slight entry, clasping him tightly around the waist with her knees. Walter added throttle and they rolled out on the taxiway. He discovered that the faster he went, the more the beautiful young señorita tightened her grip, the more she clenched him with her legs.

The tower at Hermosillo International Airport had been briefed that Comandante Fran Carlo's daughter's would be flying the funny contraption that had brought the gringo. Walter was quickly given the green light. He rolled out on the runway and gave the 'Zilla full throttle. Carla's legs were like a vise; squeezing tighter and tighter, the faster they went the tighter they squeezed. Suddenly, the 'Zilla lifted off and, as it did so, Carla's leg-vise sprung apart, the clamp relaxed, and her legs opened like a dam had burst. Walter settled back into her crotch like the trike had been made for it all along, and off they flew, into the Heavens.

Walter reached back and grabbed one of her hands, pried it loose from the seatrail. He pulled it over his shoulder and hollered, "¡Agarra me aqui!" *Hold me here!* Carla complied. She reached around Walter and hugged him tight with both arms, squeezed him.

Ahh now, reflected the triker. *This is flying. This is Heaven. This is Mexico. Maybe I will stay forever, just never leave...*
Nunca jamas.

THE ROAD NOT CLOSED or
That First Step's a Doozie!

Mean nasty Ol' Mr. Southwesterly had been blowing down Slide Mountain for weeks on end. Meanwhile, the only remedy for standing-around-on-the-ground-itis for an air horny glidehead was Daydreams, which is a spectacular flying site above Crystal Bay, Nevada but is rather boring after a few flights, or out at Zulu Ridge, which can also be great fun, but it just can't be compared to Slide Mountain. Slide is a big-mountain, lee-side launch, which means that when the prevailing southwest winds blow strong there is just no flying at Slide. This is because launch is on the wrong side of the mountain. When the prevailing southwest winds blow strong, all except the most indifferent buzzards and redtail hawks get flushed from the Slide Mountain sky.

Every glidehead in the Tahoe area, or in North America so far as Walter knew, carried a 'weather cube' close at hand, so at the touch of a button to be constantly updated to the winds aloft. The weather cube is about four inches on a side, has only two controls—an on/off switch and a volume knob—and picks up but one station; the National Oceanic and Atmospheric Administration: NOAA weather, for short. Fortunately for Tahoe glideheads, NOAA maintains a weather station atop Slide Mountain, which sits at something just under ten thousand feet above sea level, and with a touch of the button the wind report is always at hand.

"...at 9am Wednesday June 3, winds atop Slide Mountain are 270 at 22 gusting to 32..."

"Shit!" swore Gordy.

"Shit!" cursed Mork.

"Shit!" cried Rooster.

"Worse!" said Matthew. "This place really sucks." A 22 mile-an-hour wind atop the mountain at such and early hour meant there would be no flying at Slide for yet another day. "Anybody wanna make the ride out to Zulu?" he asked. Matthew was considering driving from Tahoe, over the mountain to Truckee, down along the Truckee River, through the Truckee River canyon and out past Verdi and Boomtown through Reno, then turning north and taking highway 395 out through the desert for about twenty miles to a secondary paved road that he would follow for several miles to a dirt road that he would climb to launch at Zulu Ridge. The trip took at least an hour and would deposit a glidehead at a spot where he might likely fly the southwesterly, if it wasn't too southy, and if he waited for the fearsome afternoon dust devils on the dry lakebed below to mellow out towards evening.

"Ahh, maybe," came a weak answer from someone. There just wasn't much enthusiasm.

"...Saturday, June 19 will bring an end to strong southwesterly flow aloft and the possibility of light easterly surface winds with an upper-level low pressure area." Walter could scarcely believe his ears. He turned the volume up on his weather cube as he lay in bed in the early-morning pre-dawn. "At 5am the winds atop Slide Mountain are light-and-variable, temperature is sixty two degrees and visibility is unlimited."

"Wahoo!" hollered Walter from under thye covers. Happily, he rolled over for a bit more shut-eye. He had taken the weather cube to bed with him last night due to a forecast of changing weather and diminishing winds. Who knew what the future holds for a bunch of fanatic glideheads? But it seemed certain there would be flying this afternoon in the Heavens high above Lake Tahoe. Walter dozed peacefully with visions of strong smooth thermals lofting him to tremendous altitudes. He twitched a few times as he lay dreaming, and he drooled a bit. In his slumbers he was near frozen solid and diving his wing to stay out of the clouds and maintain visual reference with Mother Earth.

In his slumbers Walter was skyed-out and at peace.

"What's with the barriers at the bottom of the Slide road?" asked Gordy. "Have you seen 'em?"

The phone had rung as Walter sat on the throne taking his morning constitutional. He was perusing a Hang Gliding Magazine at the time, and was totally happy to sit upon the throne and talk hang gliding with a buddy. Gordy's voice droned through the phone line. "I saw them yesterday when I drove down to Reno. The Nevada Department of Transportation has the road closed."

"I've seen 'em," replied Walter. "They put 'em up several days ago. I guess they're doing some road work up there, not sure what."

"Light winds on Slide this morning. You goin' up?"

"Shit yes! I wouldn't miss it, been waiting two or three weeks for this friggin' wind to stop. Seemed like it'd never stop. Hell yes I'm flyin' Slide today."

"What about the barriers?" asked Gordy. "Can we get around 'em? I didn't look to see."

"Oh Hell yes. They're easy to get around. You just drive right around 'em. There're work trucks going up there all the time."

"I don't guess they mean us anyway."

"Just for tourists," agreed Walter.

"All right then. See you up there. We'll have a safety meeting."

About an hour later Walter negotiated the barriers at the bottom of the Slide Mountain road. The road itself is only about a mile long and it winds along a precipitous mountain—the same mountain that Walter, and every other glidehead for fifty miles in every direction, was even then converging on. The Slide Mountain road services the Slide Mountain Ski Area where it dead-ends in a parking lot. There is considerable traffic on this road in the winter months when the ski lifts are running, but almost none during the off-season months when the Slide Mountain road services the local flying community almost exclusively, a rather fringy element, to put it mildly. The barriers that had been thrown up at the bottom of the Slide Mountain road had giant DOT signs that warned ROAD CLOSED and NO VEHICULAR ENTRY and LOCAL TRAFFIC ONLY. They did not specify NO GLIDEHEADS though, nothing about NO FLYERS, or NO HANG GLIDING. No HUCKING YOURSELF OFF THESE CLIFFS PROHIBITED BY LAW signs, so Walter just swung the Ford From Hell around them and sped on. It immediately became quite evident why the Nevada DOT, in their wisdom, had closed the road to the turkeys, because as Walter blazed up out of the forest and onto the road that clung to the cliff side, he was happy to discover that the guardrail had been removed.

No guardrail!

Gone!

It was like a dream come true!

No guardrail...

Wahooo!

The Slide Mountain guardrail is a bit of an issue as it were. Many fliers new to Slide are intimidated by the guardrail because it presents a formidable obstacle, at first glance anyway, right where a flier is most vulnerable to the whim of the wind—right there on launch.

The Slide fliers however, understand that once you had lifted the wing over the rail and then clambered over yourself, the guardrail offers a small measure of security against the whim of the wind because you can grab the guardrail in case of a wayward gust, and anchor yourself quite effectively. Nonetheless, once over the guardrail the only easy way out is to jump off that cliff which is something you only care to do when you are completely good and ready for it.

Having no guardrail to deal with was not going to be a big problem; more like a cakewalk, decided Walter. He stepped on the gas and sped to launch. When he pulled around the last curve in the road it looked like the Woodstock Nation had arrived in advance—Woodstock with wings. There were long-haired fliers strung out all along the cliff, everyone quite gleeful about the missing guardrail, the sweet smell of tasty safety-meetings-in-progress filled the air.

"Can you believe this?" asked Terry, who ran up to Walter's window and waved at the cliff edge.

"I won't even have to lift it today," cried Wingnut happily. He was a diminutive sort who always had to struggle a bit awkwardly to lift his wing over the rail. "It'll be a cakewalk!" he hollered. He was playing air guitar with a wing batten, strumming along to the Outlaws on the radio.

"Maybe we can talk them into leaving it like this," suggested Kelly, which seemed highly unlikely. Kelly was busy stuffing battens and tensioning his sail. "This is awesome!" he laughed.

Napper's brother Dougal was ready to fly, so he picked up his wing and strolled off launch. It was a cakewalk all right!

Several fliers had already punched off launch and were holding their own about a grand or so above launch level over in the sand chutes. He noticed Gordy soaring around right out front, so he hurriedly untied his wing from the roof rack and pulled it down for set up. He didn't want to be late! He was turning the wing over to spread the sail when the proverbial shit hit the proverbial fan, in the persona of a Nevada

Department of Transportation head-honcho himself, who came speeding around the corner in a shiny new pickup and discovered the Slide Mountain fliers colorful pre-flight party hoedown. He slammed on the brake and sat in the middle of the road for a moment as if bewildered, and then jumped out in a highly agitated state.

"CAN'T YOU SONS O' BITCHES READ?" he yelled.

He was standing next to the Napper at the time and so the Napper gave it to him straight;

"Not one of my more successful subjects," he replied. "How did you know?" It was true, the Napper is a helluva flier-there are just none better at Slide—but reading skills are far down on his list of priorities.

Honcho pulled his ball cap off his head in frustration and turned to Roderick, who at least looked somewhat more cerebral, even if he wasn't actually. "Can't you guys READ?" he reiterated. He strode over to Roderick and stood in his space. "THE DAMN ROAD IS CLOSED!" he bellowed.

Roderick continued his preparations for flight, and looked at Honcho with disinterest. He just shrugged his shoulders as though to ask, "What's the Big Deal?"

"What's the big deal?" he asked.

That stopped Honcho in his tracks. His arms were windmilling over his head and he was turning colors like a chameleon with high blood pressure. "What's the big deal...?" he asked. "WHAT'S... THE... BIG... D...!"

"Why close the road?" asked Roderick with great nonchalance. "It's gonna be great flying today."

"Why close the road? Why...!" Honcho pulled his ball cap off and stomped about launch. "In case you guys haven't noticed," he roared, "THE GUARDRAIL HAS BEEN REMOVED!" Nobody moved. Nobody said anything. Honcho windmilled his arms some more and his color remained highly unlikely. Finally, he got his second wind. "THE ROAD IS CLOSED BECAUSE THE GUARDRAIL HAS BEEN REMOVED!"

"Ummm..." mumbled Roderick. He turned and grinned at his flying buddies, as though soliciting support. "We don't need the guardrail," he said. "We don't miss it at all."

Honcho was nearly inarticulate at this observation. "Gack," was about all he could spit out. Then he sucked some air and lit into the Slide Mountain fliers once again. "You sons o' bitches," he cried. "I'm calling headquarters, I'm calling the

Highway Patrol. You'll see how much you miss it!" With that, he stomped back to his shiny pickup and sped off.

"Now there goes a guy who is entirely unclear on the concept," said Roderick as he fastened his helmet.

"I'm guessin' it's time to bail," observed Rooster with a wild grin.

"I think we outta all bail while the bailin's good," agreed Airwreck.

It was unanimous then; they were the Slide Mountain fliers, and it was a beautiful day. No guardrail would have stopped them anyway.

Photo by Geoffrey Rutledge

"¡Compra los Señor!" or,
A Gringo Makes a Purchase

Walter took two giant steps down the launch ramp and was yanked upward from Mirador Santa Caterína, and into the sky over Lake Atitlán, in the central Guatemala highlands. The gringo had the day off- not a single tourist to worry about, and had decided to go flying anyway, sort of a busman's holiday he thought happily while he circled out over launch. He was free, he was white, and he was flying...

WAHOOO!

In preparation for his day off he'd stashed his glider bag in his wing, a quart of water and two cervesas in his harness, and with that and the joint he kept in his wallet, Walter knew he could just disappear into the tropical blue sky and land anywhere. Today appeared to be an excellent day to fly, with cumulus clouds popping over the volcanoes and behind launch too. So Walter was not too surprised to take the first thermal to cloud base and head out over the lake.

As he glided out Walter noticed a curious thing: instead of descending as usual over Lake Atitlán, Walter continued a gentle climb- the variometer chirped a slow steady melody. There were wispy clouds forming below him too now, another unusual circumstance in a hang glider; usually you don't get higher than the clouds. Walter decided to see how far he could penetrate and how high he could go before these peculiar conditions would dissipate and the air commence to subside. He was glad he had worn his flight suit and, passing through nine thousand feet he zipped up the collar and pulled on his gloves. At ten grand he was still climbing, and now had the pleasure of navigating through several layers of clouds. At ten-five Walter continued to climb, now looking over the summit of Volcan San Pedro, and down into the hazy depths of the coastal plains far below.

At eleven grand he was beginning to top-out and his adrenaline level was peaking too, flying through cloud tops and enormous fluffy cloud canyons. Still, Walter did not worry- his variometer showed a very manageable climb rate of only two hundred feet per minute and Walter knew he could get twelve hundred down from his glider, if he had a mind to. Escape from the clouds should be no problem.

At eleven-six Walter's climb leveled off and the air became silky smooth. Keeping an eye on his position over the lake, Walter played hide and seek with his shadow against the clouds around him. He reveled in the spectacle and regretted he'd not thought to bring his camera. This was an uncommonly good day to fly Atitlán, thought Walter, and he almost wished there were other pilots here to witness this day. Letting go of the control bar, Walter spun his harness around backwards and let the glider fly where it would. Through the holes in the clouds Walter could see patches of the north shore of the lake, where he had come from, and patches of the south shore too, where he was slowly approaching. There was nowhere to land there Walter knew, at least nowhere he'd care to land, and he would have to turn back soon to the safety of the north shore. Looking down, Walter saw the deep blue waters of Atitlán through holes in the sky. They were being tossed by a north wind and white caps were visible: El Norte! These winds were known for being strong and unpredictable. Boatmen on the lake avoided El Norte, which can stir up and muddy the big blue lake. They call the north wind *El Chocomil.*

Spinning back to the control bar Walter was suddenly gripped by an urge to wring the glider out. He was flying an Airwave K2, very nice handling, and so he stalled the glider nose-high for a moment then pulled it back down into a steep dive. Down, down through the cloud canyons, the glider quickly built up maximum air speed. Adding a touch of bank angle, Walter suddenly released the energy and his K-2 ripped into a climbing wingover. Walter stuffed the bar and ripped off another wingover, and another...

Up and over and down again went Walter and his glider, just a gringo, skyed out and invisible in the wild blue yonder, he blew off five thousand feet in minutes through sheer exuberance. He eased off the control bar to let the K-2 fly at trim. He was low now and far out over the lake, farther than he'd ever been before; time to head for safety. He turned the glider towards Panajachel to tailwind it home when it suddenly dawned on him that something was terribly... wrong.

Walter looked down and studied the water below him to confirm his suspicion: the south wind had changed due to the arrival of a strong El Norte and Walter would have to fight a headwind to glide home. How could he have been so stupid? Feeling suddenly very small and very vulnerable over a very large and very deep lake, Walter pulled the nose down to penetrate the Chocomil. This effort produced not the effect he'd hoped for- an improved glide- but instead the glider just sank faster. The adrenaline rush Walter had experienced moments ago now left him weak and confused. What should he do now for Chrissake? He felt as though he was on a down elevator in the middle of the ocean.

Walter glanced over his shoulder at the south shore of Lake Atitlán, beckoning behind him. There really was nowhere friendly to land there, only steep volcano flanks dropping straight into deep water. A jumble of shacks clung to the lakeshore cliffs and a few docks stuck into the lake here and there.

Still... if I'm going to land in water, I might as well land in water near shore, thought Walter. He gave one more longing look towards Panajachel and home, and then he cranked a turn downwind.

The lake waters zipped by under Walter's wing now as he glided downwind with the Chocomil. Santiago Atitlán lay straight beyond his nose and Walter would be there in no time at all. Only trouble was, he could see no possible place to land there and it looked as though a water landing was imminent. For once Walter wished he'd flown with an inflated inner tube tucked onto his wing, a 'flotador', like he required of his clients. Maybe today he could use it.

Pulling up over Santiago, Walter scanned desperately for somewhere, anywhere, to land. As his brain kept dismissing one possibility after another, his eye kept turning back to a boat dock, which jutted out into the lake and stopped in a 'T'. Impossibly narrow and short, it seemed like the only opportunity for some kind of miraculous landing. If the approach was not perfect, Walter could then turn slightly, one way or the other, and drop into the lake.

One other problem confronted Walter however: a lake ferry, just one of the many that ply the lake, was headed for the same dock and would arrive there soon. Perhaps too soon. There were people standing on the end of the dock awaiting the boat. He'd have to overfly the dock and yell a warning, then turn around for his approach and quickly land, hope the Hell they'd stay out of the way. Walter could afford to wait no longer. He was very confident in his abilities to spot land the K-2, and now was the time to prove it.

Turning out over the lake again Walter flew over the dock below. The boat was slowing engines now, and he could see a deck hand, with halyard in hand, standing by to go ashore.

"¡Aguas!" yelled Walter from above: *Look out!* "¡Voy aterrisar por el muelle!" *I am going to land on the dock!* He yelled it twice as loud as he could and waved his arm in alarm as he flew overhead. The natives on the dock stopped and looked up but didn't seem to register the peril from above. Walter noticed one lady look up and wave a happy greeting in return. Did she understand? He tried once more, "¡Aqui vengo!" he hollered. *Here I come!*

With a hope and a prayer, Walter cranked his last turn and dove in for the dock. He skimmed down over the waves, actually below dock level for some seconds as he neared the dock. He planned to budget his last bit of energy to pop up onto the dock in full flare. He saw the rotten old pilings of the dock coming at him and for a moment imagined how ugly the K-2 would look if he had miscalculated just a bit and smacked in below deck. But with his airspeed and control at near end, Walter flared and popped up above the wharf. For a moment he saw the boat and all the passengers standing with jaws agape as he flashed past. Then he was looking down at a native woman, in colorful local costume, also with jaws agape and eyes wide. Then she too flashed past and Walter saw nothing but the end of the dock coming, and the cold blue of Atitlán beyond. Using his last bit of airspeed, he gave a mighty flare. The K-2 stood on end and stopped a few feet above the boards, then settled to the dock with a clank.

He'd done it! He landed on his butt and skinned a knee, but he'd done it!

Imagining he'd just performed the only successful landing in the history of Santiago Atitlán, Walter reached into his harness and pulled out a beer.

A crowd quickly assembled around the gringo and pressed closed to each other there on the dock as he popped the top and slaked his thirst. He could feel the structure shaking under the weight of a gringo and so many tiny Guatemalans, but there was little he could do about that. He realized as he yelled a warning that most of these people didn't speak Spanish anyway, speaking instead various ancient Mayan dialects. Perhaps they had not even understood his fly-by warning?

Walter also realized that the old lady he'd flown over moments before touchdown was now standing nearly on top of him and waving guipiles in his face. If the old lady had been standing any closer, she would have pushed Walter off the dock in her zeal to merchandize. Standing only about half Walter's height, she posed little problem, otherwise.

Walter concentrated on bagging his glider quickly there on the dock. He had barely enough room to walk around it without falling off. The crowd that had gathered was in a festive mood and all seemed to want to touch the wild and colorful contraption that had brought the winged gringo from the sky. The old Indian woman would not lay off Walter either, and pursued him as he went about his chore. She may have been much smaller than the gringo, but she made up for her stature with resolve.

"¡Compra lo señor, compra lo!" she implored. *Buy it mister, buy it!* It was the same chant from all the clothing vendors in all corners of the lake: "¡Compra lo señor!" Walter had no wish to purchase guipiles, especially these that this woman held forth.

The guipil is the native dress of the Mayan women throughout Central America. For centuries the guipil was woven on a handloom. Each village has a different pattern and indeed, the women in Santiago Atitlán could be easily recognized by their distinctive guipiles wherever they went. Supposedly, you could read the family history of triumphs and tragedies by the patterns woven therein. Walter had often admired the skill and beauty with which the genuine guipil was crafted, but the stuff pedaled on the streets to the tourists was typically cheap and quite unauthentic. This one was no different. With a wave of his hand Walter dismissed the tiny peasant lady. Not to be outdone, she came on even stronger in return. Walter had seen the pattern before- the determined Guatemalan clothing vendor was a force to be reckoned with.

"¡Compra lo!" she said again. Perhaps, aside from counting money, the only two words of Spanish she knew. "¡Compra lo!"

"Señora..." Walter began, but he knew it was no use to reason. The old woman was still in his face, he realized he would have to use different tactics to deal with her. With a look of scrutiny at the genuine article worn by the old lady herself, Walter went for it: "No quiero esos..." he said of the offered goods. *I don't want these.* Then, pointing at the old lady's authentic garment said: "¡Yo quiero esto!" *I want this one!* The exchange continued:

"¡Compra lo, señor!"

"¡Esto!"

"¡Compra lo, señor!"

"¡Esto!" This time he gripped the sleeve of her blouse garment between his fingers. At that the old woman looked taken aback. She stood aside and admonished Walter with a wagging finger. Putting her nose under her raised arm, she took a whiff of her own sweat. Then, with a sour look, she admonished Walter again: "¡Ouele feo!" she pointed out: *It stinks!*

Walter took a discreet step back for further negotiations. Gripping again the garment by the cuff he leaned close to the smelly old lady, "¡Limpios!" he stated: *'Clean!* "¡Limpios!" With that he turned back to bagging his wing.

The old lady had apparently had enough, and turned away. With her bundle of garments perched atop her head, she hurried off the dock and up the well-worn path towards town on some private mission. Walter thought he had gained a small victory.

"¡Señor!" heard Walter and he turned to see the boat captain beckoning. "¿Usted quiere raite?" he asked. *Do you want a ride?*

Of course Walter wanted a ride. All tourists come from and eventually return to, Panajachel, the boatman knew, even the winged ones he supposed and Walter now entered into another negotiating session with the boatman. The fellow wanted Walter to pay double because he had a glider and so the gringo agreed, but only if the captain would promise not to leave the dock until he was able to replenish his supply of cervesa, which was by now exhausted, from the nearby cervesaria, which was full of it. It was as he had returned to the boat, and had settled comfortably atop decks, stretched out with a tattered copy of <u>Azteca</u>, and with the vessel about to depart, that Walter again noticed the tiny old lady, this time hustling down the footpath towards the boat. It looked like she was moving about as fast as her stubby old legs could carry her. From a hundred meters, they established a moment's eye contact and then the ol' gal made the bottom switchback and hustled straight for the loading ramp. With a holler to the skipper, she motioned him to wait.

Hustling up the ramp and onto the boat like a seasoned deckhand, she quickly navigated the ladder to the upper deck and again stood before Walter, slightly out of breath for her efforts and a look of triumph on her face as though to say, *"Ok gringo, put your money where your mouth is!"* Stretching out her arms she held forth three authentic Santiago Atitlán guipiles, quite used, but one more beautiful than the next. Freshly laundered, the old' gal must've grabbed them off the clothesline and hustled them straight back to the gringo.

"¡Compra los!" came her litany, anew: "¡Compra los, señor!"

Walter found himself quite at odds over how to respond. The guipiles were exquisite by any standards, with the Santiago Atitlán pattern under embroidered quetzal birds. They were worn and tattered in places and had been hand repaired many times. Still, they may belong to someone else, Walter speculated. Perhaps the ol' gal had just this afternoon seen them hanging on some neighbor's clothesline and returned, at Walter's prodding, to swipe them for resale...?

"¡Compra los!" she demanded with an anxious look over her shoulder to the skipper. She shook the beautiful garments in the gringo's face. Walter felt a little foolish as the other passengers looked on. The old Mayan woman was determined to sell the gringo something, that much was obvious. But Walter was accustomed to flying with only a few small bills and some coins in his pocket. Now, having already purchased beer and passage home, he was left with slight resources to purchase souvenirs.

The captain hollered something in the Maya tongue, obviously warning the old lady that departure was imminent: she'd have to get off now... "¡Compra los!" she implored yet again.

Walter pulled his hidden money pouch from under his shirt and counted out all the quetzal bills and a few centavos, which was all he had left to spend. He shrugged his shoulders as if to indicate: 'Oh well... too late'.

The old lady stared hungrily at the wrinkled bills. Walter wondered if she could really BE hungry? He briefly considered just giving the old lady the cash, but before he could she swiped the money from his grasp and tossed the guipiles in his lap.

"¿Bueno?" It was half question, half answer. And without waiting for any response, she turned from the gringo, made a hasty exit down the boat ramp. As the boatman cast off the mooring Walter watched as she hustled back up the same ancient path, counting her take all the while. As the boat slowly departed the dock, Walter watched her secrete her new bounty deep within her skirts, and disappear towards town without ever a look back. Without even an "¡Adios!"

The Goat From Hell or,
Bathtime in Ol' Mexico

The flying gringos had been landing in a field about midway between the mountain launch on La Cumbre, and headquarters at the Hotel Costeño. It often took most of your glide to get there from La Cumbre, but once over the field there was ample room for even the most novice pilot to make a conservative approach.

One day in the landing field a pilot from New Jersey- a cop known as Carlos Campana, came to Walter with an observation: "Walter, have you noticed that beautiful lizard living in the drain pipe over yonder?" he inquired. Walter had indeed. "He's enormous", continued Carlos, "with an incredible orange crown and orange feet!"

Iguana

"He's an iguana, Carlos, and sure I've seen him," said Walter. "I've been keeping his presence secret since the locals find them very tasty. I don't want Bomfilio getting any ideas."

Bomfilio- yes that really was his name- was the Safari Sky Tours chauffeur. Walter had flagged him down in his taxi one day and hired him on the spot. Bomfilio was skeptical at first, as Walter explained that he could just leave his cab at the hotel and drive the Ford-From-Hell. He soon proved adaptable though, and after Walter paid him for his first day he became downright enthusiastic. Walter could imagine him describing his day to his señora over dinner. How the gringos spread their colorful wings and jumped off the mountain. How the local buzzards appeared quite enamored of the graceful flyers and would follow them around for hours. How he could drive the macho truck with the stereo playing loud rock 'n roll and then drink cervesa with the gringos when they settled back to Earth.

At the moment, Bomfilio was standing out in the field waving a ribbon on the end of a long pole, in an effort to advise the incoming flyers of the wind direction. There was little point in this exercise really, since the wind was quite strong and obvious and everyone knew where the wind was. But Bomfilio enjoyed standing there waving the pole, so Walter let him. He knew it made him feel part of the action and besides- it kept his attention away from the cooler full of cervesa, of which he was quite fond. Walter wanted to explain to him that there was no point in waving the flag back and forth though, that this would only confuse the flyers overhead. Better to just hold the flag still, let the wind blow the ribbon.

"What say we try and catch that iguana?" insisted Carlos. "We could use a mascot, and we'll let him go later."

It was this simple challenge that led to Carlos and Walter awakening the next morning before dawn. They had consulted briefly with Bomfilio about lizard capturing techniques, and he told them the easiest way was to pump a round of birdshot into him from as close as you could get. Failing that, you might sneak up close to his lair before he awakes and then bash his head in when he pokes it out. Bomfilio also offered a delicious recipe, should we be successful, but seemed doubtful of our abilities. Maybe we could fly like the birds, but iguana hunting was another matter, best left to the locals.

So the next morning found Carlos and Walter on their bellies, silently crawling through the pre-dawn grayness, through cow pies and tall grasses, towards the lizard's roost. This particular field had an irrigation ditch running through it and every hundred meters or so dropping about ten feet into a small pool from whence the water would flow level again and repeat the process in steps. These pools had often provided the gringos with a refreshing dip, like a cool fresh Jacuzzi. Small drainage pipes about six inches in diameter led into the ditch and were open-ended to drain the fields during times of flood. The coveted iguana was holed up in one of these and was always seen at the same pipe.

Obviously, this was his lair.

Carlos and Walter, crawling on their bellies now, inched towards the sound of cascading water. Carlos had suffered a major dose of sunburn poolside back at the hotel some days ago, and even in the predawn light Walter could see him peeling. He looked as though he was about to molt.

Cautiously, they parted the last vegetation beside the ditch only to be met with a startling sight: a goat had fallen into the canal somewhere up stream and been unable to escape. Now the unfortunate critter was quite dead and floating upside down in the ditch. All four feet stuck out of the water and pointed at the gray Mexican dawn. His head dangled invisibly below the surface, and his bloated stomach kept the poor beast afloat. The whirlpool formed by the water spun him around and around...

Walter didn't know who was more startled by the sight- himself or Carlos- but one of them flinched and made a retching sound. The next thing Walter saw was the whiplash of the lizard's tail as the critter spun and slipped back into his nest. The beast had been several inches from his nose and easily within his grasp, but Walter was too startled by the unexpected sight to notice and react in time. Disappointed, Carlos and Walter returned empty handed to the hotel and found the rest of the gringos having breakfast. Walter thought some of them might have lost their appetite as he related the story of the bloated goat and the lizard's narrow escape from gringo clutches.

Some years later, the Great Iguana Hunt quite forgotten, Walter made a solo journey from Lake Atitlán in Guatemala back to Colima, driving up the coast highway, a route not recommended to anyone who has any hurry. Each town you travel through has topes- Mexican for speed bumps- some of them rather viscous, and all of them requiring an almost complete stop. There are thousands of topes along the way. Also, Walter was carrying a large sum of small, unmarked bills, mostly in dollars, from a successful season for Safari Sky

Tours. These were secreted in the gliders, in the toolbox, in a pillow, under the seat, hidden in small bundles here and there.

When Walter finally arrived in Colima, it felt like a homecoming and he was ready to party down with his Mexican compadres. He was also thinking of Nanci- lovely Nanci who must be nearing the age of consent. The last time Walter had seen Nanci, he nearly threw himself on the ground at her feet, and covered them with kisses. Nanci was in mid-bloom, yet still very naive. She was too young to take back to Gringolandia, even though her parents might approve. Nanci had been central to many of Walter's fantasies since then. Perhaps now was the time to make a move, to confess his everlasting love and devotion. First, however Walter would need to clean up some...

So he headed for the ditch.

Arriving at the landing field Walter drove the Ford-From-Hell on up the dirt road a couple of pools, until the road entered a stretch of citrus trees. This would afford him some privacy. His truck was very well known in and around Colima. Everyone was curious about the crazy gringos who jump off the mountain and fly up to the clouds. Quickly, Walter slipped into a swimsuit and headed for the refreshing coolness of the pool. His last thought before jumping in was how thankful he was that no disgusting dead goats were floating therein. He might have noticed that the water level was higher than normal, but he was too fixated on the cool, refreshing cascade. He dove in with a splash that took his breath away. He lay on the bottom being swirled by the water 'till his lungs felt about to burst. The whirlpool tumbled him several times.

It was not until he floated to the surface that Walter noticed anything amiss. In the past years the water had always been about waist deep. It was always a little difficult exiting the pools, due to the rather swift current. Slippery algae growing on the walls of the pool added to the problem. But now the water was shoulder deep and the extra buoyancy combined with the stronger current made it quite impossible to get any footing. Walter made a lunge for the canal wall and fell pitifully short of his objective. He had a sudden vision of that drowned goat swirling around and around, with his horrible bloated belly, his head spinning around and around for eternity.

Desperate now, he slipped back into the whirlpool for another attempt. He gulped a bit of water on the way down and thought of the Ford-From-Hell parked safely just a few meters away. He made another lunge and again fell short, this time resubmerging immediately. The current pinned him momentarily and Walter gulped more water. He had another vision, this time of the local Federáles being alerted of his drowned and bloated carcass floating in the whirlpool, then searching the Ford and finding his cash. The gliders being divvied up amongst the local pilots; they always did covet his wings. It was as though his life flashed before his eyes. So much left unfinished...

As he gathered himself on the bottom of the pool for one last desperate attempt to save his sorry ass, Walter thought of Nanci and how he may never caress her budding breasts, might never know the secrets of those satin thighs, and the delights waiting for him. May never know if she truly loves him.

So close yet so far!

Walter coiled his body for the leap. His ears were pounding with the sound of the rushing water. He thought briefly of man's ancient struggle against nature and what an ultimately undignified way this would be to make the Grand Salida. This just wouldn't do at all... he could see the headlines in the Colima morning press: Gringo Found Floating, Drowned In Ditch.

His feet touched the bottom and he exploded towards the surface. The tip of his index finger found a desperate grip on the slimy canal wall. Painfully, and with great effort, he wrenched the other hand up and found another grip. He hung there briefly as the current clutched at his body. He thought: *Oh shit Carlos! If you could see me now!*

Slowly Walter pulled himself from the frothy waters. One hand lost purchase and for a second, it looked as though he would plunge back below the surface, but he held on and pulled himself back up. The gringo figured this was the last try. If he couldn't extract himself from the clutches of the ditch this time, he would have to push off and float down stream, take his chances with the current. Maybe the next pool would offer a better chance at survival.

With all his remaining strength Walter heaved again and got himself up to shoulder height and now the adrenaline kicked in. With a groan of effort he hoisted himself kicking and thrashing out of the Canal-From-Hell. He lay panting on the bank. Exhausted, he lay in the dirt with his eyes closed, and thanked the Gods his life had been spared.

Sometime later- a moment? An eternity? Walter rolled onto his side and then stood uneasily to his feet. He sat on the tailgate of the Ford, quite shaken. He looked down the farm road to see a small Mexican boy pedaling his bicycle in his direction. When the child saw Walter look up he waved at him and redoubled his efforts. Now Walter could recognize Pedro, one of the local farm kids and one of his admirers. Pedro skidded to a stop at his feet and jumped towards him to slap hands.

"¡Hola Walter!" he shouted gleefully, "¡Bienvenidos!" Welcome back!

"Hola Pedrito," Walter returned, weakly shaking his small grubby hand. "¿Como haz estado?" Walter intoned feebly. *How have you been?* Walter felt light-headed from his resent wrassle with Eternity.

"Bien gracias" replied Pedro , "y gusto que ver te." Pedro, for one, was glad to see the gringo. "Quando llegaste?" He asked. *When did you arrive?*

"Ahorita," Walter explained. *Just now.* Trying to act cool and nonchalant, he grabbed a cervesa from the cooler and cracked the lid. But he had no stomach for beer, and as he tried to swallow, the stuff came right back up, exiting through his nose with a nasty fizz.

"Fuiste a nadar?" asked Pedro. *Did you take a swim?* He could see the gringo was all wet, and had put one and one together.

"Sí" said Walter weakly, "Fui a bañar." *I took a bath*, he explained.

Pedro looked at the ditch and then back at Walter. "Mucho agua," he said. "Peligroso." *Much water. Dangerous.*

Tell me something I don't know kid!

Pedro looked from the gringo to the distant mountain of La Cumbre, and the launch where he had often accompanied Walter and his flyers. "Ahora vas a volar?" he inquired. *Now you go flying?*

No tellin' about these loco gringos. Always seeking out danger. Cheating the odds.

"No Pedro, no voy a volar." *Enough peligro for one gringo for one day.* "Por que no vamos por un refresco?" Walter suggested: *What say you and I go for a soda pop.* Pedro liked nothing better than a cherry soda from the tienda up the street.

"¡Hora le!" he agreed, "¡ya nos vamos!" and tossed his rusty bicycle on the tailgate. *We're outta here!*

Glidehead Lemmings at Hotel Costeño or, Reefer Madness in Ol' Mexico

With the sun settling towards the Mexican Riviera, Team Tahoe was frolicking in the pool at Hotel Costeño, refreshing themselves after a dusty day of flying.

They'd had a reasonably successful day at La Cumbre, the local flying site just outside of old colonial Colima town. They'd all gotten off and into the ridge lift and boated around hooking the small thermals that were drifting too fast to take very high. But they'd flown for a couple hours and then they'd landed in the tiny village below, a place called Pisila. They drank their fill of chilled cervesa in liter bottles called 'caguamas', and they generally had a great day. The ride back to the hotel had become more and more rowdy under the effects of many Mexican cervesas.

So far, the only dark cloud in Sky Tours sky was the one hanging over the head(s) of Walter's partner(s) Rodney (and Beth). Earlier, one of Team Tahoe, considered a good solid pilot back home, came diving into the LZ at Pisila and never even tried to flare, wasting a downtube on Rodney's Wills Wing AT, when he just flew it into the ground. Another had set up too short for final and flown into a thorn bush, leaving myriad tiny scratches over the leading edge of another of Rodney's wings, and Rodney had had a stressful day in general- another tough day to add to the growing list. So while the group of flyers frolicked poolside at the hotel, Rodney and Beth had sequestered themselves in their room and fired up a big fat joint. If they couldn't get rid of these rowdy drunks who called themselves Team Tahoe, they would ignore them as best as possible. A refreshing dip in the pool was out of the question.

Bobby Carter bobbed to the surface near Walter who was hanging on the rim of the pool under some banana trees while he gazed up at the hotel roof overhang, a second floor platform that jutted out towards the pool. Bobby, a paleface redhead gringo was beet-red in the face from the Mexican sun, but with a cold can of cervesa Tecate in hand, he didn't seem to notice. Bobby, like the rest of Team Tahoe, was ready to let the good times roll. This was VACATION, after all. This was Mexico.

Later, Walter would realize that his next words were the cause of much of his trouble, trouble that would only serve to widen the approval gap he suffered with his erstwhile partners Rodney and his wife, just as surely as if he'd shot himself in the foot. But they seemed like clever words at the time, innocent enough, the obvious question which begged to be asked:

"Hey Bobby," he inquired, "do you think we could make it off the roof?"

"Huh?" asked Bobby, then followed Walter's gaze. The Hotel Costeño offered a delightfully beckoning overhang up there, it looked as though just one strong stride for an approach would send a jumper straight into the deep end of the pool with an enormous kerslpash. "Why SURE!" replied Bob. "Perfect!" His face lit up with sudden insight.

Team Tahoe was a bunch of skiers who'd found hang gliding after all. These guys were not strangers to jumping, there was a bit of lemming in them all. Lead these guys to a jump, to a cliff or to any sort of precipice whatsoever, and they were just likely to bail. Back at Squaw Valley, which had some notable drops indeed, these guys were The Locals. But Walter wasn't exactly anxious to be first. Turning to Bobby, he gave him the dare;

"Well... give it a try," he suggested. "I dare ya."

"ME?" questioned Bobby. "ME? Why me? YOU'RE the guide!" He pointed his can of Tecate up at the overhang. "Now get UP there!" Walter just submerged, ducked under the water and swam off to the other end of the pool. When he re-surfaced Bobby Carter was there, exhorting him. "Do it Walter!" he demanded. "You're the guide. Do it!"

Beth sucked heartily on the pipe they had smuggled into Mexico. Actually, Walter had done the smuggling, he'd brought the pipe and the dope too, when he'd discovered that his partners were too paranoid to cross the border while holding. This issue had become apparent just before the Sky Tours caravan had loaded-up for the journey south and Rodney and Beth had consulted Walter about the pot:

Should they bring it?

Was it safe?

Would they be thrown in a Mexican hoosegow to languish forever?

Was there pot available in Mexico?

Should they leave their stash at home and buy some there?

Walter considered it all ridiculous- the Mexican authorities would never guess that gringos came to Mexico with the 'yerba'. As everyone knew, gringos came to Mexico to GET the yerba. When it was agonizing decision time over the stash back in California, Walter had snatched the baggie from Beth's hand and climbed atop the Ford-From-Hell to stash it. There, he had unzipped the nearest wing bag, to insert pipe and pot- the obvious hiding place. But Rodney had vetoed that idea too; it was one of his own gliders that Walter chose to stick the dope in. So Walter had unzipped his own personal wing bag and hidden the pot in there. Rodney was finally satisfied. Subsequently, the lovely couple had followed that bag closely in their Volkswagen Thing for five hundred miles as the gringo caravan headed south. But after the whole troop had traveled one hard day south of the border, Rodney had quietly retrieved the dope and was now hoarding it, refusing to share it, dismissing any requests. "Why didn't you bring yer own?" he asked. That was okay with Walter, who knew serious potheads when he saw them.

Now, Beth passed the reefer to her man, who licked a run, then sucked on it too. They were hiding in the small bathroom of their lodgings in the Hotel Costeño, huffing on the joint and blowing the smoke out the tiny window. They were forced to stand atop the toilet with the lid down so they could get close enough to the window for their plan to be effective. They traded places as they traded tokes. From here, the prevailing winds would send the smoke northward, and away from the hotel, so they hoped.

Through clenched teeth Beth said, "Ssssssss can you believe these guys?"

Rodney huffed the joint and rolled his eyes. He took a couple short breaths of wind and held on, hic, hic. Finally, he exhaled a mighty cloud of sweet smoke, carefully blowing it out the vent. "Bunch of crazy drunks bwaaah," he confirmed.

"We've gotta get rid of that guy Walter," said Beth. "He's a menace." This was an unfair judgment Walter would have felt, had he been there to defend himself rather than out in the pool with his buddies where he belonged. "He just eggs these guys on. Did you see he bought three cases of beer?"

"How can we get rid of him?" wondered Rodney. The stack of wings, after all, was on Walter's huge truck, the Ford-From-Hell. In fact, this entire wild adventure, this Safari Sky Tours, was originally Walter's idea. It would be hard to get rid of him now. He was the guide.

"Merle," came Beth's one-word reply. She was already huffing another toke from the joint, which was burning nicely now. "Fuppt... we fuppt... get Merle... fuppt... to volunteer fuppt... bwaaahhh his truck," she finished. The tiny bathroom had become a hazy dopers' den, filled with spent pot smoke, despite their best efforts. Merle, otherwise known by Team Tahoe as "Farmer", had tagged along with the Safari Sky Tours caravan on the southbound journey in his mighty Mitsubishi Montero. The Montero could hold only the Farmer's wing- there would be no room for more even if he would agree to their entreaties. Beth passed the joint to Rodney. "We put half the wings on our Thing, half on Merle's Montero, and we fire Walter."

Beth was disregarding a couple of facts, not the least of which was that the Farmer was a lost soul in Mexico, could not speak a single word of Español, and could not even calculate the rate of exchange between dollars and pesos. Merle had actually asked, one night at dinner: "Hey Walter, how many pesos in a dollar?" which precipitated yet another outburst of raucous laughter from Team Tahoe. Merle was truly a stranger in a strange land.

But Beth's brain was scheming, turning and bursting, looking for a solution. Somehow she would get rid of that Walter. She had been keeping a journal of the journey, which was turning into an itemized and detailed collection of Walter's screw-ups and social blunders. "We don't need that guy. Or the rest of 'em," she added between tokes. "Just listen to 'em...!"

Outside, one of the three drunks who called themselves The Borracho Brothers was hollering something at Walter. "Do it!" he exorted. "Do it!" The others joined in and it became a chant...

"DOIT!DOIT!DOIT!"

"That incident with the cop on the street was way too much," Rodney shook his head. "I could have killed him." He was referring to an episode just that morning when Walter had skillfully swerved the Ford, loaded with gringos and gliders, around a pedestrian policía who tried to flag them over while they were driving through the narrow streets of Colima. Walter had learned long ago that no one stops for beat cops if they can avoid it. Why should they? You step on the gas and *vamanos*, the cop is left behind. This particular cop had jumped nimbly out of the way, almost as though he'd been expecting such disrespect, and then he'd turned his attention to Rodney and Beth who followed in their Thing. In the rearview mirror Walter could see the cop throw up his hand, could see the Thing brake to a stop. He'd stepped on the gas and just left them there to deal with an irate cop. What else could he do? Rodney and Beth could learn the hard way, just as Walter had done. It was called PAYING YER DUES.

The cop had stopped them for no apparent reason, had extorted some dollars from them, also for no apparent reason, and then happily let them go. But the victims were not happy. That episode had cost Rodney and Beth time, trauma, and a twenty-dollar bill. Team Tahoe and the Borracho Brothers had found it quite hilarious of course, and Walter was their temporary hero.

"We've got to get rid..." but Beth's ruminations were cut off by a particularly rowdy outburst from the gringos frolicking in the pool.

"Wal-TER, Wal-TER, Wal-TER," they hollered. As a litany, it was the ultimate insult to Rodney and Beth, who wanted only to part company with their 'guide'.

"Wal-TER, Wal-TER!"

"What the Hell is he doing NOW," wondered Beth aloud. She handed the joint to Rodney, slipped out from the bathroom dope den, and closed the door behind her. She walked over to the door to the outside and tossed it open. The pool and the frolicking gringos were but a few feet away, but they didn't seem to notice Beth stride out of the room. Apparently their attention was drawn to something at roof-top level. Beth stepped to the edge of the pool and peered up. Suddenly a body came streaking down from above, a body balled-up in a move known to children everywhere as a 'cannonball'. The body hit the deep end of the pool just about perfectly centered, with an gigantic kersplash. It raised an enormous wall of water that washed over the gringa and drenched her thoroughly. The chant continued:

"Wal-TER, Wal-TER, Wal-TER!"

When the water settled, and Walter's grinning head bobbed to the surface, the gringos went wild with glee, but Beth gasped in fury. The cannonball roof jump precipitated a 'lemming effect' with the rest of Team Tahoe, who all clambered from the pool, dashed joyfully up two flights of stairs to the roof and, with a few giant steps, threw themselves happily, recklessly, gleefully, into the air. This was what they lived for, found unexpectedly right here at their hotel, and conquered.

"Wahoo," they yelled.

"Cannonball!"

"Jack the kife!"

"Daffy!"

"Air time!"

"Flying Gringos!"

Beth sloshed inside her room and slammed the door. She hurried to the bathroom and stepped quickly inside, grabbing a towel. "What's going on?" asked Rodney, concerned. By now, his eyes had that completely stoned look. "What are they yelling about? What happened?"

"You don't wanna know," said his wife. "But that guy Walter is a menace. He's gotta GO!"

Photo by Lorenzo Sherman

Sacrifices Will Be Made or,
How Can I Miss You If You Won't Fly Away?

Imagine my surprise when I opened my door one morning in Valle de Bravo to find a paraplegic parked in his van out front, with a hang glider on his roof. It was not so surprising to find a hang gliding paraplegic; I know a few paras who hang glide, and I've launched a few too— shoving them off the cliff on wheels. More surprising was the fact that he was a good three hard days drive south of the border- and traveling solo at that! You've got to hand it to the guy- that takes a lot of nerve and determination to pull off. Yet there was Butch Sonso, dragging his wheelchair out of his old Chevy van and onto the steep rocky streets of Valle de Bravo.

As I stood in front of Casa Cabrónes that morning, Butch began a conversation, which developed into a ramble, grew into a harangue, and then launched into a full-on tirade. He talked about every subject under the sun and never stopped from that day on. As far as I know he continues on today in the same manner.

Butch hung out and followed me around Mexico for a couple of weeks, flying from El Peñon del Diablo, and doing a good job. When we all headed south into Guatemala we had four vehicles in the caravan, and plenty of gringos, so someone always rode shotgun with Butch until he'd bored us all, one by one and collectively, to tears. For the last day of that journey Butch traveled alone again, conversing vociferously, I must assume, as we climbed up into the Guatemala highlands.

Butch talked whenever there was someone to talk to, and even when he was alone. At least, when any one of us came upon Butch accidentally, there he would be, carrying on a conversation with himself. This would not be a mumble or a whispered chat, but a full-blown oration, complete with arm-waving gesticulation.

The guy could talk.

Butch would happily talk a blue streak to any Mexican or Guatemalan or Quiche Indian, even though of different tongues. If only they would listen, Butch would do the rest. He spoke not a word of Spanish, but the indigenous folks seemed very intrigued by Butch. They listened carefully, grinning, nodding their heads and offering him help.

Well... we got him down to Guatemala, or I guess I should say that he got himself there, and we were throwing him off the cliff in his ancient Magic 3, rolling him off the launch on the wheels he'd equipped his wing with. Once in the air, he flew very well and we could stand on launch and hear him talking to himself, even as he climbed into the firmaments above. It was a mantra that was really getting on my nerves, and I found myself seeking places to hide from Butch Sonso.

As usual, Butch rode up to launch in the Ford-From-Hell with us on the day that the Guatemalan Army decided to check out our airshow in the sky above Lake Atitlán. When we arrived atop the mountain we found them sprawled around at company rest, in the shade of a few trees, or laying on the grass. A few were on their feet as the Ford From Hell arrived, and they all quickly formed columns and came to attention as their commander presented ranks. There were a few words of welcome and introduction, and then we gringos set to work assembling gliders. It was strange, to say the least, to be setting up and making ready with a flock of diminutive soldiers, all in full combat gear and rather in the way.

I, for one, was interested in getting airborne before the local revolucionístas got word that the Federáles would be easy pickings on a cliffside above Lake Atitlán, and we became target practice for rebel anti-aircraft fire. I wanted to get myself, and all my gringos, with the possible exception of Butch, out of there.

But Butch was happily entertaining the soldiers with a steady "Yadda, yadda, yadda", he finally had a captive audience. This- even though it was obvious that the soldiers had not a clue about what the gringo spoke. They just looked amazed at the sight of him scrambling around in the dirt setting up his wing. They nodded their sweaty heads and lent an occasional hand stuffing a batten or tensioning a wire. When he began to squirm into his harness, their speculation intensified; *Was this gringo really going to jump?*

We made ready to fly, and as usual it fell to me to shove Butch off the hill. I was chosen because Butch refused to let anyone else in my company have the job. There were other pilots present who were capable and certainly up to the task, but Butch would yell for me whenever he needed a push. For my part, I was more than happy to comply, if for no other reason than to be rid of the guy for a while, however fleeting the solitude. The technique is to hold the glider's keel at a flying angle of attack and keep it there as you move closer and closer to the edge, accelerating all the while. Then, heave as hard as possible and roll him off the cliff on his wheels and I mean- you gotta really shove.

With soldiers standing anxiously on both sides of the launch, I grabbed Butch's stinger on his Magic 3 and began walking at the edge. I shoved harder and took a jogging step. Next I put all my weight into the wing and strained for all my might at the cliff edge. Just about then I guess, and for reasons I still can't fathom, Butch changed his mind and commenced to holler. Worse- he bellowed the only word in his entire Spanish vocabulary, simply because it happens to be identical in English as well.

Butch yelled the first word that I'll bet ninety percent of the soldiers up there had understood from him for their entire visit, as I was pushing him at that cliff edge.

In fact, Butch started yelling the one word that everyone up on the cliff that day, gringos, soldiers and Indios alike understood perfectly well" "NO!" he screamed "NOOOO! NOOOO! NOOOOOOOO!"

I don't understand to this day why he was yelling so. I must assume he had suddenly changed his mind and he wanted me to stop shoving. This was not a good idea and, in fact, we had discussed (at great length I might add), about the point-of-no-return, and that once the glider started moving rapidly towards the edge and once it reached a certain point, there was just no "NO!" about it. Once the glider reaches that point, the only solution to ANY problem was more airspeed. Everything looked fine to me and besides, I wanted him out of there.

So Butch did not get his wish, but I got mine; a beautiful launch with hardly any dive at all, a launch that left me dangling at the cliff edge, scrambling on tiptoes in the dirt to avoid falling myself into the abyss. As he floated away on the gentle breeze we could all hear Butch exclaiming more inanities. Then I turned and beheld the reaction of the Guatemalan commandos.

It was a mixed response. Most of the soldiers were grinning in stunned but happy disbelief. Some of them still held their heads in excitement. Everyone continued to listen carefully. Then a quiet cheer went up for their hero in the sky. But the Commander himself looked at me as though I was a monster.

Did I really have such little regard for my fellow gringos? Or was this some kind of new-age torture or right-of-passage that these gringos inflict on each other? Kind of like the Aztecs tossing virgins to the volcano? You mean to say that all along the poor crippled gringo DIDN'T want to fly? What hapless innocent soul might be sacrificed next?

Butch soared away into the Heavens until his voice became distant, faded still more, and finally shut up altogether. The rest of us gringos suited up and got the hell out of there, much relieved.

Hell is a River Canyon or, Dang Fool Flyer

Clearly, not every journey begins with a single step as is often said. Walter's journey, for example, had begun with a single lousy decision, and soon he was gazing down on his own frightful destiny, his own personal Hell.

The day had started out nicely enough... After a very pleasant soaring flight along the Sierra Nevada, the flyer found himself over the verdant fields of Verdi, California. It would have ended as a very successful and enjoyable afternoon if he had simply landed right then and there along Highway 80, and hitchhiked his way home. But as he gazed west up the Truckee River canyon a Heavenly vision crept into his brain and clouded his judgment. Suddenly Walter saw Julie in all her glory, Julie of the welcoming arms and luscious kisses. The vision that crept into Walter's brain was Julie... in her birthday suit. It was a vision that drew him west, what mortal man could resist?

Julie loved to sunbathe on her terrace on sunny afternoons just like this one. Her back yard was only about ten miles away now, as the gringo flies. Looking west from Walter's lofty perch, it seemed like such an easy glide and such a splendid idea. Imagine Julie's surprise, her delight, thought the *flier,* when my shadow falls across her, when she gazes up into the sky, and when she sees her winged hero on high. Won't she be impressed?

That was all it took. Walter banked the wing for a westerly heading, pulled the nose down slightly for his best-glide airspeed and pointed his toes behind him to minimize his drag profile. Leaving Verdi at fourteen thousand feet, Walter began a long glide for Martis Valley, with a song of joy in his heart.

> *Love lift us up where we belong*
> *Where the eagles fly on a mountain high*
> *Love lift us up where we belong*
> *Far from the world below*
> *Where the free winds blow*

Walter was daydreaming along the sky, happily recalling how he had met Julie across the counter at a North Tahoe watering hole. He remembered that first brilliant smile she had offered him, that first flight they had made together, that first kiss and then, inevitably, Walter's thoughts turned to that first round of lovemaking, high in a Sierra meadow, just the two of them surrounded by wild flowers, birds and bees. Another song came to Walter's lips, and so he sang along, just a skyed-out fool in love. It was the Beatles now:

> *Julia*
> *Song I sing*
> *Calls me*
> *So I sing a song of love for*
> *Julia*

But about halfway to Martis Valley Walter encountered massive sinking air, which startled him and woke him from his reverie. Perhaps this was just the down-cycle left behind from a thermal updraft. Perhaps this was cool air that had spilled over the mountains from the west. Perhaps it was just the prevailing winds that had finally set in for the afternoon and were flowing down the canyon like the Truckee River herself. Whatever it was, Walter had failed to account for such an event in his foggy mental calculations, and about halfway to Martis Valley it became horribly evident that Martis Ridge, lying directly in his flight path, would be the most formidable obstacle to his happiness and fulfillment. If he could but top Martis Ridge, then he would arrive happily in Martis Valley—an easy glide from Julie's fulfilling embrace. He dropped his chin onto his chest and stared under his knees—back the way he'd come from. Clearly he was beyond the point-of-no-return and turning around was not going to help. There was no choice now but to press on.

It was the possibility that Walter would not glide over Martis Ridge that disturbed him, focusing him on his immediate future. If he were unable to glide over the ridge that was even now looming up before him, he would be stuck like some lovesick fool, in the Truckee River canyon, and there would be no welcoming arms to fly to, no sweet kisses to welcome.

The flyer tried not to look down upon the territory he was traversing as he held his sights on Martis Ridge. But he knew well enough what lay in store for him if he should go down there. The Truckee River is a delightful sight for a tourist. It is a beckoning paradise for a kayaker or a fly fisherman. But if you are hang gliding, or if you are flying anything but a helicopter or a magic carpet, the Truckee River canyon is appallingly forbidding.

Deep within the canyon, alongside the blue and green river, there also run the twin strips of Highway 80, one of the busiest trucking routes in America. In his mind's eye, Walter pictured himself and his wonderful wing, his beautiful yellow Comet 185, splattered all over a Mac truck like some sick hood ornament. Next to the highway run the twin rails of the Union Pacific Railroad, not a welcoming prospect either. In his mind's eye Walter glimpsed himself flattened to the thickness of a flour tortilla by the Trans Sierra Express, left behind like some gruesome high-tech lunch for the local coyote crowd. To top it off, Pacific Gas and Electric also run their power lines along the river. Once again, Walter's fertile imagination betrayed him; this time grim visions left him dangling and sparking, hopelessly tangled in high-tension power lines. Why, there was one hazard after another in the Truckee River canyon. Even the Truckee River herself was high with spring runoff. Landing in the river would really be a disaster. Truly, this was no place for landing an aircraft, even something as slow and highly maneuverable as a UP Comet 185.

In a desperate effort to maximize his glide, Walter practiced what the textbooks recommend- he flew slow when his flight deck beeped, a bit faster when it was silent, and faster still when the sink alarm toned. He tucked his elbows in toward his chest, concentrated fully on a steady glide, and began a bit of a prayer. But the stress level and pulsing sound in his brain grew louder with each passing minute as he sunk towards his adversary. It just wasn't looking good for the Home Team. The song that came to Walter's lips now was more desperate, and he wasn't sure where it came from:

> *He's got you'n me brother*
> *In his hands*
> *He's got you'n me brother*
> *In his hands*
> *He's got you'n me brother*
> *In his hands*
> *He's got the whole World in his hands*

In a last-ditch effort to top the ridge Walter slowed the wing, swapping airspeed for a bit of altitude, but also approaching stall speed as a result. Still, all he could see were treetops and pinecones. He flew so close to the trees that he startled a squirrel, who was so astonished to see the big gringo that he dropped his nut and flung himself from his perch. The flyer might have broken down in tears right then and there but... well, airmen are not supposed to be whiners after all, and it would also be counter-productive. He still had a chance to make something of his future, but it was looking grim. A curse may have issued from his lips just then, something like "Shit oh Dear!" or "I'm lookin' like toast now!" but there was no way to tell.

With no room to glide over Martis Ridge, with a crash atop the forest imminent, Walter shoved the wing hard a larboard and gave her a one-hundred-eighty degree turn. Pointing her away from the Heaven in Julie's arms now, he looked down and beheld the Purgatory that confronted him. Another song came to Walter just at that moment, a song from his youth, a song he had not heard for twenty years, a song that seemed to say it all:

> So high you can't get over it
> So low you can't get under it
> So wide you can't get around it.
> Oh rocka my soul!

Walter had indeed made a single foolish decision—fly to Julie's arms—yet suddenly his mind was washed clean of all his apprehensions, there were no tears of fears, there was not even any feeling sorry for himself anymore. Out of the blue, Walter was abruptly calm and composed, and he had a bit of a pledge to himself.

I can do this, *he thought.*

I can handle this.

No sweat captain.

Piece of cake!

His pulse rate returned to normal, his stress fell away like precipitation into the canyon below him, and he began to plan an emergency approach to Hell. If he could just get his feet safely on the ground somewhere down there, Heaven would wait. Down, down and down the flyer glided. With about two thousand feet of air between himself and the river, at about three or four hundred feet per minute sink rate, he had about five minutes to plan his escape from the jaws of death at worst, or serious injury at least. He spotted what looked like a tiny meadow surrounded by all the obstacles on one side—river, highway, train tracks and power lines—and tall forest on the other. If he could make an approach up the canyon and over the train tracks perhaps he could wedge that wing into that tiny meadow. It was worth a try. Anything was worth a try. One try. One single try.

That was all he had left.

Putting the wing in a gentle bank Walter circled down into the Truckee River canyon, every sense focused now, on that tiny patch of safety, every nerve tingling with anticipation. It was time to put all his landing skills to the test. Reaching a pattern altitude he flew a classic aircraft approach focused on a spot landing, holding the bar down by his belt buckle.

He whistled along downwind with lots of airspeed.

He turned base leg and sized up his target.

He banked the wing hard to turn final right over the railroad tracks.

He pulled the nose down to skim low over the tracks yet avoid the powerlines, and he dropped down into the meadow.

It was a tight meadow, only about the size of half a football field, and narrow too. Out in the middle, two deer were munching the green grass like Bambi and son. They turned and took one look at the flyer, and bounded into the forest, their white tails flashing. Walter was burning up the field now, and had too much speed, too much distance. He tried to get low enough to drag his boots in the dirt but the trees were coming at him too fast. With all other options exhausted Walter did the only thing left: he flared. Hard!

The wing pitched up and climbed into the sky. Walter held the flare for all his might, and looked down in dread of what was to come. His boots were about twenty feet in the air as gravity took over and Walter plunged to earth with a resounding clanging thud and a cloud of dust.

The Happy Hour crowd at the Beachhouse tavern was rather raucous as Walter ordered a refreshing beverage. He had been out flying with the local gang at Daydreams, the beautiful hang gliding site over the beach at Lake Tahoe and the Tahoe flyers had all landed at the tavern for the beer and the glory. They could land on the beach amid all the bikinis, belly up to the bar, order a designer beer and carry it outside to help with bagging their wings. Life was good. Walter reflected on how lucky he was to be participating in such an awesome activity when up walked Dan, one of his non-flying buddies. Dan was always interested in the flying, and full of questions. Walter bought Dan a beer and they were enjoying the good life when Dan slapped his leg.

"Oh!" he declared. "You won't believe what I saw last week!"

"Really," replied Walter. "What was that?"

"Ha!" laughed Dan. "I was driving down to Reno and going through the Truckee River canyon and I looked up and there was some dang fool hang gliding in there!"

"No!" said Walter with a catch in his throat. He cleared his windpipe and continued. "Who the Hell would be that dang stupid?"

"Can you believe it?" asked Dan. He knew enough about flight to know that this was really foolish. "I don't know," he speculated. "Obviously some dang fool! Sheesh!"

Walter could only agree, he took a good swig of the refreshing suds, and changed the subject.

¡Adios México!
A Lucky Gingo, a Polka, the Sky

It was my last day of flying in Mexico for the winter; ten days had not been enough. So I was mildly disappointed when I could not follow my amigos Jim and Tim as they curled upwards at The Wall. I flew right under Jim, maybe a hundred feet below him, but I found no lift at all, just a bunch of rowdy air. I was amazed and dismayed then, as each time I glanced at Jim he was noticeably higher. But I was really in no hurry. I knew that if I left The Wall now I wouldn't be back here for many months, this was my last day of Mexican flying until next year. So I took a little cruise.

The Wall has a reputation as a serious lift source, so I was sure to encounter my thermal somewhere, my ticket to ride, right? I worked a couple of thermals here and a couple there, but nothing meaningful. I flew circles over The Slot without success, and cranked and banked over the Dinner Plate, but never got anywhere. Each time I glanced over my shoulder at my fellow pilots they were smaller and smaller, as they topped out thousands of feet above me. Finally they were goners, headed for Valle de Bravo, and they had left me far behind, sweat on my brow.

I didn't care though. I cranked and banked the Falcon and just joyed in my last few hours of flight in México. I was in no hurry, remember? The air had been so good the past week that I had no doubt I would pilot my slow boat back to town, a México farewell flight. I flew out over the imposing fluted mass of El Peñon himself and circled there with a couple of buzzards. The Rock of the Devil was always good for some pucker-factor.

But suddenly, I noticed something disturbing: the clouds that had been on the horizon in the morning had quickly advanced across El Peñon, casting all in shadow. Had I waited too long? The big solar cooker was shutting down; now it didn't look so good anymore. I was a long way from town, I was flying a very slow wing, and here comes the shade! There were yet a few holes in the cloud cover so my confidence was still high, but it was not completely un-shaken. I would need some luck indeed, to get home to Valle de Bravo.

I glanced over at launch, about a mile away, and I was surprised to see the glint of sparkling sunlight, as if reflected from a windshield.

Huh?

Was the truck still on launch? I wondered.

Were they waiting for me to make a move?

I had no radio, so I had no means of contacting our driver, no means of telling him to get going and don't wait for me, except maybe to fly low over launch and yell something like a dang fool gringo. But I didn't want to do that because I would have to relinquish my hard-earned position at The Wall to fly all the way back to launch. I was angry, more like frustrated really, at our driver Antonio for waiting for me.

I was even angrier with myself for not having explained things more clearly to him from the start; there was no reason for Antonio to wait for me. I had ropes in my harness, I can speak the language, and I've got a thumb. I had retrieved myself many times in México and it's all part of the adventure. Furthermore, Antonio had three of our clients who had chosen not to fly that day waiting in the truck with him. Two of them are a couple of seniors, George and Nora Rich. They must have been watching me doing my yo-yo impression at The Wall for the last hour and a half or so, wondering if I would shit or get off the pot! They must be hoping I would just land somewhere, anywhere, so they could pick me up, get on with life, and head back to town.

With each circle I concentrated on looking back towards launch again and yes, saw another glint off the windshield. Sure enough, the truck was still on launch.

Fudge! I exclaimed to the sky.

Puta Madre!

Chingales!

Looking more carefully, I thought I saw two tiny dots on the launch itself: that could only be people, friends, amigos. They were standing on launch waiting for me and it was ruining my flight.

Shoot!

With my mind in a quandary, I hooked a couple more weak Wall thermals, just hoping Antonio would read my vibes and leave me there, to fend for myself. But finally I decided I had to make a move. Each thermal at The Wall was weaker than the previous anyway. I might be stuck here all day and still piano. The cloud cover was now complete and there was no solar heating at all. In the distance the snowy peak of the Nevado was slipping into shade.

Rats!

I had three options: 1)I could fly back to launch, probably sinking all the way, and either head obviously down to the Piano where they could retrieve me, or 2) maybe just holler my fool head off to Antonio to head back to town, or 3) I could make the bold move and a beeline over the back to the first landing fields at Las Peñitas where they would find me on the way home. There was only enough altitude for these three options. I didn't want to piano, so I pointed the Falcon over the back and concentrated on best glide. I hoped Antonio was watching for me because I WAS OUTTA THERE.

Vamanos cabrónes!

I glided straight for the first of two lava domes at Las Peñitas and along the way I found nothing resembling lift, not even a ripple. All was in shade. I pointed the Falcon at the second lava dome, aiming it at the small bowl in the rock- the last chance before entering a landing pattern for the cornfield below. Suddenly, just in front of the bowl, I felt a tiny nudge on my nose.

Could it be lift?

I let up on the nose and flew as conservative as I knew how. A wing lifted and I made a tentative circle, trying to keep it flat. I flew along, staring the rock wall in the face, so to speak. Below me lay several fields where I could land, but I tried not to look at them, tried to concentrate on the here, on the now. I still wanted Valle de Bravo though it seemed unlikely.

I must concentrate...

My variometer made a timid groan and I checked the altimeter, which showed sixty-nine hundred feet above sea level. I completed the turn and checked again. Now it read sixty-nine hundred and ten. I was maybe four or five hundred feet above the fields below and climbing, however slowly.

Don't look down! I told myself.

Don't look down!

Don't look down!

I circled there and I looked up, but I couldn't believe I was climbing. It was time for some good ol' fashioned FAITH! These rocks are not known as reliable lift sources, and the whole valley was now in deep shade from the clouds above. The heat had been turned off. Yet, each time I checked my altimeter, the instrument confirmed that I was another ten feet higher.

Eventually I climbed through seven grand on a silky-smooth thermal. Better yet, I was slowly drifting... drifting... I was drifting towards a wooded ridge that is a noted lift source: El Zacamecáte.

Gradually, the lift got fat and smooth and, passing through eight thousand feet, I felt more confidence. I had only gained eleven hundred feet so far, but something magical was happening, one of those inexplicable events that happen exclusively to Those Who Wait.

Or maybe to Those Who Want It Badly Enough.

Or maybe just to Them Who're Foolish Enough to Go There and Give It a Try!

What ever it was, suddenly, I tingled from head to toe with excitement; I had waited, I had wanted, I had worked. And now... here I was! I resolved to hang tight with this thermal 'till there weren't no more! 'Till it was all used up. I was excited, I was thrilled, and I was free as a bird! I was hopeful too; that the gang I had left on launch would head back towards town, and forget about me.

I climbed through nine grand and the thermal dissipated. So I headed out, pushing for Valle again, flying out the far end of the Zacamecate and looking for more lift. I arrived over Casa Morada where I found buoyant air, and a few more bashful beeps from the vario. I circled ever so carefully, in the shade all the while, and I was astonished and pleased to hear the variometer begin to chirp again, and then to tone solid; it was music to my ears! I tightened up the turns and pushed out: the lift was getting stronger!

I squeaked back to nine thousand feet and suddenly the thermal turned on. Soon came ten thousand feet, and I was beginning to cool off in more ways than one: the sweat I had generated over the last hour felt good as it evaporated in the high cool mountain air and, at eleven grand, the view of distant Valle was improving. It looked like I might make it after all! I was still climbing when I spotted a family of buzzards enter my thermal below me, coming in from all directions. I zipped up my jacket and pulled on my gloves and soon I was at twelve thou and climbing, the thermal fat, the air incredibly smooth, the sun nowhere in sight and all was shadow below me. Yet, since arriving over the landing fields at Las Peñitas I had climbed more than a mile.

A song came suddenly to brain, a simple and happy Ranchero that I had heard in Flaco's truck, a song I could not avoid, a silly, catchy tune that I could not deny, a Mexican polka:

> Adios México! Adios México!
> How I got along without you,
> I'll never know and it's
> Adios México!"

First I hummed a few bars, then I sang it, and then it came strong from my lips. I was a flying fool, skyed out, singing a simple song.

At twelve-seven my blessed thermal slowed. I did a wingover to aim the Falcon at Valle, and I started to glide. I tucked in my arms, pointed my toes, and I waited, watching the magic land of the central Mexican highlands slip beneath my wings. Glancing under my left wing I bid a fond farewell to launch behind me... and to The Rock of the Devil in the distance.

¡Adios México!

Somewhere over Casas Viejas, approaching the village on a marginal glide, I found yet another thermal at around eight grand and took it back to ten-five. From this position it was obvious that I could glide well beyond the landing field beside the lake, I had made it! In fact, I could take a leisurely little farewell tour of Valle de Bravo and La Peña beyond.

I could also see two tiny gliders in the landing field. These would be Tim and Jim, and they were undoubtedly gloating over a cold beer, probably laughing about having left me, their guide after all, far behind in some cornfield or worse- the Piano field.

Wahaahaa, the joke's on us all!

But I was a foolish little dot in the sky, singing a silly song! I glided over town and found smooth, strong winds and buoyant air over the village and over La Peña. I mapped-out the narrow streets and alleys of Valle, spotted the narrow corner where I lived, admired the Zocalo and the Estrella. I watched tiny toy-like cabs poking slowly past the central camionera below me. I maneuvered into a position where I could quickly tail wind it to the LZ when I got low.

All the while, I had that giddy feeling in my head and the song in my heart: ¡Adios México!

I worked my way down to approach altitude with no hurry, then stuffed the bar to my knees and turned a blazing final. I touched down on one foot and let out a whoop of joy!

Tim and Jim were quite surprised to see my Falcon on final over the lake. They came out to carry my wing the last few feet to the picnic tables. They stuck a cold cervesa in my claw and we all stood around grinning. The gringos were all sore and sunburned and very satisfied with their week of Mexican flying. As for myself, my last flight in México had been pure magic!

"Goodbye,
If you hear of my being stood up against a Mexican stone wall
and shot to rags please know that I think that a pretty good
way to depart this life. It beats old age, disease, or falling
down the cellar stairs. To be a gringo in Mexico, ahh- that is
euthanasia!" – Ambrose Bierce 1913

Down on the border...

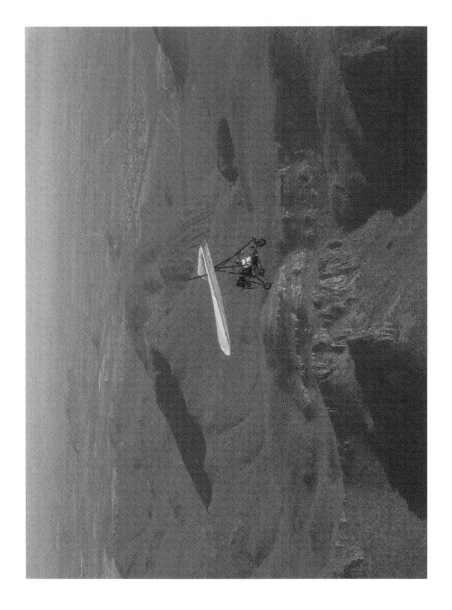

Lost gringo, old Mexico...

Hang gliding in Mexico, Colimótl on the horizon.

Until next time amigos, happy trails!

Made in the USA
Charleston, SC
09 February 2010